NICOLAS ESTRADA

········

NEW RINGS

········

500+ DESIGNS

WITH OVER 600
ILLUSTRATIONS

Thames & Hudson

On the cover:
front: Jorge Castañon, *Colour Ring*. Photograph by Damián Wasser.
back: A selection of images from throughout the book.

Translated from the Spanish *Anillos: 500 creaciones artísticas de todo el mundo* by Satèl·lit bcn – Inma Alavedra and Hugo Steckelmacher

All the images in this book have been reproduced with the knowledge and prior consent of the artists concerned. Every effort has been made to ensure that credits accurately match the information supplied. In the event of any omissions or errors, the publisher would be pleased to make the appropriate correction for future editions of the book.

First published in the United Kingdom in 2011 by
Thames & Hudson Ltd, 181A High Holborn, London WC1V 7QX

www.thamesandhudson.com

First published in 2011 in paperback in the United States of America by
Thames & Hudson Inc., 500 Fifth Avenue, New York, New York 10110

thamesandhudsonusa.com

This revised edition published in 2016

Original edition © 2011 Promopress, Barcelona
Revised edition © 2016 Promopress, Barcelona
This edition © 2016 Thames & Hudson Ltd, London

British Library Cataloguing-in-Publication Data
A catalogue record for this book is available from the British Library

Library of Congress Catalog Card Number 2015953661

ISBN 978-0-500-29240-2

Printed in China

CONTENTS

Elizabeth Shypertt

Sandra Duarte | P. 110

At its most basic, a ring is a circle. However, this familiar shape can represent many concepts that are difficult to define, such as infinity and perfection, and has intrigued scholars for at least five millennia. It was this fascination that led to the discovery of pi – the numerical value of the ratio of the circumference of a circle to its diameter – and the quest for its true value, which ultimately illuminated and advanced an entire branch of mathematics: geometry. We now know that pi is an irrational number; it cannot be represented exactly and is always an approximation, even when calculated on a computer to millions of decimal places. Consequently, the circumference and area of a circle cannot be measured with absolute accuracy, and the circle retains some of its original mystery.

Jimena Rios | P. 36

Joan Codina | P. 184

Augousta Themistokleous | P. 223

The pieces in this collection all fall within the basic definition of a ring: all are essentially circular and can be worn on a finger. However, it would be wrong to label them as traditional. They are anything but simple and are sometimes more than a little unconventional, pushing our basic concept of the ring beyond its established associations and into another category entirely: miniature sculpture.

Through the ages, artists and jewelers have tested the boundaries of their disciplines, inspired by a host of different motivations and goals. Some have set out to break new ground, to shock, to invent or hone techniques; others, to explore new materials, or simply to see whether something is possible

and where it ultimately leads. Once you step outside the boundaries of traditional ring-making, there are no guarantees that the finished product will be a success. In the hands of an experienced and capable practitioner, however, the results can be very exciting indeed.

Many rings in this collection use themes and media that defy simple definition. The use of real animal parts, anatomical imagery such as skulls, and even insects has resulted in some particularly striking examples. Some are made of materials not commonly used for rings. Others approach traditional media in a non-traditional way: by mounting diamonds, for example, on the inside of the band so that only the wearer – and whoever might see it on

the nightstand – knows the ring's true value. Some are not truly wearable at all, pushing beyond the rational to the irrational – rather like pi, in a manner of speaking.

This book is a blend of the avant-garde, the unconventional and the delightful. It showcases rings that stimulate the imagination by challenging traditional practices and standard definitions. The finished products are sculptures for the hands, and range from simple to complex, from rings you could wear every day to those that you can hardly wear at all. Without exception, they are all beautifully made and intriguing in their own way. This stunning collection provides a snapshot of the creations of the best art jewelers working today.

PREFACE

Carles Codina Armengol

Catalina Brenes | P. 19

Emily Watson | P. 30

Fabrice Schaefer | P. 126

When primitive man first saw a thread of gold, perhaps the simplest object that came to mind was a plain hoop or ring around a finger. Since gold was too soft and malleable to be made into tools or weapons, it seemed from the start to be destined for purely ornamental use. I believe that giving this metal a circular form was the most automatic and intuitive gesture, but this mechanical act brought with it the far-reaching consequence of giving this rudimentary shape a symbolic value, turning it into both a piece of jewelry and a form of currency.

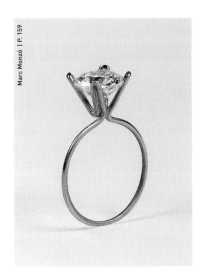

Marc Monzó | P. 159

backs on technology and work with fewer resources, in an attempt to make their pieces much more anthropological, closer to everyday life and what it means to be human.

Of course, a ring is no more complicated to create than any other piece of jewelry, but it does possess some characteristics that make it particularly interesting.

From my perspective, making a ring is a challenge because it is worn at one of the body's extremes, somewhere that involves a great deal of movement. The fingers are also highly expressive, playing a vital role in communication and language. A ring lives on the part of us that touches other people, the part we use to hug or to hit, and without it, we feel unprotected.

Creating a piece of jewelry is always an act of communication between the maker and the wearer, a relationship that is enmeshed in a social context that may affirm, strengthen or criticize it. The ring,

positioned on the anatomical extremes of our hands, plays a special role in this relationship, in a way that pieces such as brooches and necklaces do not, perhaps because they are compositionally easier to resolve, especially for the many jewelry-makers who egocentrically forget that jewelry should have a communicative relationship with the body.

Nowadays, the situation is very different: a huge range of available tools are available to us, the process of jewelry-making can be completely mechanized or even carried out digitally. The materials and techniques we have at our disposal are potentially limitless. Faced with this reality, what continues to surprise and fascinate me most when teaching the art of jewelry-making is seeing how many emerging artists prefer to turn their

INTRODUCTION

WHAT'S IN A RING?
Marjorie Simon

Julia deVille | P. 125

Dauvit Alexander | P. 16

Michal Oren | P. 234

Seated at his table, St Eligius, the patron saint of goldsmiths, glances up as he weighs the gold wedding ring for the elegant medieval couple behind him. In the background on the right is a box of thirteen rings of gold and gems, whose designs continue to be worn more than five hundred years later.

A ring is a line without end that both encloses (a finger) and excludes (everything else, the rest of the hand). Do you put your finger in the ring or put the ring on your finger?

Since the dawn of humanity, symbolic objects worn on the body have mediated between the known and unknown. Rings are a navigational aid for life in a capricious and uncertain universe. Evidence suggests that jewelry dates back tens of thousands of years, to the agricultural revolution and the domestication of dogs. Was the first ring made from the femur of a mammal, emptied of its marrow, or a coil of grass, a perforated shell or the vertebra of a large fish?

History and legend are rich in ring lore. Aristotle, Helen of Troy and Ulysses all wore rings. A mummy from Thebes, dating back over 3,000 years, wears a dozen rings. A 16th-century portrait of Cardinal Albrecht von Brandenburg shows him wearing twice as many. In Venice, the Doge threw his ring into the Adriatic on Ascension Day to symbolize the union of the city with the sea. In folklore, magical rings appear in Sanskrit, in Chaucer's tales and in the stories collected by the Brothers Grimm, evidence of a timeless desire to control the behaviour of others, talk to animals, be invisible, or rule the world.

Rings may have different functions: signet rings, often with a swivel top of engraved gold or carnelian, were used with melted wax to seal documents and other items. Signet rings were so important that early Christian women, who were otherwise forbidden adornments, were permitted rings to seal up household goods. Poison rings, notably favoured by the Borgias, the family of Italian nobles who rose to power during the Renaissance, were little vessels of death, while cramp rings of the 14th century were thought to protect against the intestinal scourges that ravaged medieval Europe. Teething rings, a circlet of ivory with a silver charm, soothed many a fretful infant. The wearing and exchanging of rings of remembrance, friendship and mourning, many containing the braided hair of the beloved, peaked during the Victorian age.

Even the materials have their own narratives. In medieval folktales, Reynard the Fox had a ring studded with three magical gemstones: red for light, white for health, green for protection. In Roman times, only ambassadors, and later aristocrats, were allowed to wear gold rings. Free Roman men wore iron rings, thereby creating a material hierarchy that has been gradually challenged ever since. With the development of substitute materials such as glass and enamel to imitate gemstones and porcelain to replace carved agates, no hand

needed to be naked of adornment, regardless of social status.

Rings commemorate life events: birth, marriage, death, affiliations, achievements and attachments. Intimate, portable objects of beauty, rings have a protective power that extends to our hands with their marvellous digits and opposable thumbs, source of our miraculous dexterity and proof of an indissoluble link to our even more miraculous brains. Our first tool, the hand symbolizes membership of the human community. Temperate climates support the wearing of rings, where hands are exposed to the elements and to the eyes of others. The decline in harsh physical labour, the disappearance of gloves in bourgeois society, and the emergence of nail salons in recent decades all favour a culture of rings.

All of these things and more have become fodder for contemporary ring-makers, from ironic commentaries to solemn homages to all of jewelry's history, from Egyptian inlays to Etruscan granulation, from Victorian braided hair to the 'Dutch smooth' movement.

More than just a hand ornament, rings are part of the world we can wear. They trumpet the enthusiastic embrace of materials and technology. The rings in this book are makers' rings, created by fine

craft artists. Not strictly functional, they express the artists' intentions in the same media in which rings have been crafted for millennia – metal, gemstones, glass, enamel and wood, as well as some that St Eligius would never have heard of: rubber, plastics, resins, paper, polymers and lab-grown gems.

What's in a ring? Unlike a brooch, you don't need clothing to wear it. Unlike earrings, you only need make one. Unlike a neckpiece, you can compress an entire narrative into a tiny package. The physical limitations of ring design create a tiny window through which a vast landscape may be revealed. Come on in – take a look.

For scholarship and interpretation, the author is indebted to Sylvie Lambert's indispensable book *The Ring*.

THE SYMBOLISM OF RINGS

ELEMENTS OF IDENTITY AND INDIVIDUALITY
Carolina Hornauer

Mari Ishikawa | P. 63

Who I am, what I am and what I want to be are some of the questions that stay with us throughout our lives, inextricably bound up with our identities. We want to be ourselves, we seek to hide our personality, but we also strive to identify with a particular group. There is within us a profound need for recognition.

Since the beginnings of mankind, ornamental jewelry has served to express the feelings and personality of its wearer, as well as those of the wider community and its environment. Mythology, religion, customs and class differences are just some of the aspects that can be revealed by studying the form and function of a ring. In this regard, the ring as a primitive decorative object has been instrumental in historical and anthropological studies of a number of different cultures.

As a cultural and artistic artefact, the ring can paint a portrait of its creator (the jeweler), its wearer, the viewer and the ring itself. In this sense, it is an object of dialogue, and this is the role it has played historically for kings, emperors, priests, the bourgeoisie and the aristocracy, and, following the secularization and industrialization of fashion, for people in general. Is it possible for a ring, through an aesthetic and symbolic discourse, to reinforce self-awareness and heighten consciousness of what makes its wearer different from others? Can a small, circular adornment really bolster the identity of the person wearing it? If we

assume that jewelry is, broadly speaking, a way of standing out, of setting oneself apart from other people, then the answer to these questions is a resounding yes.

The 'Ring of the Fisherman' provides one of the best examples of the ring's symbolic power. Used since at least the 13th century, the Annulus Piscatoris forms a vital part of the Pope's regalia. During his coronation ceremony, the Pope receives a gold ring made especially for him, with his name inscribed around the figure of St Peter. Through ritual and iconography (the fisherman as a symbol of the foundation of the Church), the ring expresses a sense of supremacy and power that belong to its wearer alone. The ring represents God's authority being transferred to his representative on earth, who holds the highest rank within the Church. This ring reinforces its wearer's identity by virtue of the wearer appropriating the symbolic values contained in the object itself. The immense power it confers is reflected in the fact that the Pope is not a Pope without his ring. Indeed, he uses the ring to stamp bulls and letters; one greets the Supreme Pontiff by kissing his ring; and, upon its bearer's death, the ring is solemnly destroyed by the Camarlengo.

With all due respect to the mouth and eyes, the hand is without a doubt the body part that expresses itself most eloquently, and a ring can speak along with it. During the 1960s, jewelry became more open and reflective, and pieces began to be made for the rest of the body. Aesthetically speaking, the ring began to be regarded as a second skin; no longer a mere adornment, it instead became an intrinsic part of the finger, part of a whole, ourselves, Jung's Self.*

Contemporary jewelry, which can make use of practically unlimited materials, forms and meanings, enables us to reinterpret its wearers. We see the emergence of expressive rings, such as those made by Chris Irick, who plays with the size of the jewel to push the limits of the body using innovative proportions. At the same time, the ring continues to be the most intimate of jewels. The rings of Katja Prins, which contain sensuous materials such as pearls and polyurethane rubber and are in direct contact with the skin, can

possess erotic overtones. Mari Ishikawa, meanwhile, delves into the images of nature to recreate an inner world, depicting the relationship between nature and our lives. It should not therefore surprise us that the ring, an intimate and symbolic object, has itself become an identity marker.

Some rings are made to be looked at, some can be worn on two or more fingers, some conceal their more poetic side, some require their wearer to move in order to function, some interact with and reflect the observer, some leave messages or can write, and some have to be inflated. These small, user-friendly and sometimes extremely simple objects represent the search for a new identity, and since no two people are alike, perhaps this fact is only to be expected.

Flora Bhattachary | P.112

Chris Irick | P. 62

* The Self is defined by Carl Gustav Jung as the central archetype of the collective unconscious, the whole of the individual psyche. The Self is represented symbolically by the circle. It is the product of the process of individuation.

INDIVIDUALITY

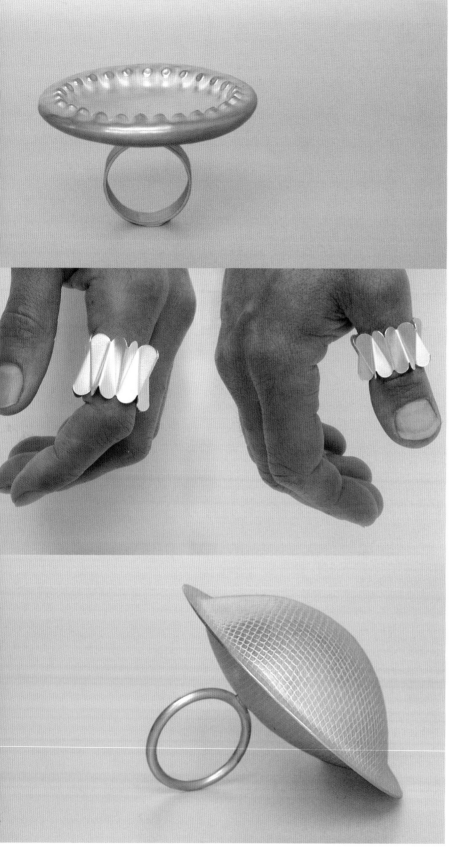

ELS VANSTEELANDT
Alchemila

Media	925 silver
Dimensions	5.0 × 5.0 × 4.0 cm
	(2 × 2 × 1⁵⁄₈ in.)

Photo: Els Vansteelandt

ELS VANSTEELANDT
Heartwork

Media	925 silver
Dimensions	2.5 × 2.5 × 2.0 cm
	(1 × 1 × ¾ in.)

Photo: Els Vansteelandt

ELS VANSTEELANDT
Untitled

Media	925 silver
Dimensions	6.0 × 6.0 × 5.0 cm
	(2³⁄₈ × 2³⁄₈ × 2 in.)

Photo: Els Vansteelandt

GIOVANNI CORVAJA
The Golden Fleece: Fidelity

Media	18ct gold: 104,272 single threads (2.085 km / 1¼ miles of thread in total)
Dimensions	2.4 × 1.8 × 1.6 cm (1 × ¾ × ⅝ in.)

Photo: Giovanni Corvaja

GIOVANNI CORVAJA
Untitled

Media	18ct gold: 26 alloys, shading from white to red to yellow
Dimensions	1.6 × 1.1 cm (⅝ × ⅜ in.)

Photo: Giovanni Corvaja

GIOVANNI CORVAJA
Untitled

Media	18ct gold: enamel
Dimensions	1.7 × 1.3 cm (⅝ × ½ in.)

Photo: Giovanni Corvaja

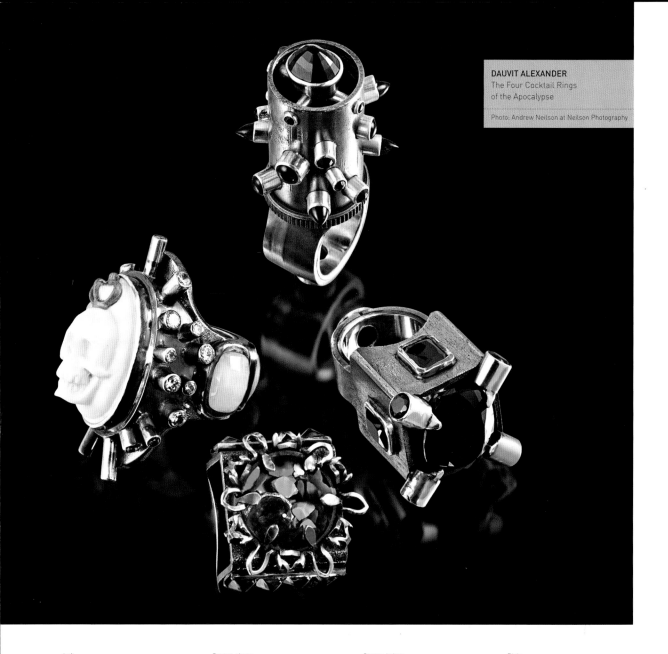

DAUVIT ALEXANDER
The Four Cocktail Rings
of the Apocalypse

Photo: Andrew Neilson at Neilson Photography

Left		Centre, above		Centre, below		Right	
Pestilence, the White Horse		War, the Red Horse		Death, the Pale Green Horse (Thanatos)		Famine, the Black Horse	
Media	silver, hand-made unglazed porcelain with 24ct gold detail, quartzite, cubic zirconias, corroded iron gas pipe	Media	silver, steel, garnets	Media	silver, corroded steel, green quartz, found lens, peridot, enamel chips	Media	silver, etched steel, black tourmaline, black onyx, black zircon
		Dimensions	6.0 × 2.5 × 2.5 cm (2⅜ × 1 × 1 in.)				
Dimensions	4.0 × 3.5 × 3.0 cm (1⅝ × 1⅜ × 1⅛ in.)			Dimensions	4.0 × 3.5 × 2.5 cm (1⅝ × 1⅜ × 1 in.)	Dimensions	5.5 × 3.0 × 3.0 cm (2⅛ × 1⅛ × 1⅛ in.)

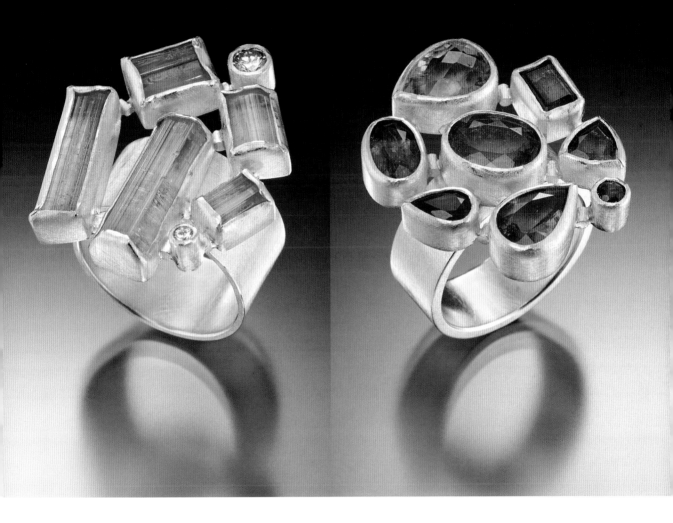

PETRA CLASS
Big Green Ring

Media	22ct gold, 18ct gold,
	diamond, tourmaline
Dimensions	2.5 × 2.5 × 2.5 cm
	(1 × 1 × 1 in.)

Photo: Hap Sakwa

PETRA CLASS
Big Red Ring

Media	22ct gold, 18ct gold,
	ruby, red tourmaline
Dimensions	2.5 × 2.5 × 2.2 cm
	(1 × 1 × 7/8 in.)

Photo: Hap Sakwa

DAPHNE KRINOS
Big Flower Ring

Media   silver, amethyst, patina
Dimensions   3.8 × 3.0 cm (1½ × 1⅛ in.)

Photo: Joel Degen

DAPHNE KRINOS
Ring

Media   18ct gold, silver,
             diamonds, quartz, patina
Dimensions   2.2 × 2.0 cm (⅞ × ¾ in.)

Photo: Joel Degen

CATALINA BRENES
Rimani

Media   silver, aquamarine
Dimensions   3.5 × 2.0 cm
             (1⅜ × ¾ in.)

Photo: Riccardo Rivello

MICHELLE KRAEMER
Le P'tit Noir

Media   lead, Japanese paper,
             lacquer
Dimensions   4.0 × 3.0 × 3.0 cm
             (1⅝ × 1⅛ × 1⅛ in.)

Photo: Federico Cavicchioli

CATALINA BRENES
Baila, Baila (Dance, Dance)

Media   silver, aragonite, fluorite
Dimensions   4.5 × 2.5 cm
             (1¾ × 1 in.)

Photo: Riccardo Rivello

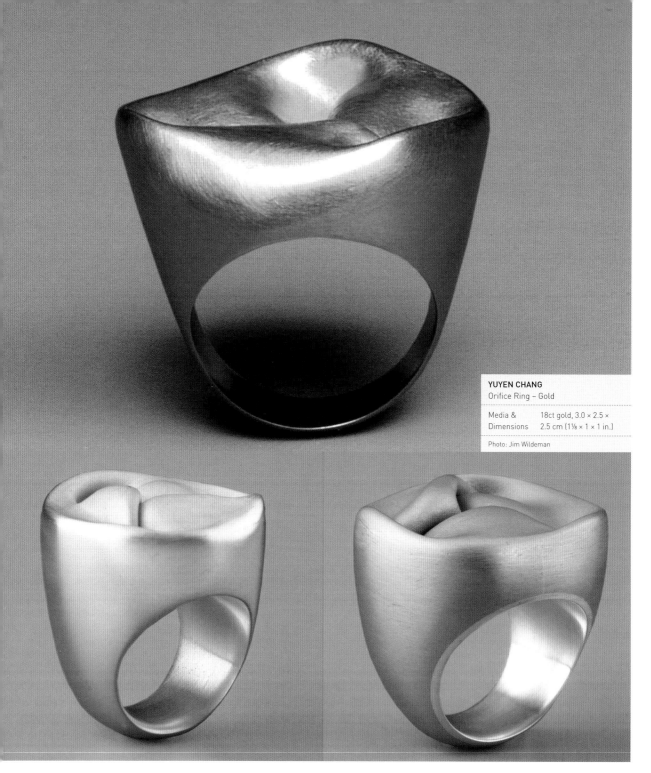

YUYEN CHANG

Orifice Ring – Silver

Media   fine silver, 925 silver
Dimensions   3.0 × 2.5 × 2.5 cm (1⅛ × 1 × 1 in.)

Photo: Jim Wildeman

YUYEN CHANG

Orifice Ring – Copper

Media   925 silver, copper
Dimensions   3.0 × 2.5 × 2.5 cm (1⅛ × 1 × 1 in.)

Photo: Jim Wildeman

CHARITY HALL
Cicada Wing Ring

Media & Dimensions	silver, peridot, yellow sapphire, cicada wing, resin, 3.9 × 2.6 × 2.6 cm (1⅝ × 1 × 1 in.)

Photo: Charity Hall

ALEJANDRA SOLAR
Untitled

Media	silver, polyurethane, synthetic lacquer
Dimensions	6.0 × 3.5 × 1.7 cm (2⅜ × 1⅜ × ⅝ in.)

Photo: Joan Soto

ALAN REVERE
A New Twist

Media	18ct gold, pearls
Dimensions	4.2 × 4.0 × 3.8 cm (1⅝ × 1⅝ × 1½ in.)

Photo: Barry Blau

VICTORIA ALTEPETER
Sky Maps

Media	silver, brass
Dimensions	4.0 × 4.0 × 3.2 cm
	(1⅝ × 1⅝ × 1¼ in.)

Photo: Victoria Altepeter

JINA SEO
OK Ring

Media	brass, thread, glove
Dimensions	11.7 × 7.6 × 5.4 cm
	(4⅝ × 3 × 2⅛ in.)

Photo: Jina Seo

TITHI KUTCHAMUCH
Personal Space

Media	gold-plated silver
Dimensions	4.5 × 2.5 × 0.8 cm
	(1¾ × 1 × ⅜ in.)

Photo: Seng Jakoon

TITHI KUTCHAMUCH Animal and a Ring

Media	silver, gold plate
Dimensions	Cow: 3.5 × 2.8 × 0.8 cm (1⅜ × 1⅛ × ⅜ in.)
	Rabbit: 3 × 2.8 × 0.8 cm (1⅛ × 1⅛ × ⅜ in.)
	Pig: See above (Personal Space)
	Bird: 3.5 × 2.7 × 2.3 cm (1⅝ × 1⅛ × ⅞ in.)

Photo: Narut Vatanopas

ROBEAN VISSCHERS
Untitled

Media	gold, black rhodium,
	citrine
Dimensions	2.4 × 2.4 × 1.5 cm
	(1 × 1 × ⅝ in.)

Photo: Brutesque

ROBEAN VISSCHERS
Untitled

Media	white gold, aquamarine
Dimensions	2.4 × 2.0 × 1.5 cm
	(1 × ¾ × ⅝ in.)

Photo: Brutesque

ROBEAN VISSCHERS Untitled

Media	gold, diamonds
Dimensions	2.4 × 2.4 × 1.6 cm
	(1 × 1 × ⅝ in.)

Photo: Brutesque

MARIANA VISO ROJAS
Saltimbanco

Media & Dimensions	silver, textile, 3.0 × 1.2 × 0.2 cm (1⅛ × ½ × ⅛ in.)

Photo: Rosa Castells

MARIANA VISO ROJAS
Keter

Media	silver, textile
Dimensions	3.0 × 2.1 cm (1⅛ × ⅞ in.)

Photo: Rafael Tirado

MARIANA VISO ROJAS
Vulcano

Media	silver, textile, tiger eye
Dimensions	2.8 × 2.6 cm (1⅛ × 1 in.)

Photo: Rafael Tirado

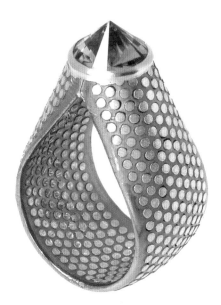

SALIMA THAKKER
Untitled

Media	18ct yellow gold, silver, garnets, patina
Dimensions	3.4 cm (1⅜ in.)

Photo: Salima Thakker

SALIMA THAKKER
Untitled

Media	18ct yellow gold, silver, tourmaline, patina
Dimensions	3.4 cm (1⅜ in.)

Photo: Salima Thakker

SALIMA THAKKER Untitled

Media	18ct yellow gold, diamonds
Dimensions	3.2 cm (1¼ in.)

Photo: Salima Thakker

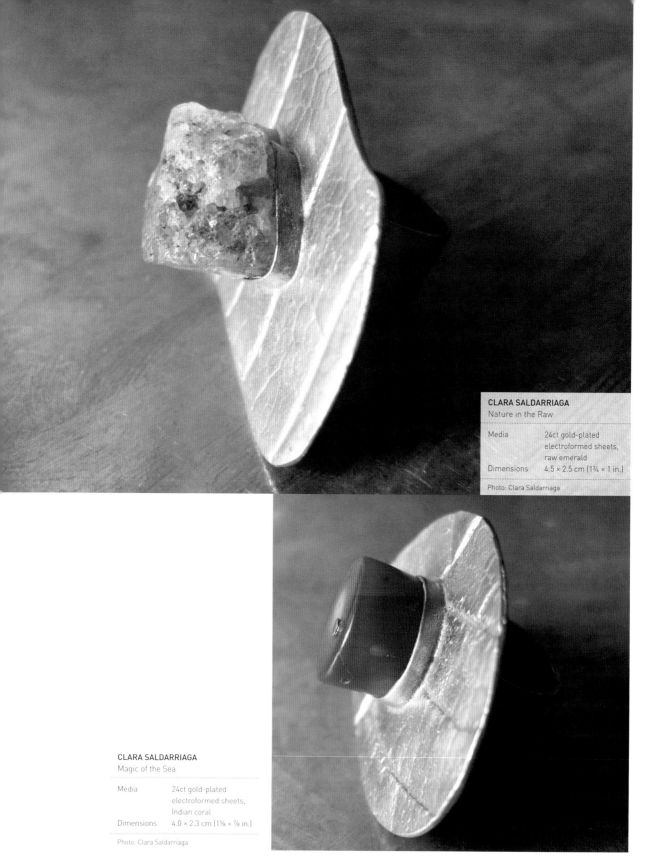

CLARA SALDARRIAGA
Nature in the Raw

Media	24ct gold-plated electroformed sheets, raw emerald
Dimensions	4.5 × 2.5 cm (1¾ × 1 in.)

Photo: Clara Saldarriaga

CLARA SALDARRIAGA
Magic of the Sea

Media	24ct gold-plated electroformed sheets, Indian coral
Dimensions	4.0 × 2.3 cm (1⅝ × ⅞ in.)

Photo: Clara Saldarriaga

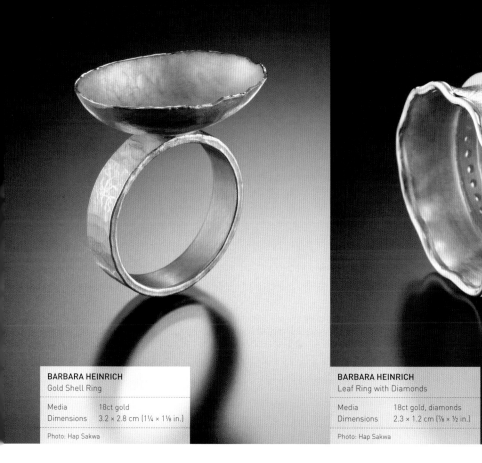

BARBARA HEINRICH
Gold Shell Ring

| Media | 18ct gold |
| Dimensions | 3.2 × 2.8 cm (1¼ × 1⅛ in.) |

Photo: Hap Sakwa

BARBARA HEINRICH
Leaf Ring with Diamonds

| Media | 18ct gold, diamonds |
| Dimensions | 2.3 × 1.2 cm (⅞ × ½ in.) |

Photo: Hap Sakwa

BARBARA HEINRICH
Hammered Gold Band with
Diamond Rims

| Media | 18ct gold, diamonds |
| Dimensions | 2.5 × 1.9 cm (1 × ¾ in.) |

Photo: Barbara Heinrich Studio

ELENA GORBUNOVA 1

Media   slver, glass
Dimensions   7.0 × 4.0 × 4.0 cm
             (2¾ × 1⅝ × 1⅝ in.)

Photo: Elena Gorbunova

JÁNOS GÁBOR VARGA Curl Ring

Media   iron
Dimensions   2.1 × 2.1 × 0.8 cm
             (¾ × ¾ × ⅜ in.)

Photo: Luca Orlandini

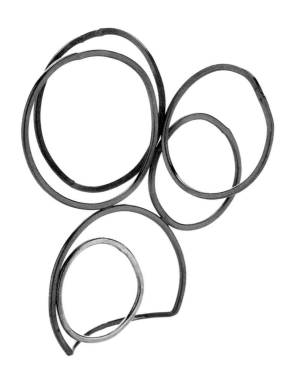

AMY TAVERN Cage Ring

Media &   pink gold, 925 silver,
Dimensions   patina, 10.0 × 7.6 ×
             5.0 cm (3⅞ × 3 × 2 in.)

Photo: Hank Drew

EMILY WATSON Antlers

Media   Corian
Dimensions   5.7 × 6.4 × 0.5 cm
             (2¼ × 2½ × ¼ in.)

Photo: Emily Watson

CINNAMON LEE Inset Rings

Media   titanium, silver, spinel
Dimensions   2.5 × 2.5 × 1.4 cm
               (1 × 1 × ½ in.)

Photo: John Lee

CINNAMON LEE Superstructure Ring

Media   titanium
Dimensions   2.4 × 2.4 × 1.2 cm
               (1 × 1 × ½ in.)

Photo: John Lee

FRANCESC OLIVERAS Recycling

Media   gold, resin
Dimensions   2.3 × 2.3 × 1.5 cm
               (⅞ × ⅞ × ⅝ in.)

Photo: David Campos Bel

FRANCESC OLIVERAS Hot Ice

Media   gold, diamonds
Dimensions   2.2 × 2.2 × 1.5 cm
               (⅞ × ⅞ × ⅝ in.)

Photo: David Campos Bel

ELVIRA GOLOMBOSI
No. 7

Media	haematite
Dimensions	8.4 × 4.0 × 3.0 cm
	(3¼ × 1⅝ × 1⅛ in.)

Photo: Evelyn Bencicova

ELVIRA GOLOMBOSI
No. 14

Media	lapis lazuli
Dimensions	11 × 5.0 × 3.0 cm
	(4⅜ × 2 × 1⅛ in.)

Photo: Evelyn Bencicova

ELVIRA GOLOMBOSI
No. 12

Media   jasper
Dimensions   5.5 × 2.5 × 2.5 cm
              (2⅛ × 1 × 1 in.)

Photo: Evelyn Bencicova

MARIA CRISTINA BELLUCCI
Ring 4

Media	silver, coloured pencils
Dimensions	2.7 × 2.7 × 1.4 cm
	(1 × 1 × ½ in.)

Photo: Maria Cristina Bellucci

MARIA CRISTINA BELLUCCI
Ring 2

Media	silver, coloured pencils
Dimensions	4.0 × 2.0 × 0.8 cm
	(1⅝ × ¾ × ⅜ in.)

Photo: Maria Cristina Bellucci

SOFIA BJÖRKMAN Untitled

Media	silver
Dimensions	3.0 × 3.0 × 2.0 cm
	(1⅛ × 1⅛ × ¾ in.)

Photo: Sofia Björkman

SOFIA BJÖRKMAN Untitled

Media	silver
Dimensions	3.0 × 2.0 × 1.0 cm
	(1⅛ × ¾ × ⅜ in.)

Photo: Sofia Björkman

GERTI MACHACEK
Figure 19

Media	18ct gold
Dimensions	3.1 × 2.3 × 2.1 cm
	(1¼ × ⅞ × ⅞ in.)

Photo: Sophie Pölzl

GERTI MACHACEK
Two to Tango

Media	18ct gold
Dimensions	3.3 × 2.2 × 2.1 cm
	(1¼ × ⅞ × ⅞ in.)

Photo: Sophie Pölzl

GERTI MACHACEK
8 Diagrams

Media	silver, patina
Dimensions	3.0 × 2.9 × 2.2 cm
	(1⅛ × 1⅛ × ⅞ in.)

Photo: Sophie Pölzl

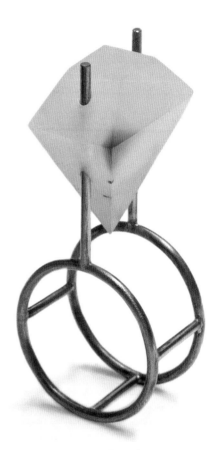

JIMENA RÍOS
Toad Skin

Media	24ct gold, silver, enamel, patina
Dimensions	6.0 × 4.0 cm (2⅜ × 1⅝ in.)

Photo: Negro Karamanian

PHILIP SAJET
Amber Ring

Media	amber, gold
Dimensions	4.6 × 2.3 × 2.2 cm (1¾ × ⅞ × ⅞ in.)

Photo: Beate Klockmann

PILAR GARRIGOSA
Untitled

Media	18ct gold, rubellite
Dimensions	3.0 × 2.5 cm (1⅛ × 1 in.)

Photo: Nos & Soto

CUCÚ RUIZ
Little Pearl

Media	gold, pearl
Dimensions	2.8 × 2.6 × 2.0 cm
	(1⅛ × 1 × ¾ in.)

Photo: Claudia Quade-Frau

BIBA SCHUTZ
Folded Box Ring

Media	18ct gold
Dimensions	3.8 × 1.7 × 1.7 cm
	(1½ × ⅝ × ⅝ in.)

Photo: Ron Boszko

BORIS BALLY
Mesh (Soulfully Synchronizing Gears)

Media	18ct yellow gold
Dimensions	3.0 × 3.0 × 1.0 cm
	(1⅛ × 1⅛ × ⅜ in.)

Photo: J. W. Johnson Photography

FABRIZIO TRIDENTI
Restricted Area Ring

Media   brass, acrylic paint
Dimensions   5.2 × 3.5 × 2.4 cm
               (2 × 1⅜ × 1 in.)

Photo: Fabrizio Tridenti

FABRIZIO TRIDENTI Untitled

Media   titanium
Dimensions   5.4 × 3.3 × 3 cm
               (2⅛ × 1¼ × 1⅛ in.)

Photo: Indaco

FABRIZIO TRIDENTI Untitled

Media   brass, acrylic paint
Dimensions   5.2 × 3.9 × 3.9 cm
               (2 × 1⅝ × 1⅝ in.)

Photo: Fabrizio Tridenti

MIKALA MORTENSEN Blind Love

Media	925 silver
Dimensions	2.2 × 2.2 × 1.0 cm
	(⅞ × ⅞ × ⅜ in.)

Photo: Mikala Mortensen

SARAH ROBINSON
Dog

Media	925 silver
Dimensions	5.0 × 2.4 × 0.9 cm
	(2 × 1 × ⅜ in.)

Photo: Sarah Robinson

FLAVIA BRÜHLMANN
Wavy Wall

Media	silver
Dimensions	3.0 × 2.0 × 2.0 cm
	(1⅛ × ¾ × ¾ in.)

Photo: Flavia Brühlmann

JIMENA BOLAÑOS Stones

Media	925 silver
Dimensions	7.0 × 2.6 × 2.3 cm
	(2¾ × 1 × ⅞ in.)

Photo: Jimena Bolaños

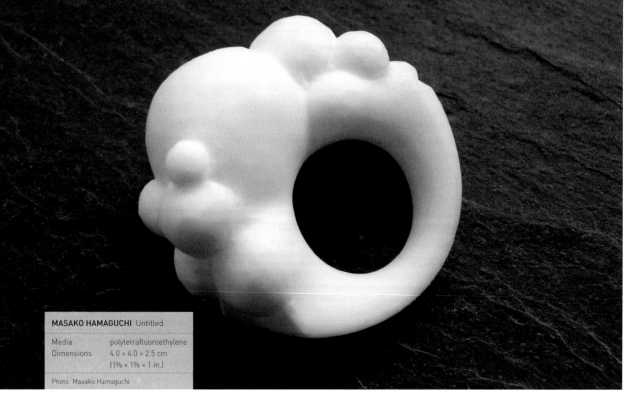

MASAKO HAMAGUCHI Untitled

Media	polytetrafluoroethylene
Dimensions	4.0 × 4.0 × 2.5 cm
	(1⅝ × 1⅝ × 1 in.)

Photo: Masako Hamaguchi

SIM LUTTIN
Stripped Naked

Media	silver, patina
Dimensions	3.8 × 3.8 × 1.0 cm
	(1½ × 1½ × ⅜ in.)

Photo: Kevin Montague

MELINDA RISK
Goodbye to the Sadness

Media	22ct gold, 18ct gold,
	925 silver, copper,
	aquamarine, diamonds
Dimensions	2.8 × 2.5 × 2.3 cm
	(1⅛ × 1 × ⅞ in.)

Photo: Melinda Risk

TANIA SKLYAR
Untitled

Media	silver
Dimensions	4.5 × 3.0 cm
	(1¾ × 1⅛ in.)

Photo: Dimitri Kireev

ROB JACKSON Orbital

Media	18ct gold, iron, steel, black diamond, uncut diamond
Dimensions	4.1 × 2.6 × 2.6 cm (1⅝ × 1 × 1 in.)

Photo: Rob Jackson

GLORIA GASTALDI
Marbles

Media	925 silver, patina, beads
Dimensions	2.6 × 2.0 × 1.3 cm (1 × ¾ × ½ in.)

Photo: Andrea Vaggione

ROB JACKSON Chanterelle

Media	18ct gold, iron, steel, ruby
Dimensions	3.0 × 2.2 × 2.2 cm (1⅛ × ⅞ × ⅞ in.)

Photo: Rob Jackson

GLORIA GASTALDI
Mobile

Media	925 silver, methacrylate
Dimensions	2.8 × 2.0 cm (1⅛ × ¾ in.)

Photo: Andrea Vaggione

TERRY WARE
Coral Finger Ring

Media	18ct yellow gold,
	925 silver, coral
Dimensions	3.0 × 2.5 × 1.9 cm
	(1⅛ × 1 × ¾ in.)

Photo: CarinKrasner.com

**ROBERTA FERREIRA &
LAURA JENER**
Vasij 8

Media	silver, raku ceramic,
	patina
Dimensions	1.9 × 1.9 × 1.6 cm
	(¾ × ¾ × ⅝ in.)

Photo: Ernest Brugué & Ricard Gabaldà

SHU-PING (JOANNE) HUANG
Build Ring

| Media | silver, PVC, cotton thread |
| Dimensions | 7.5 × 6.0 cm (3 × 2⅜ in.) |

Photo: Federico Cavicchioli

MANUELA URIBE PIEDRAHÍTA
Amethyst Druse

Media &	925 silver, amethyst, 3.4 ×
Dimensions	2.8 × 1.2 cm (1⅜ × 1⅛ × ½ in.)

Photo: Daniela Peters

LENKA TRUBAČOVÁ Ice Queen

Media	14ct white gold,
	Tahitian pearl
Dimensions	3.1 × 3.1 × 3.0 cm
	(1¼ × 1¼ × 1⅛ in.)

Photo: Vlastimil Bartas

MARIELLE DEBETHUNE
Ressentir (Feeling)

Media	silver, patina
Dimensions	1.5 × 1.5 cm (⅝ × ⅝ in.)

Photo: Marielle Debethune

MARIELLE DEBETHUNE
Ring with Screw Mount

Media	silver, patina, steel, quartz
Dimensions	3.0 × 1.5 cm (1⅛ × ⅝ in.)

Photo: Marielle Debethune

JAN KERKSTRA &
MARION PANNEKOEK
Sunset Boulevard

Media	silver, quartz, patina
Dimensions	2.0 × 1.6 cm
	(¾ × ⅝ in.)

Photo: Jan Kerkstra

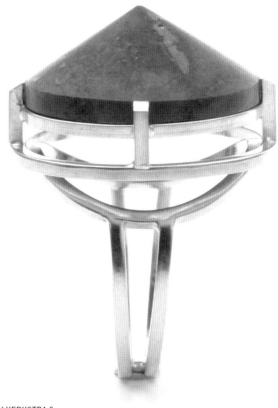

JAN KERKSTRA &
MARION PANNEKOEK
Blue World

Media	14ct gold, lapis lazuli
Dimensions	2.0 cm (¾ in.)

Photo: Jan Kerkstra

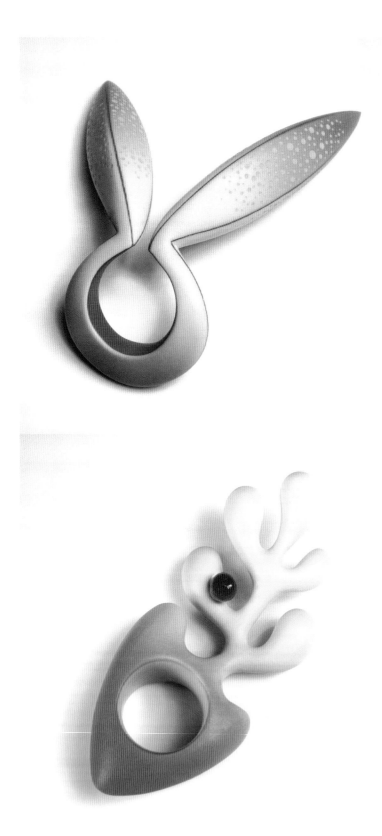

JEFFREY LLOYD DEVER
Convergence

Media	polymer clay, steel
Dimensions	7.6 × 7 × 2.5 cm
	(3 × 2¾ × 1 in.)

Photo: Gregory R. Staley

JEFFREY LLOYD DEVER
Matisse Revisited

Media	polymer clay, reclaimed
	glass bead, steel
Dimensions	8.9 × 3.8 × 0.7 cm
	(3½ × 1½ × ¼ in.)

Photo: Gregory R. Staley

POLLY HORWICH
60 Rings

Media	iron, plastic
Dimensions	various sizes

Photo: Polly Horwich

THEO SMEETS Danzig Potato

Media	amber, gold, plastic
Dimensions	8.2 × 3.2 × 2.2 cm
	(3¼ × 1¼ × ⅞ in.)

Photo: Manu Ocaña

HELEN BRITTON Untitled

Media	silver, sapphires, diamonds
Dimensions	various sizes

Photo: Dirk Eisel

VIKTORIA MÜNZKER
Phialina

Media	wood, metal granules, agate, bronze
Dimensions	5.5 × 3.5 × 1.5 cm (2⅛ × 1⅜ × ⅝ in.)

Photo: Viktoria Münzker

LITO
Untitled

Media	gold, aquamarine, Tahitian pearl
Dimensions	3.2 × 2.9 × 2.0 cm (1¼ × 1⅛ × ¾ in.)

Photo: Kostas Satlanis

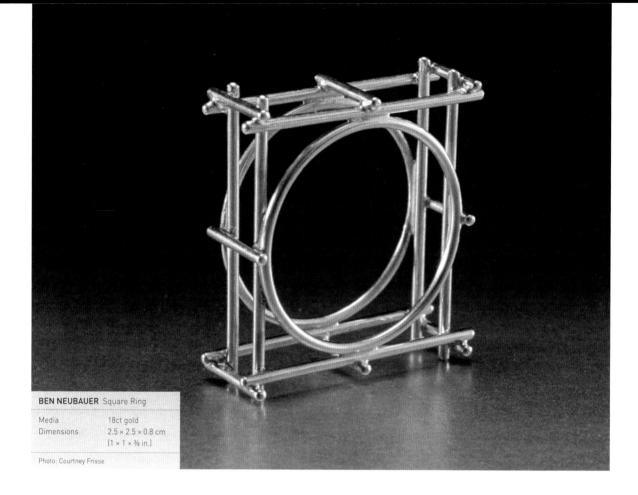

BEN NEUBAUER Square Ring

Media	18ct gold
Dimensions	2.5 × 2.5 × 0.8 cm
	(1 × 1 × ⅜ in.)

Photo: Courtney Frisse

AUGOUSTA THEMISTOCLEOUS
Untitled 5

Media	925 silver, industrial
	heatproof fibre
Dimensions	4.0 × 4.0 × 3.0 cm
	(1⅝ × 1⅝ × 1⅛ in.)

Photo: Constantinos Kyriacou

DAVID FOWKES
Citrine Ring

Media	gold, citrine
Dimensions	4.0 × 3.0 × 2.5 cm
	(1⅝ × 1⅛ × 1 in.)

Photo: Keith Leighton

DAVID FOWKES
Tourmaline Ring

Media	gold, tourmaline,
	diamonds
Dimensions	8.0 × 3.0 × 2.8 cm
	(3⅛ × 1⅛ × 1⅛ in.)

Photo: Keith Leighton

DIAN YU Statement Ring

Media	brass, glue, resin, prehnite, gold foil, paint
Dimensions	2.5 × 2 × 1.5 cm each
	(1 × ¾ × ⅝ in.)

Photo: Grond Fu

CARME FÀBREGAS BARTOK
Knight

Media	silver, patina
Dimensions	3.3 × 2.9 cm (1¼ × 1⅛ in.)

Photo: Carme Fàbregas Bartok

ISABEL MIR Construction

Media	18ct gold, 925 silver, patina
Dimensions	4.1 × 3.1 cm (1⅝ × 1¼ in.)

Photo: Isabel Mir

PETER HOOGEBOOM
Cup Ring

Media	ceramic
Dimensions	3.5 × 2.5 × 2.0 cm
	(1⅜ × 1 × ¾ in.)

Photo: Henni van Beek

EWA DOERENKAMP
Transition

Media	silver, patina
Dimensions	2.2 × 1.5 cm (⅞ × ⅝ in.)

Photo: Ewa Doerenkamp

SELDA OKUTAN
Rectangle Ring

Media	gold, silver, topaz
Dimensions	3.7 × 2.1 × 1.0 cm
	(1½ × ¾ × ⅜ in.)

Photo: Mehmet Arda

JOANNE HAYWOOD
Tree Ring

| Media | silver, textile elements, patina |
| Dimensions | 7.0 × 1.5 × 1.5 cm (2¾ × ⅝ × ⅝ in.) |

Photo: Rory Moore

GABI VEIT
Findling

| Media | aluminium |
| Dimensions | 3.5 × 2.2 cm (1⅜ × ⅞ in.) |

Photo: Federico Cavicchioli

EXPRESSION

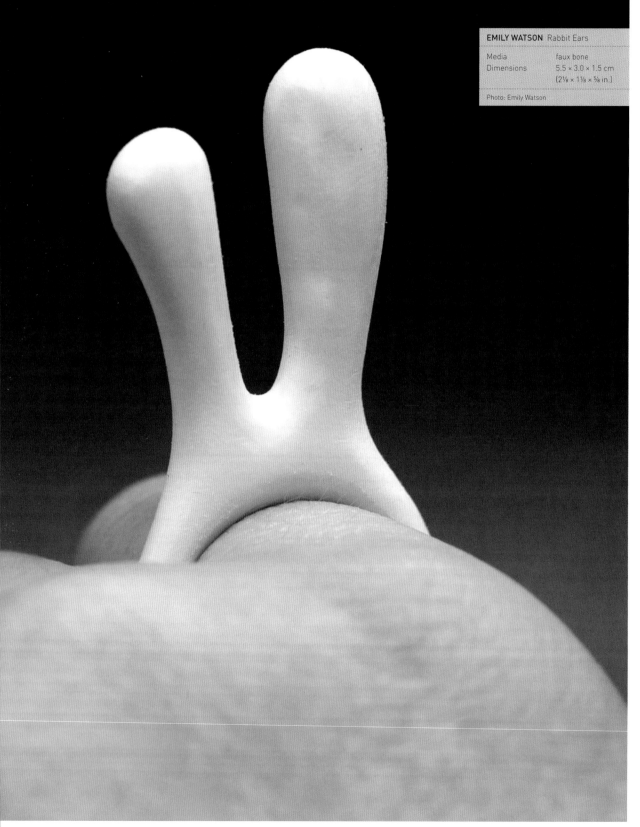

MEIRI ISHIDA
Bunny

Media   felt, resin
Dimensions   4.0 × 2.8 × 2.0 cm
              (1⅝ × 1⅛ × ¾ in.)

Photo: Meiri Ishida

MEIRI ISHIDA
Honey

Media   felt, resin
Dimensions   7.6 × 5.0 × 2.0 cm
              (3 × 2 × ¾ in.)

Photo: Meiri Ishida

MEIRI ISHIDA
Teddy

Media   felt, resin
Dimensions   5.0 × 3.0 × 2.0 cm
              (2 × 1⅛ × ¾ in.)

Photo: Meiri Ishida

MEL MILLER
Remember When

Media   925 silver, copper,
             enamel, textile
Dimensions   9.0 × 8.0 × 5.0 cm
             (3½ × 3⅛ × 2 in.)

Photo: Jeremy Dillon

PAMELA RITCHIE
Fickle Spring

Media   925 silver, plastic
Dimensions   4.1 × 2.8 × 2.8 cm
             (1⅝ × 1⅛ × 1⅛ in.)

Photo: Pamela Ritchie

SHU-PING (JOANNE) HUANG
Ring with Holes

Media   silver, rubber sponge
Dimensions   5.0 × 3.0 cm
                 (2 × 1⅛ in.)

Photo: Federico Cavicchioli

SOYEON KIM Tropicanas

Media   plastic pull tabs, leather,
                 glass, cotton
Dimensions   5.0 × 2.5 × 1.0 cm
                 (2 × 1 × ⅜ in.)

Photo: Soyeon Kim

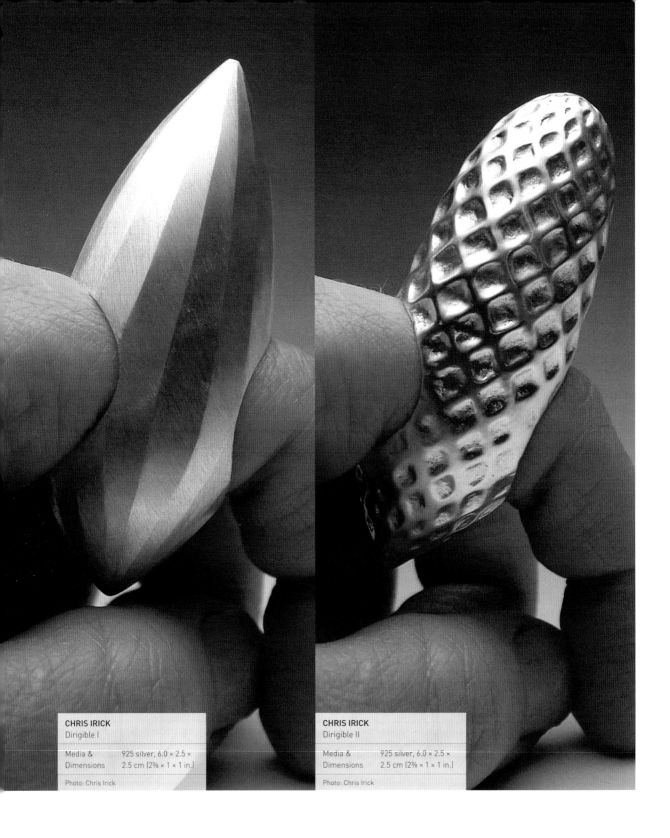

CHRIS IRICK
Dirigible I

| Media & Dimensions | 925 silver, 6.0 × 2.5 × 2.5 cm (2⅜ × 1 × 1 in.) |

Photo: Chris Irick

CHRIS IRICK
Dirigible II

| Media & Dimensions | 925 silver, 6.0 × 2.5 × 2.5 cm (2⅜ × 1 × 1 in.) |

Photo: Chris Irick

MARI ISHIKAWA Moonlight Shadow

Media	925 silver, Tahitian pearls
Dimensions	7.5 × 5.0 × 3.5 cm
	(3 × 2 × 1⅜ in.)

Photo: Frank Vetter

MARI ISHIKAWA Moonlight Shadow

Media	18ct gold, 925 silver
Dimensions	8.0 × 6.5 × 4.0 cm
	(3⅛ × 2½ × 1⅝ in.)

Photo: Frank Vetter

ELVIRA H. MATEU
Round Cactus

| Media & | silver, wood, textile, 5.0 × |
| Dimensions | 3.5 × 2.5 cm (2 × 1⅜ × 1 in.) |

Photo: Elvira H. Mateu

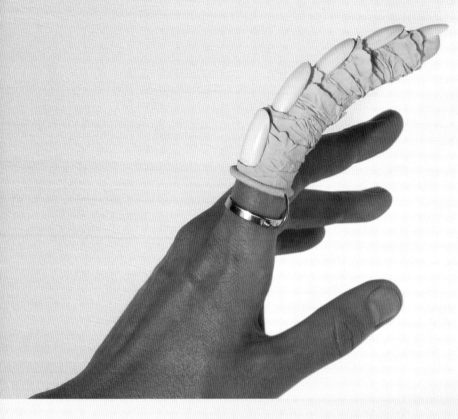

MI-MI MOSCOW Regeneration

Media	nickel silver, paper, artificial nail, paint
Dimensions	9.2 × 2.8 cm (3⅝ × 1⅛ in.)

Photo: mi-mi moscow

MI-MI MOSCOW Fire-Aquarius

Media	nickel silver, paper, artificial nail, paint
Dimensions	12.6 × 11.5 cm (5 × 4½ in.)

Photo: mi-mi moscow

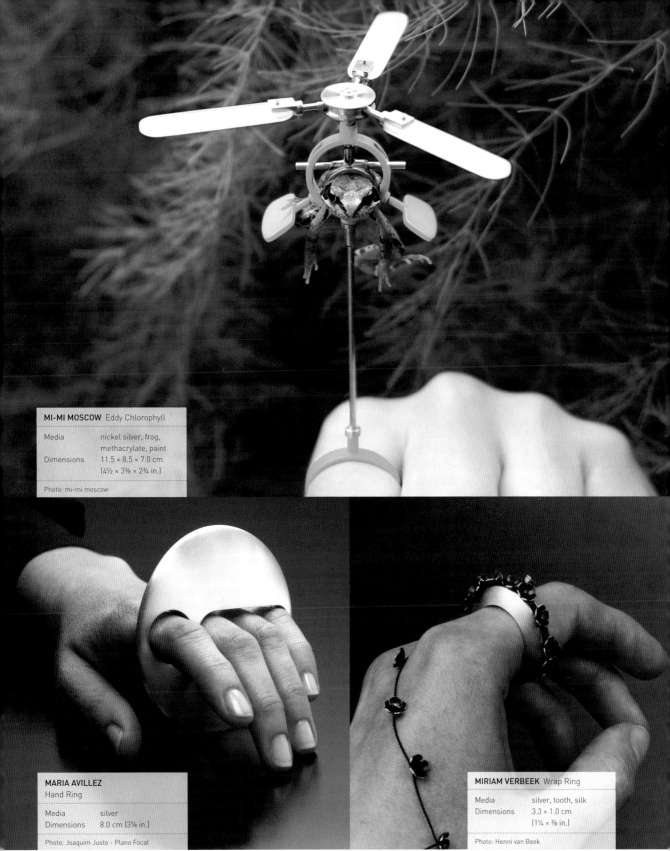

MI-MI MOSCOW Eddy Chlorophyll

Media	nickel silver, frog, methacrylate, paint
Dimensions	11.5 × 8.5 × 7.0 cm (4½ × 3⅜ × 2¾ in.)

Photo: mi-mi moscow

MARIA AVILLEZ
Hand Ring

Media	silver
Dimensions	8.0 cm (3⅛ in.)

Photo: Joaquim Justo - Plano Focal

MIRIAM VERBEEK Wrap Ring

Media	silver, tooth, silk
Dimensions	3.3 × 1.0 cm (1¼ × ⅜ in.)

Photo: Henni van Beek

STEFANIA LUCCHETTA
Crystal 32

Media	stellite
Dimensions	5.0 × 4.0 cm (2 × 1⅝ in.)

Photo: Fabio Zonta

STEFANIA LUCCHETTA
Digital 65

Media	white gold, stellite, diamond
Dimensions	5.0 × 4.0 cm (2 × 1⅝ in.)

Photo: Stefania Lucchetta

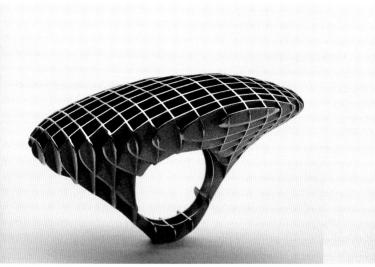
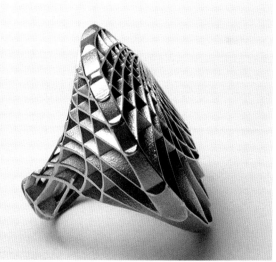

STEFANIA LUCCHETTA
Sponge 25

Media	biocompatible resin, diamonds
Dimensions	4.5 × 4.0 cm (1¾ × 1⅝ in.)

Photo: Fabio Zonta

STEFANIA LUCCHETTA
Crystal 11

Media	biocompatible resin
Dimensions	4.5 × 4.0 cm (1¾ × 1⅝ in.)

Photo: Fabio Zonta

MELISSA BORRELL
Three in One Ring

Media	gold, silver
Dimensions	4.0 × 4.0 × 3.0 cm
	(1⅝ × 1⅝ × 1⅛ in.)

Photo: Marty Doyle

MELISSA BORRELL
Folded Flocked Ring

Media	silver, flock, patina
Dimensions	4.5 × 4.2 × 3.0 cm
	(1¾ × 1⅝ × 1⅛ in.)

Photo: Marty Doyle

MELISSA BORRELL
Open Square Ring

Media	silver
Dimensions	4.0 × 4.0 × 3.5 cm
	(1⅝ × 1⅝ × 1⅜ in.)

Photo: Marty Doyle

NILS SCHMALENBACH
Space 5

Media	925 silver
Dimensions	2.2 × 2.2 cm (⅞ × ⅞ in.)

Photo: Nils Schmalenbach

NILS SCHMALENBACH
Space 4

Media	18ct gold
Dimensions	3.4 × 1.8 cm (1⅜ × ¾ in.)

Photo: Nils Schmalenbach

NILS SCHMALENBACH
Spaces

Photo: Nils Schmalenbach

TING-CHUN ARA KUO
Bird

Media	925 silver, pearls, polymethacrylate
Dimensions	7.0 × 7.0 × 4.0 cm (2¾ × 2¾ × 1⅝ in.)

Photo: Federico Cavicchioli

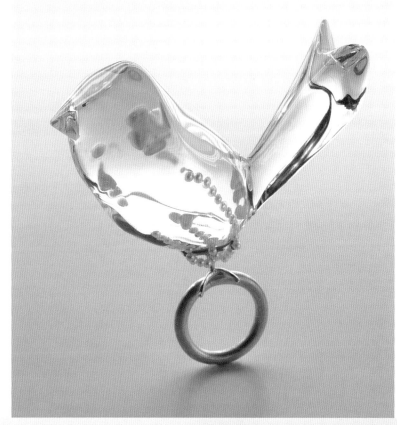

TOM FERRERO
New Zealand Journal Rings

Media	925 silver, resin, various found objects from New Zealand
Dimensions	4.0 × 3.0 × 3.0 cm (1⅝ × 1⅛ × 1⅛ in.)

Photo: Kevin Montague

ROC MAJORAL & ABRIL RIBERA
Flô

Media	yellow gold, black diamonds
Dimensions	3.3 cm (1¼ in.)

Photo: Archivo Majoral

ROC MAJORAL & ABRIL RIBERA
Pop

Media	yellow gold, white gold, diamonds
Dimensions	5.0 × 2.0 cm (2 × ¾ in.)

Photo: Archivo Majoral

STEPHANIE JENDIS On Earth

Media	silver, uvarovite, reconstructed onyx
Dimensions	5.0 × 3.5 × 3.0 cm (2 × 1³/₈ × 1¹/₈ in.)

Photo: Tivadar Nemesi

PHILIP SAJET Red Shard Ring

Media	silver, niello, crystal
Dimensions	4.0 × 2.3 × 1.1 cm (1⁵/₈ × ⁷/₈ × ³/₈ in.)

Photo: Beate Klockmann

JILLIAN MOORE Nugget Rings

Media	copper, polymer clay, plastic, epoxy resin, paint
Dimensions	3.4 × 3.2 × 3.2 cm (1³/₈ × 1¹/₄ × 1¹/₄ in.)

Photo: Jillian Moore

ARATA FUCHI Hiding Lust 3

Media	24ct gold, silver, silver dust, patina
Dimensions	6.5 × 4.0 × 3.7 cm (2½ × 1⅝ × 1½ in.)

Photo: Ichiro Usuda

ARATA FUCHI XX

Media	24ct gold, silver, silver dust, patina
Dimensions	3.6 × 3.1 × 2.9 cm (1⅜ × 1¼ × 1⅛ in.)

Photo: Ichiro Usuda

BARBARA CHRISTIE The Kiss

Media	18ct yellow gold, mandarin garnet, fire opal
Dimensions	2.2 × 1.4 × 3.4 cm (⁷⁄₈ × ½ × 1³⁄₈ in.)

Photo: Graeme Harris

BARBARA CHRISTIE Ridges

Media & Dimensions	18ct white gold, clear pink diamond, aquamarine, 2.0 × 2.6 × 3.8 cm (¾ × 1 × 1½ in.)

Photo: Graeme Harris

ROC MAJORAL & ABRIL RIBERA
Untitled

Media	yellow gold, citrine
Dimensions	2.0 × 2.0 cm (¾ × ¾ in.)

Photo: Archivo Majoral

BARBARA STUTMAN Ring Ring 2

Media	copper wire
Dimensions	5.2 × 5.0 × 2.4 cm
	(2 × 2 × 1 in.)

Photo: Anthony McLean

BARBARA STUTMAN Ring Ring 4

Media	copper wire
Dimensions	7.6 × 5.8 × 0.8 cm
	(3 × 2¼ × ⅜ in.)

Photo: Anthony McLean

FRANCESCA VITALI
Sunflower

Media	glass beads, paper
Dimensions	4.0 × 4.0 × 2.0 cm
	(1⅝ × 1⅝ × ¾ in.)

Photo: Francesca Vitali

MARINA MASSONE Beehive Rings

Media   silver, patina
Dimensions   5.0 × 5.0 × 3.0 cm
              (2 × 2 × 1⅛ in.)

Photos: Marina Massone

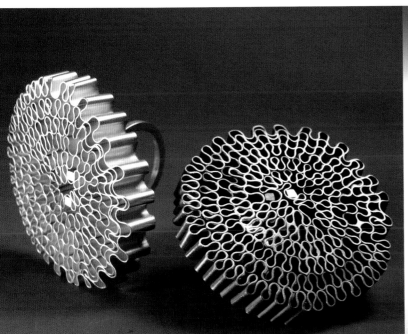

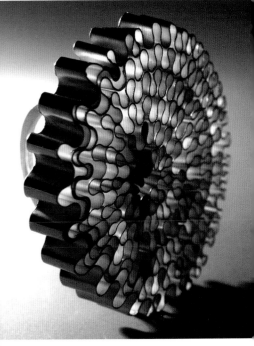

KARIM OUKID
Olympia

Media   silver, enamel, coral
Dimensions   3.0 × 2.8 × 2.8 cm
              (1⅛ × 1⅛ × 1⅛ in.)

Photo: Pau Esculies

DANIEL DICAPRIO
Orifice Ring 5

Media   22ct gold, blackwood
Dimensions   2.5 × 2.5 × 5.1 cm
             (1 × 1 × 2 in.)

Photo: Daniel DiCaprio

DANIEL DICAPRIO
Orifice Ring 3

Media   22ct gold, blackwood
Dimensions   3.8 × 3.8 × 3.8 cm
             (1½ × 1½ × 1½ in.)

Photo: Daniel DiCaprio

JACQUELINE CULLEN
Hand-Carved Ring with 18ct Gold
Granulation

Media	18ct gold, Whitby jet
Dimensions	4.0 cm (1⅝ in.)

Photo: The Goldsmiths' Company

JACQUELINE CULLEN
Hand-Carved Ring with Inlaid
Fine Gold

Media	18ct gold, Whitby jet
Dimensions	4.0 cm (1⅝ in.)

Photo: Nick Turner

CECILIA RICHARD Asomador IX
(Something that Pokes Out IX)

Media	18ct gold, silver, patina
Dimensions	3.0 cm (1⅛ in.) in diameter

Photo: Facundo Di Pascuale

ANGELO VERGA
Sintered Nature 2

Media	mokume gane steel, wood, enamel
Dimensions	6.0 × 5.0 cm (2⅜ × 2 in.)

Photo: Giuseppe Bisceglia

ANGELO VERGA
Sintered Nature 7

Media	mokume gane steel, wood, enamel
Dimensions	6.0 × 5.0 cm (2⅜ × 2 in.)

Photo: Giuseppe Bisceglia

ANGELO VERGA
Sintered Nature 4

Media	mokume gane steel, wood, enamel
Dimensions	6.0 × 5.0 cm (2⅜ × 2 in.)

Photo: Giuseppe Bisceglia

ANGELO VERGA
Sintered Nature 5

Media	mokume gane steel, wood, enamel
Dimensions	6.0 × 5.0 cm (2⅜ × 2 in.)

Photo: Giuseppe Bisceglia

BRONWYNN LUSTED
Riverwood Leaf

Media   salvaged river wood
Dimensions   6.0 × 4.0 × 3.0 cm
               (2⅜ × 1⅝ × 1⅛ in.)

Photo: Bronwynn Lusted

BRONWYNN LUSTED
Riverwood Swirl

Media   salvaged river wood
Dimensions   6.0 × 4.0 × 3.0 cm
               (2⅜ × 1⅝ × 1⅛ in.)

Photo: Bronwynn Lusted

BRONWYNN LUSTED
Cocobolo Twist

Media   cocobolo wood
Dimensions   4.0 × 2.5 × 2.0 cm
               (1⅝ × 1 × ¾ in.)

Photo: Bronwynn Lusted

BARBARA HEINRICH
Dogwood Ring

Media   18ct gold, diamonds
Dimensions   5.0 × 3.2 cm (2 × 1¼ in.)

Photo: Hap Sakwa

LENKA TRUBAČOVÁ
Diploria Blok

Media   925 silver
Dimensions   2.5 × 2.2 × 0.8 cm
             (1 × ⅞ × ⅜ in.)

Photo: Vlastimil Bartas

LULU TEHILA FEINSILVER
Sira

Media	925 silver
Dimensions	6.8 × 4.1 cm (2⅝ × 1⅝ in.)

Photo: Lulu Tehila Feinsilver

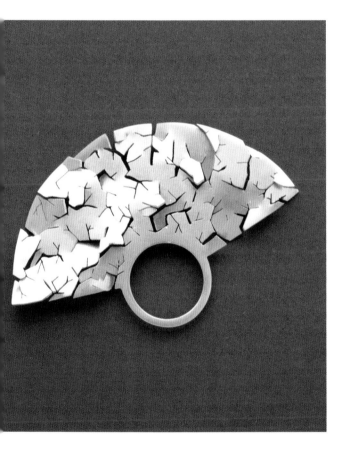

MARILÈNE MORENCY
Untitled

Media	925 silver
Dimensions	2.0 × 2.0 × 2.0 cm (¾ × ¾ × ¾ in.)

Photo: Marilène Morency

MARILÈNE MORENCY Untitled

Media	925 silver
Dimensions	2.0 × 2.0 × 2.0 cm (¾ × ¾ × ¾ in.)

Photo: Marilène Morency

NANCY NEWBERG
Rectangle Web Ring

Media   silver, diamonds
Dimensions   3.7 × 1.0 × 1.0 cm
               (1½ × ⅜ × ⅜ in.)

Photo: Justin Diamond

NANCY NEWBERG
Various

Media   gold, silver, diamonds
Dimensions   various sizes

Photo: Peggy Wong

NANCY NEWBERG
Untitled

Media   silver, diamonds, pearls
Dimensions   4.2 × 1.8 × 1.8 cm
               (1⅝ × ¾ × ¾ in.)

Photo: STK Photography

CLAUDIO PINO
Oceanid, Nymphe de la Mer

Media	platinum, 18k gold, Tahitian pearl, amethyst, prehnite
Dimensions	2.0 × 4.0 × 1.5 cm (¾ × 1⅝ × ⅝ in.)

Photo: Claudio Pino

CLAUDIO PINO
The Kym Double Ring

Media	platinum, gold, tanzanites, diamonds, Tahitian pearl
Dimensions	5.0 × 3.5 × 1.5 cm (2 × 1⅜ × ⅝ in.)

Photo: Claudio Pino

ALIDRA ALIĆ Iris

Media	925 silver, plastic
Dimensions	10.0 × 10.0 cm (3⅞ × 3⅞ in.)

Photo: Dorte Krogh

BABETTE VON DOHNANYI
Imagination

Media	silver with 3D printed corn starch
Dimensions	6.5 × 5.0 × 5.0 cm (2½ × 2 × 2 in.)

Photo: Federico Cavicchioli

ALINA LÓPEZ
Flowing

Media	silver, copper, enamel, patina
Dimensions	3.4 × 1.5 cm (1⅜ × ⅝ in.)

Photo: Julio César Gómez

ANA CHECA
Manzana (Apple)

Media	925 silver, crystal
Dimensions	2.5 × 2.5 cm (1 × 1 in.)

Photo: Ramón Outon

EDITH BRABATA Apples

Media	925 silver, rhodium, coral
Dimensions	4.0 × 2.7 × 2.7 cm (1⅝ × 1 × 1 in.)

Photo: Pablo Fernández de Valle

CÉDRIC CHEVALLEY
Life

Media	silver, crystal, enamel, soil
Dimensions	4.2 × 3.1 cm (1⅝ × 1¼ in.)

Photo: Cbijoux

TITHI KUTCHAMUCH Vase Garden

Media	silver, glass
Dimensions	24 cm × 13 cm × 13 cm
	(9½ × 5⅛ × 5⅛ in.)

Photo: Petr Krejci

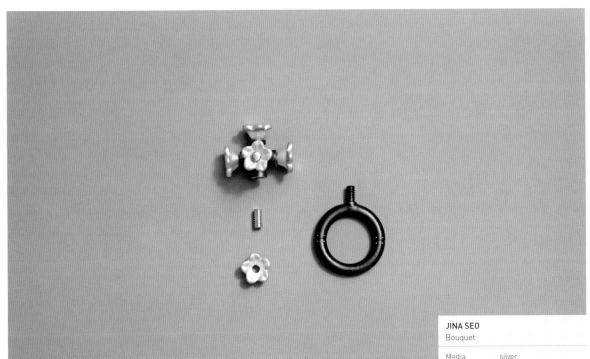

JINA SEO
Bouquet

Media	silver
Dimensions	12.7 × 3.8 × 2.5 cm
	(5 × 1½ × 1 in.)

Photo: Jung-Soo Park

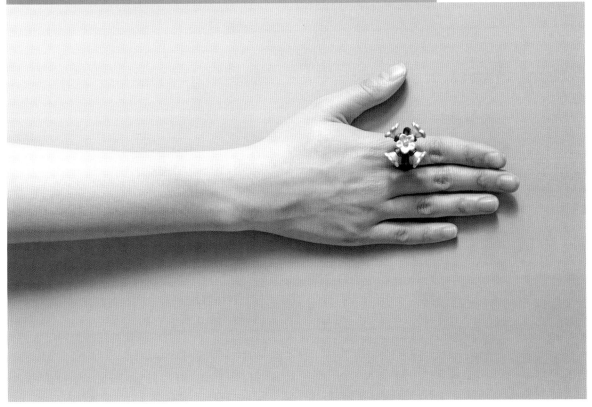

MARJORIE SIMON
Clover/Tangerine

Media	22ct gold, 925 silver, copper, enamel
Dimensions	3.0 cm (1⅛ in.)

Photo: Ken Yanoviak

CARACTÈRE (GEMA BARRERA & PASCAL CRETIN) Ellipse

Media	silver, lacquer
Dimensions	3.2 × 2.7 × 2.3 cm (1¼ × 1 × ⅞ in.)

Photo: Caractère

MARJORIE SIMON
Marigold

Media	22ct gold, 925 silver, copper, enamel
Dimensions	3.0 cm (1⅛ in.)

Photo: Ken Yanoviak

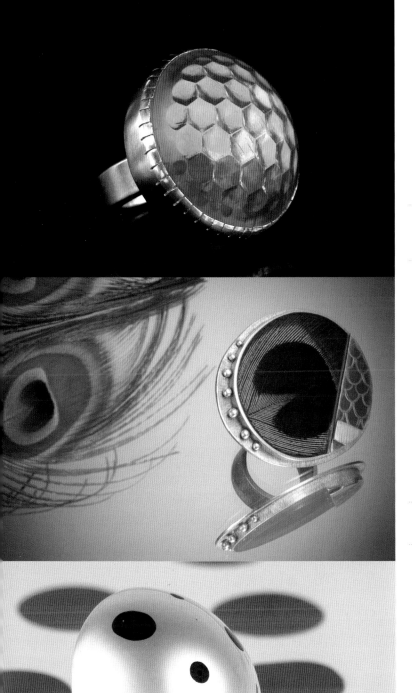

JENNY WINDLER
Reflecto-Dome

| Media | 925 silver, vintage bike reflector, glass beads |
| Dimensions | 2.5 × 2.5 × 2.5 cm (1 × 1 × 1 in.) |

Photo: Jenny Windler

ISABEL MIR
Peacock

| Media | 925 silver, peacock feather, resin |
| Dimensions | 3.0 × 2.8 cm (1⅛ × 1⅛ in.) |

Photo: Isabel Mir

JUANA ORTIZ
Toadstool Ring

| Media | 950 silver, polyester resin |
| Dimensions | 3.4 × 2.5 cm (1⅜ × 1 in.) |

Photo: Juan Carlos Rendón

KARIN SEUFERT
Untitled

Media	22ct gold
Dimensions	2.8 × 2.8 cm (1⅛ × 1⅛ in.)

Photo: Karin Seufert

LEE HYE RAN
Farfalle

Media	brass, gold plated
Dimensions	3.0 × 2.7 cm (1⅛ × 1 in.)

Photo: Studio

TOBY COTTERILL
Unwrapped Explosion

Media	925 silver, 24ct gold foil
	3.0 × 3.0 × 0.6 cm
Dimensions	(1⅛ × 1⅛ × ¼ in.)

Photo: Toby Cotterill

COLLEEN BARAN
Cloud Ring

Media	925 silver
Dimensions	4.7 × 3.6 × 2.5 cm
	(1⅞ × 1⅜ × 1 in.)

Photo: Colleen Baran

SOFIA BJÖRKMAN Ring

Media	silver
Dimensions	9.0 × 7.0 × 3.0 cm
	(3½ × 2¾ × 1⅛ in.)

Photo: Sofia Björkman

SOFIA BJÖRKMAN Ring

Media	gold
Dimensions	6.0 × 5.0 × 4.0 cm
	(2⅜ × 2 × 1⅝ in.)

Photo: Sofia Björkman

SOFIA BJÖRKMAN Ring

Media	wood
Dimensions	11.0 × 4.0 × 2.0 cm
	(4⅜ × 1⅝ × ¾ in.)

Photo: Sofia Björkman

MARIE MARCANO Osteoporosis

Media   bone
Dimensions 4.0 × 2.5 × 2.0 cm
            (1⅝ × 1 × ¾ in.)

Photo: Marie Marcano

ELS VANSTEELANDT
Eleonora

Media	925 silver
Dimensions	4.4 × 2.7 × 2.7 cm
	(1¾ × 1 × 1 in.)

Photo: Els Vansteelandt

ELS VANSTEELANDT
Let's Fly

Media	22ct gold
Dimensions	3.8 × 2.5 × 2.5 cm
	(1½ × 1 × 1 in.)

Photo: Els Vansteelandt

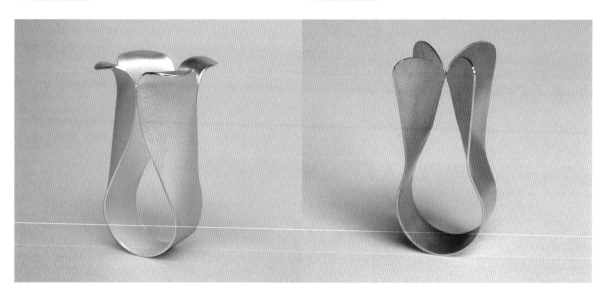

TOMOYO HIRAIWA Peace Wave

Media	950 silver, patina
Dimensions	5.0 × 4.5 × 3.8 cm
	(2 × 1¾ × 1½ in.)

Photo: Yoshitaka Uchida

TOMOYO HIRAIWA Peace Wave

Media	950 silver
Dimensions	4.5 × 3.8 × 3.3 cm
	(1¾ × 1½ × 1¼ in.)

Photo: Yoshitaka Uchida

EMILY CULVER
Membrane Ring

Media   photopolymers, silver,
             bronze
Dimensions   4.5 × 3.8 × 3.8 cm
             (1¾ × 1½ × 1½ in.)

Photo: Emily Culver

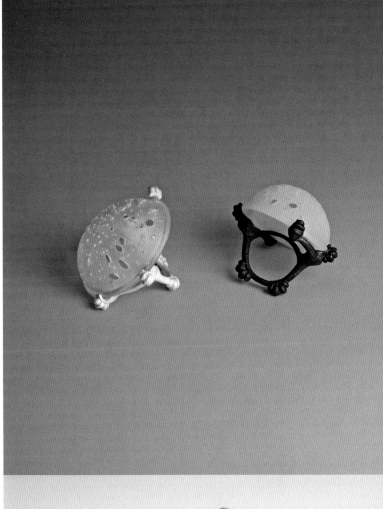

SARAH DE GASPERIS
Untitled

Media   925 silver, pearls, zircon
Dimensions   2.8 × 2.3 × 0.9 cm
             (1⅛ × ⅞ × ⅜ in.)

Photo: Jonás Manzanares

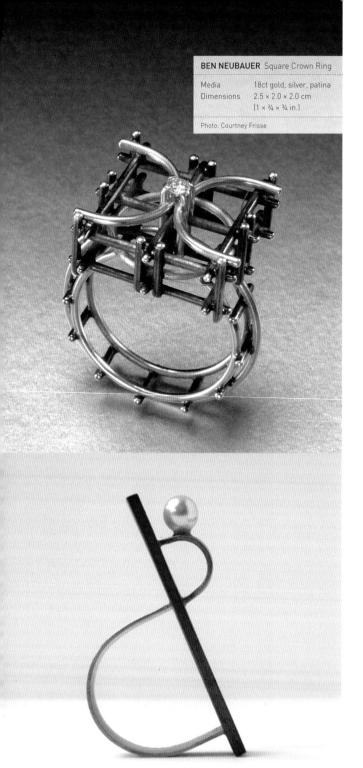

BEN NEUBAUER Square Crown Ring

Media	18ct gold, silver, patina
Dimensions	2.5 × 2.0 × 2.0 cm
	(1 × ¾ × ¾ in.)

Photo: Courtney Frisse

ROBEAN VISSCHERS
Untitled

Media	silver, copper, pearl
Dimensions	4.0 × 4.0 × 2.9 cm
	(1⅝ × 1⅝ × 1⅛ in.)

Photo: Brutesque

BLANDINE LUCE
Bridge Ring

Media	silver, copper, pearl
Dimensions	4.0 × 2.5 cm (1⅝ × 1 in.)

Photo: Imagitram

ROBERTO CARRASCOSA
Marks in the Water I

Media	silver, coral, citrines, vintage earring
Dimensions	4.0 cm (1⅝ in.)

Photo: Pere Peris

SEBASTIAN BECK
Frog

Media	silver, rhodium, jasper, tourmaline
Dimensions	2.6 × 2.5 cm (1 × 1 in.)

Photo: Sebastian Beck

ROBERTO CARRASCOSA
Barroc&Roll I

Media	silver
Dimensions	3.0 cm (1⅛ in.)

Photo: Roberto Salmó

YAEL KRAKOWSKI
Flower Ring #1

Media	925 silver, glass beads, thread
Dimensions	7.5 × 7.5 × 5.0 cm (3 × 3 × 2 in.)

Photo: Yael Krakowski

YAEL KRAKOWSKI
Flower Ring #9

Media	925 silver, glass beads, thread
Dimensions	7.5 × 7.5 × 7.0 cm (3 × 3 × 2¾ in.)

Photo: Yael Krakowski

RAMÓN PUIG CUYÀS Utopos

Media	silver, quartz, paper, resin
Dimensions	3.0 × 2.5 cm (1⅛ × 1 in.)

Photo: Ramón Puig Cuyàs

RAMÓN PUIG CUYÀS Cap de Creus

Media	silver, quartz, paper, resin
Dimensions	3.0 × 2.5 cm (1⅛ × 1 in.)

Photo: Ramón Puig Cuyàs

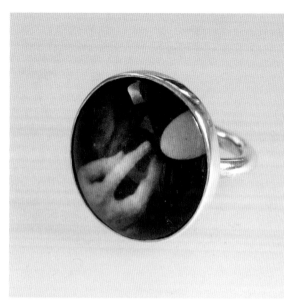

DRILLING LAB
Clamp Ring

Media   stainless steel
Dimensions   7.5 × 1.9 × 1.9 cm
             (3 × ¾ × ¾ in.)

Photo: Lu-Wei Chen

EDGAR MOSA
Untitled series

Media   wire, sourced materials
Dimensions   c. 5.0 × 2.0 × 2.0 cm
               (2 × ¾ × ¾ in.)

Photo: Joseph McShea

VICTOR SALDARRIAGA
Tropical Mountain Forest

Media   gold, silver
Dimensions   8.0 × 6.0 cm (3⅛ × 2⅜ in.)

Photo: Andrés Gómez

MOTOKO FURUHASHI
Never Get Bored

Media   silver, copper, steel,
               acrylic
Dimensions   5.5 × 5.5 × 4.0 cm
               (2⅛ × 2⅛ × 1⅝ in.)

Photo: Motoko Furuhashi

BIBA SCHUTZ
Doodling Ring

Media	silver
Dimensions	7.0 × 3.8 × 3.2 cm
	(2¾ × 1½ × 1¼ in.)

Photo: Ron Boszko

DIAN YU
Real or Fake Isn't the Problem 3

Media	brass, resin, gold foil
Dimensions	2.5 × 2.5 × 1.7 cm
	(1 × 1 × ⅝ in.)

Photo: Grond Fu

DIAN YU
Real or Fake Isn't the Problem 1

Media	brass, moonstone, quartz
Dimensions	2.5 × 2.0 × 1.5 cm
	(1 × ¾ × ⅝ in.)

Photo: Grond Fu

FEDERICA PALLAVER
Skiagraphia

Media	silver
Dimensions	2.0 × 2.0 × 1.8 cm
	(¾ × ¾ × ¾ in.)

Photo: Federica Pallaver

JENNACA LEIGH DAVIES
Folded Ring

Media	925 silver, paper
Dimensions	3.5 × 3.0 × 3.0 cm
	(1⅜ × 1⅛ × 1⅛ in.)

Photo: Katja Kulenkampff

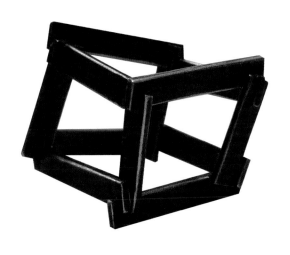

KENNETH C. MACBAIN Swoosh

Media	925 silver, dyed resin
Dimensions	8.5 × 3.0 × 1.7 cm
	(3⅜ × 1⅛ × ⅝ in.)

Photo: Kenneth C. MacBain

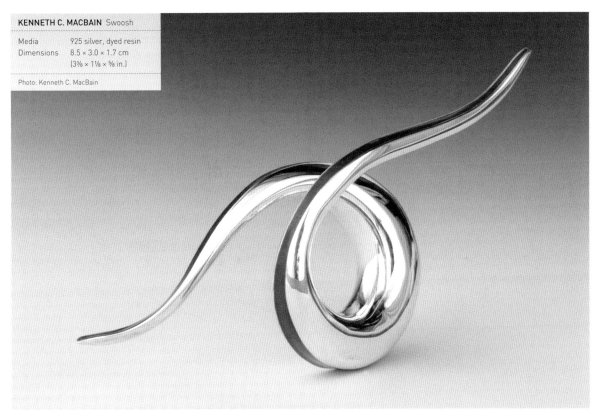

REBELLION

COLLEEN BARAN | I Miss You

Media	925 silver, rubber, ink
Dimensions	4.0 × 3.5 × 2.3 cm
	(1⅝ × 1⅜ × ⅞ in.)

Photo: Colleen Baran

I miss you the second you leave

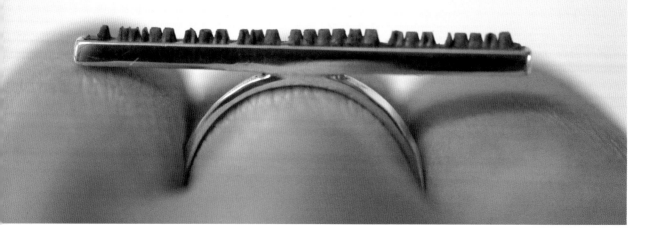

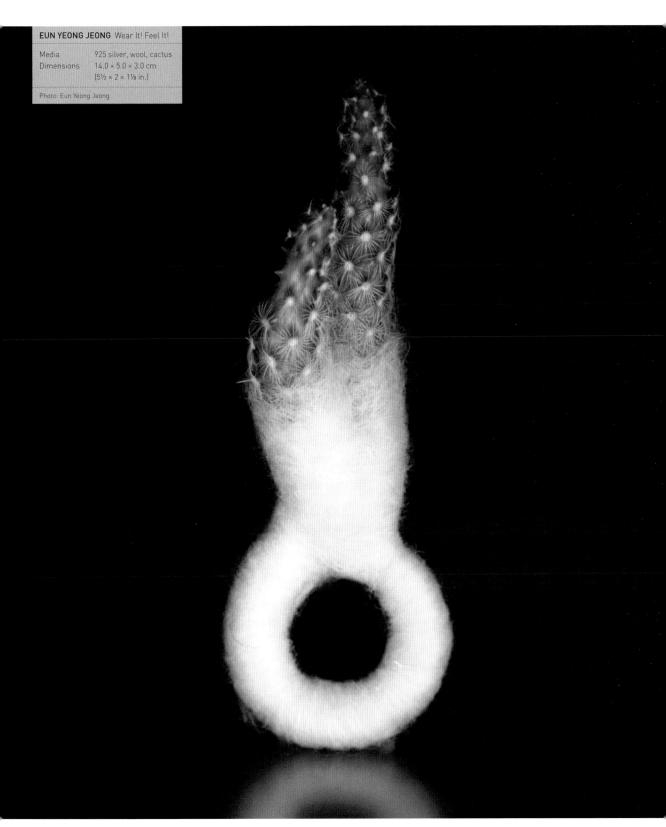

EUN YEONG JEONG Wear It! Feel It!

Media   925 silver, wool, cactus
Dimensions   14.0 × 5.0 × 3.0 cm
             (5½ × 2 × 1⅛ in.)

Photo: Eun Yeong Jeong

JIM COTTER
Ring with an Image

Media   925 silver, brass, wood,
               screws, zircon
Dimensions   5.1 × 4.4 × 3.2 cm
               (2 × 1¾ × 1¼ in.)

Photo: J. Cotter Studio

**BANDADA (ANA MARÍA RAMÍREZ
& ADRIANA DÍAZ)** Pyrite

Media   925 silver
Dimensions   3.1 × 2.0 × 1.0 cm
               (1¼ × ¾ × ⅜ in.)

Photo: Ana María Ramírez & Adriana Díaz

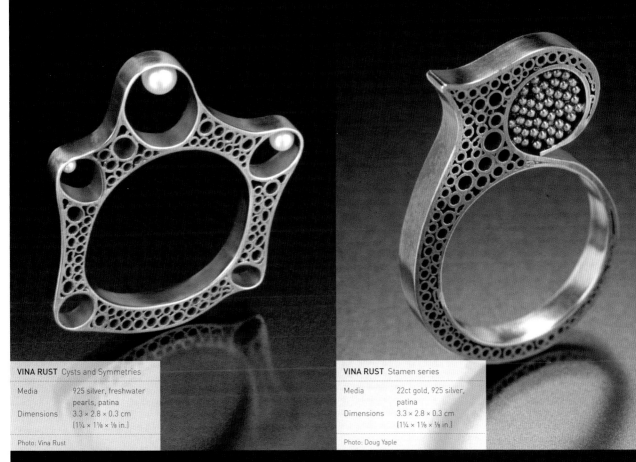

VINA RUST Cysts and Symmetries

Media	925 silver, freshwater pearls, patina
Dimensions	3.3 × 2.8 × 0.3 cm (1¼ × 1⅛ × ⅛ in.)
Photo: Vina Rust	

VINA RUST Stamen series

Media	22ct gold, 925 silver, patina
Dimensions	3.3 × 2.8 × 0.3 cm (1¼ × 1⅛ × ⅛ in.)
Photo: Doug Yaple	

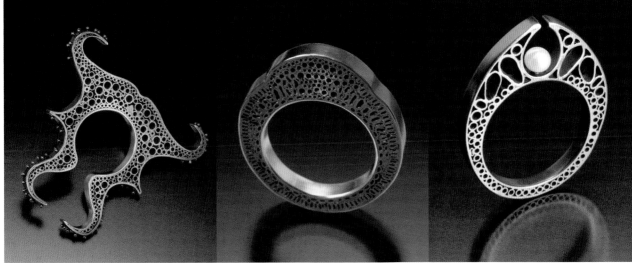

VINA RUST
Stamen series

Media	22ct gold, 925 silver, patina
Dimensions	5.6 × 5.0 × 0.3 cm (2¼ × 2 × ⅛ in.)
Photo: Doug Yaple	

VINA RUST
Stained Cell series

Media	14ct gold, 925 silver, patina
Dimensions	3.0 × 2.7 × 0.4 cm (1⅛ × 1 × ⅛ in.)
Photo: Doug Yaple	

VINA RUST
Cysts and Symmetries

Media	925 silver, freshwater pearls, patina
Dimensions	3.0 × 2.4 × 0.3 cm (1⅛ × 1 × ⅛ in.)
Photo: Vina Rust	

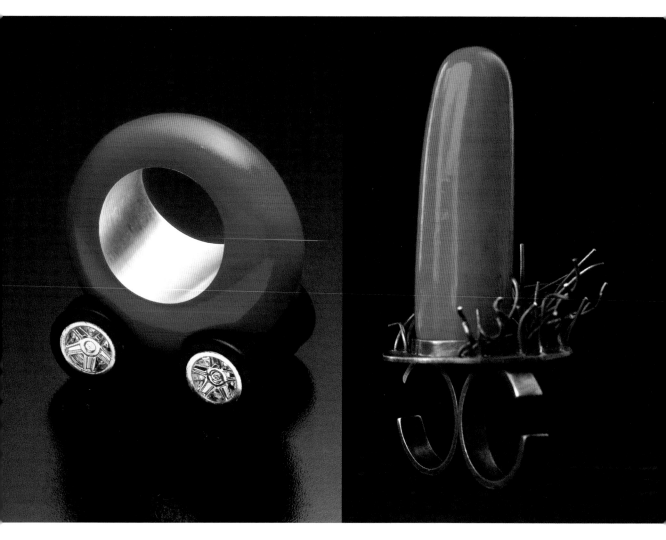

SANDRA DUARTE
Wheels

Media	silver, plastic, rubber, acrylic paint
Dimensions	3.8 × 3.8 × 2.0 cm (1½ × 1½ × ¾ in.)

Photo: Contacto Directo

ROBERTA FERREIRA
& LAURA JENER
Priapus

Media	silver, pottery, patina
Dimensions	6.9 × 4.0 × 3.3 cm (2¾ × 1⅝ × 1¼ in.)

Photo: Ernest Brugué and Ricard Gabaldà

ARATA FUCHI Magic Mushroom

Media   24ct gold, silver,
             silver dust
Dimensions   4.7 × 3.7 × 3.7 cm
             (1⅞ × 1½ × 1½ in.)

Photo: Ichiro Usuda

ARATA FUCHI Hallucination

Media   24ct gold, silver,
             silver dust, niello
Dimensions   6.5 × 4.6 × 4.3 cm
             (2½ × 1¾ × 1⅝ in.)

Photo: Ichiro Usuda

JANICE PEREZ Untitled

Media   Wood, tourmaline
Dimensions   4.0 × 2.5 × 1.5 cm
               (1⅝ × 1 × ⅝ in.)

Photo: Henrique Gualtieri

JANICE PEREZ Untitled

Media   wood, copper
Dimensions   10 × 3.5 × 2.5 cm
               (3⅞ × 1⅜ × 1 in.)

Photo: Henrique Gualtieri

FLORA BHATTACHARY
Jyamiti Swirl Ring

Media   gold, amethyst, pearl
Dimensions   3.5 × 2.7 × 2.7 cm
               (1⅜ × 1 × 1 in.)

Photo: Sylvain Deleu

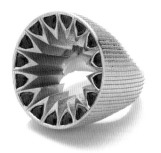

FLORA BHATTACHARY
Yantra and Taxila Rings

Media   Yantra: gold, silver;
               Taxila: vermeil, amethyst
Dimensions   3.4 × 3.4 × 3.4 cm
               (1⅜ × 1⅜ × 1⅜ in.)

Photo: Sylvain Deleu

LISE SCHØNBERG Autumn

Media	silver, seeds, resin
Dimensions	5.0 × 4.0 cm
	(2 × 1⅝ in.)

Photo: Lise Schønberg

LISE SCHØNBERG Doubting Hen

Media &	silver, seeds, enamel,
Dimensions	resin, plastic, 7.0 ×
	3.0 cm (2¾ × 1⅛ in.)

Photo: Lise Schønberg

CARLES CODINA ARMENGOL
Untitled

Media	gold, silver, patina
Dimensions	3.0 × 2.0 × 1.0 cm
	(1⅛ × ¾ × ⅜ in.)

Photo: Joan Soto

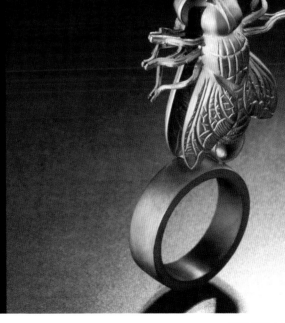

MI-MI MOSCOW
Under Construction

Media	nickel silver, paper, artificial nail, paint
Dimensions	8.3 × 6.3 cm (3¼ × 2½ in.)

Photo: mi-mi moscow

MI-MI MOSCOW Dualism

Media	nickel silver, paper, artificial nail, paint
Dimensions	11.5 × 3.0 cm (4½ × 1⅛ in.)

Photo: mi-mi moscow

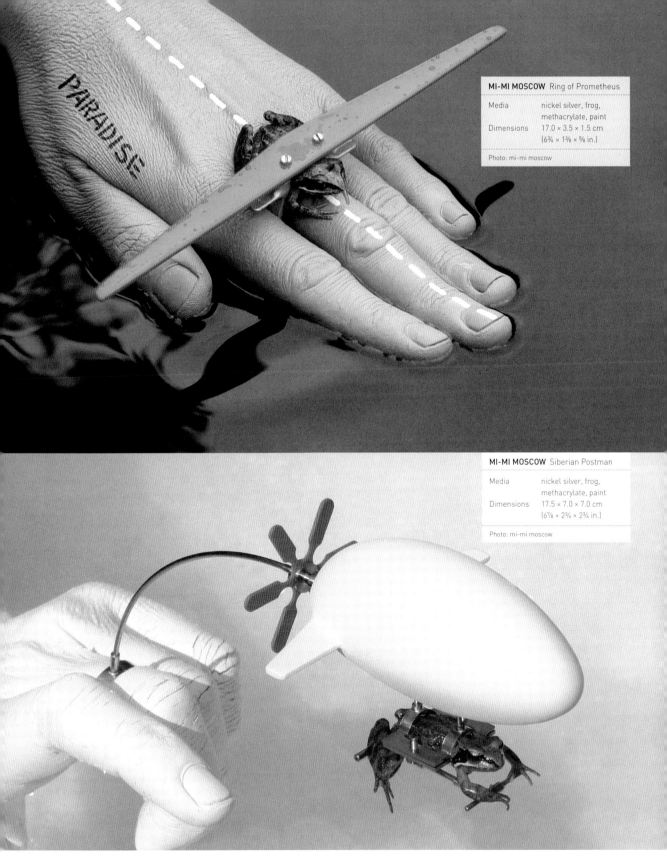

MI-MI MOSCOW Ring of Prometheus

Media	nickel silver, frog, methacrylate, paint
Dimensions	17.0 × 3.5 × 1.5 cm (6¾ × 1⅜ × ⅝ in.)

Photo: mi-mi moscow

MI-MI MOSCOW Siberian Postman

Media	nickel silver, frog, methacrylate, paint
Dimensions	17.5 × 7.0 × 7.0 cm (6⅞ × 2¾ × 2¾ in.)

Photo: mi-mi moscow

SOPHIE BOUDUBAN
Capsules

Media	rusted iron
Dimensions	5.5 × 3.8 cm (2⅛ × 1½ in.)

Photo: Fabrice Schaefer

SOPHIE BOUDUBAN
Reliquary

Media	rusted iron, brass, bone from a pig
Dimensions	5.5 × 4.0 cm (2⅛ × 1⅝ in.)

Photo: Christian Balmer

ENRIC MAJORAL Sand Jewelry III

Media	silver, acrylic paint
Dimensions	5.3 × 3.5 × 0.4 cm
	(2⅛ × 1⅜ × ⅛ in.)

Photo: Archivo Majoral

ENRIC MAJORAL Sand Jewelry II

Media	silver, acrylic paint
Dimensions	6.0 × 4.5 × 3.0 cm
	(2⅜ × 1¾ × 1⅛ in.)

Photo: Archivo Majoral

ENRIC MAJORAL
Sand Jewelry

Media	silver, acrylic paint
Dimensions	5.8 cm (2¼ in.)

Photo: Archivo Majoral

JOSÉE DESJARDINS A Jeweller's
Travel Memorabilia: Udaipur #3

Media	925 silver, chrysoprase, lapis lazuli, polymethacrylate, antique Indian coins
Dimensions	4.5 × 3.0 × 3.0 cm (1¾ × 1⅛ × 1⅛ in.)

Photo: Anthony McLean

JOSÉE DESJARDINS
A Jeweller's Travel Memorabilia:
Udaipur #4

Media	925 silver, polymethacrylate, antique Indian coins
Dimensions	5.0 × 2.5 × 2.0 cm (2 × 1 × ¾ in.)

Photo: Anthony McLean

RIKE BARTELS Untitled

Media	22ct gold, cornelian, sapphire, ruby, tourmaline, crystal, fire opal, amethyst
Dimensions	3.5 × 3.0 × 3.0 cm (1⅜ × 1⅛ × 1⅛ in.)

Photo: Jens Mauritz

RIKE BARTELS
Untitled

Media	22ct gold, tourmaline, chrysoberyl, jadeite, ruby
Dimensions	3.5 × 3.0 × 3.0 cm (1⅜ × 1⅛ × 1⅛ in.)

Photo: Martin Fengel

ROC MAJORAL & ABRIL RIBERA
Creature

Media   silver, patina
Dimensions   4.0 × 2.5 × 2.0 cm
               (1⅝ × 1 × ¾ in.)

Photo: Archivo Majoral

SANDRA DUARTE Tunies

Media   silver, plastic, lapis
               lazuli, garnet, agate,
               coral
Dimensions   5.0 × 3.0 × 3.0 cm
               (2 × 1⅛ × 1⅛ in.)

Photo: Contacto Directo

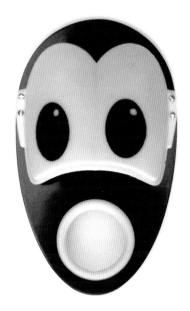

KEPA KARMONA
The Jazz Singer

Media	PVC, screws, prefabricated material
Dimensions	8.0 × 4.8 × 2.0 cm (3⅛ × 1⅞ × ¾ in.)

Photo: Kepa Karmona

KEPA KARMONA
Donkey Kong

Media	silver, prefabricated material
Dimensions	8.0 × 5.0 × 2.5 cm (3⅛ × 2 × 1 in.)

Photo: Kepa Karmona

KEPA KARMONA
Peach Stone Solitaire

Media	peach stone, tourmaline
Dimensions	3.5 × 3.0 × 1.2 cm (1⅜ × 1⅛ × ½ in.)

Photo: Kepa Karmona

CINNAMON LEE
Black Solitaire rings

Media	(clockwise from top left) gold, spinel; gold, spinel; gold, spinel; gold, diamond
Dimensions	3.0 × 2.3 × 1.1 cm (1⅛ × ⅞ × ⅜ in.)

Photo: John Lee

CINNAMON LEE
Super Solitaire ring

Media	titanium, silver, spinel
Dimensions	3.0 × 2.4 × 1.2 cm (1⅛ × 1 × ½ in.)

Photo: John Lee

CINNAMON LEE
Covert Romantic ring

Media	titanium
Dimensions	3.0 × 2.3 × 1.1 cm (1⅛ × ⅞ × ⅜ in.)

Photo: John Lee

JULIA DEVILLE Claw Ring

Media	925 silver, black diamonds
Dimensions	2.5 × 2.0 cm (1 × ¾ in.)

Photo: Terence Bogue

JULIA DEVILLE
Nanna's Engagement Ring

Media	18ct white gold, diamonds, black rhodium plating
Dimensions	2.2 × 2.2 cm (⅞ × ⅞ in.)

Photo: Terence Bogue

JULIA DEVILLE Prey Ring

Media	925 silver, black sapphire, black rhodium plating
Dimensions	8.5 × 3.0 cm (3⅜ × 1⅛ in.)

Photo: Terence Bogue

JULIA DEVILLE Mourning Ring

Media	18ct white gold, vintage diamonds, black rhodium plating
Dimensions	2.2 × 2.0 cm (⅞ × ¾ in.)

Photo: Terence Bogue

JULIA DEVILLE Medieval Wedder

Media	18ct gold, ruby
Dimensions	2.0 × 2.0 cm (¾ × ¾ in.)

Photo: Terence Bogue

FABRICE SCHAEFER
Untitled

Media	titanium, amethyst
Dimensions	3.5 cm (1⅜ in.)

Photo: Fabrice Schaefer

FABRICE SCHAEFER
Cow

Media	fine silver, titanium
Dimensions	3.0 cm (1⅛ in.)

Photo: Fabrice Schaefer

FABRICE SCHAEFER
Nail

Media	24ct gold, titanium
Dimensions	2.8 cm (1⅛ in.)

Photo: Fabrice Schaefer

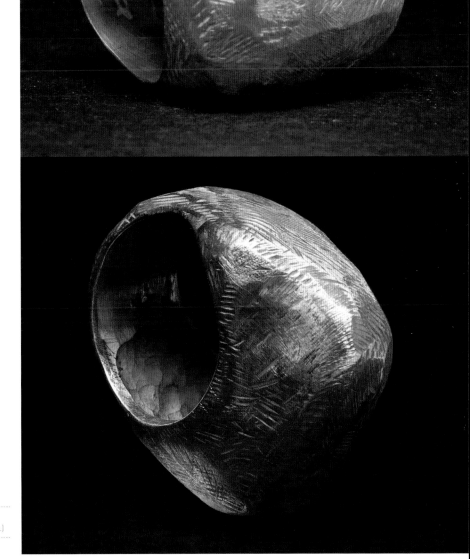

RANA MIKDASHI
Bombo 2

Media	925 silver, gold plated
Dimensions	3.3 × 2.5 cm (1¼ × 1 in.)

Photo: Toufic Araman

RANA MIKDASHI
Bombo 4

Media	925 silver
Dimensions	3.4 × 1.7 cm (1⅜ × ⅝ in.)

Photo: Toufic Araman

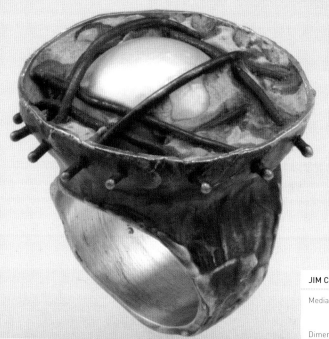

JIM COTTER Katrina Ring

Media	925 silver, steel, concrete, mabe pearl, patina
Dimensions	3.0 × 2.8 × 2.5 cm (1⅛ × 1⅛ × 1 in.)

Photo: J. Cotter Studio

JAN ARTHUR HARRELL
Cameo Ring

Media	24ct gold-plated copper, painted tin, faux pearls
Dimensions	1.8 × 1.8 × 1.5 cm (¾ × ¾ × ⅝ in.)

Photo: Jack Zilker

JAN ARTHUR HARRELL
Trophy Wife Ring

Media	24ct gold-plated copper, rusted steel, faceted glass
Dimensions	1.8 × 1.8 × 1.0 cm (¾ × ¾ × ⅜ in.)

Photo: Jack Zilker

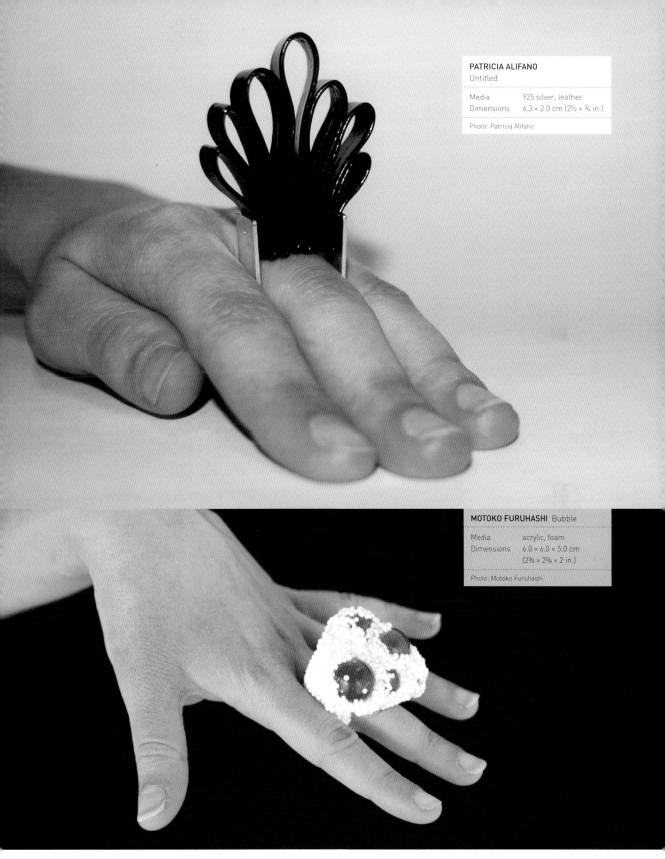

NICOLAS ESTRADA Abstract

Media	silver, amethyst
Dimensions	various sizes

Photo: Joan Soto

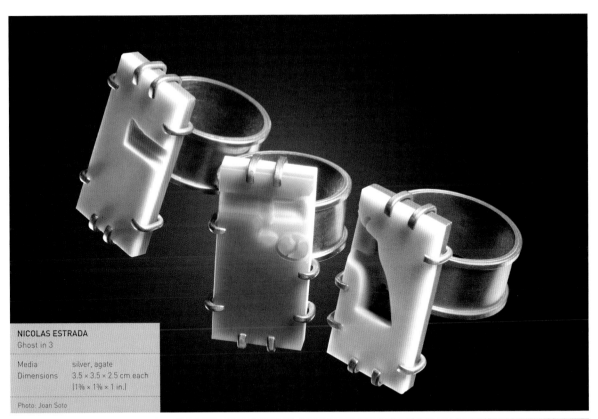

NICOLAS ESTRADA
Ghost in 3

Media	silver, agate
Dimensions	3.5 × 3.5 × 2.5 cm each
	(1⅜ × 1⅜ × 1 in.)

Photo: Joan Soto

NICOLAS ESTRADA Skull & Pearls

Media	silver, rock crystal, pearls
Dimensions	3.5 × 3.0 × 3.0 cm
	(1⅜ × 1⅛ × 1⅛ in.)

Photo: Joan Soto

NICOLAS ESTRADA Skull & Lapis

Media	silver, gold, citrine, lapis lazuli
Dimensions	1.5 × 3.0 × 3.0 cm
	(⅝ × 1⅛ × 1⅛ in.)

Photo: Joan Soto

BEN NEUBAUER
Dish Ring

Media	18ct yellow gold, 18ct
	white gold, blue zircon
Dimensions	4.0 × 3.5 × 3.5 cm
	(1⅝ × 1⅜ × 1⅜ in.)

Photo: Courtney Frisse

BABETTE VON DOHNANYI
Ring 128

Media	silver, patina
Dimensions	4.4 × 3.0 × 1.9 cm
	(1¾ × 1⅛ × ¾ in.)

Photo: Federico Cavicchioli

MICHAEL BERGER
Kinetic Ring

Media	18ct white gold, stainless steel, 12 diamonds, micro ball bearings, patina
Dimensions	3.5 × 3.4 × 1.0 cm (1⅜ × 1⅜ × ⅜ in.)

Photo: Michael Berger

MICHAEL BERGER
Kinetic Ring

Media	18ct yellow gold, stainless steel, micro ball bearings, patina
Dimensions	3.6 × 2.4 × 1.0 cm (1⅜ × 1 × ⅜ in.)

Photo: Michael Berger

MICHAEL BERGER
Kinetic Ring

Media	18ct white gold, stainless steel, Tahitian and freshwater pearls, patina
Dimensions	4.1 × 3.7 × 1.0 cm (1⅝ × 1½ × ⅜ in.)

Photo: Michael Berger

FLORIAN WAGNER
Proud People

Media	gold, diamonds
Dimensions	4.5 × 4.1 × 2.0 cm
	(1¾ × 1⅝ × ¾ in.)

Photo: Florian Wagner

  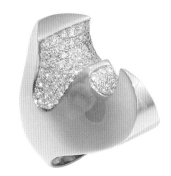

FLORIAN WAGNER
Overcast Heaven and Hell Ring

Media	gold, diamonds
Dimensions	3.5 × 3.0 × 2.6 cm
	(1⅜ × 1⅛ × 1 in.)

Photo: Florian Wagner

RIKE BARTELS
Untitled

Media	22ct gold, coral, jade, diamond
Dimensions	3.2 × 3.0 × 3.0 cm (1¼ × 1⅛ × 1⅛ in.)

Photo: Jens Mauritz

RIKE BARTELS
Cubist Bouquet

Media	22ct gold, coral
Dimensions	3.5 × 3.5 × 3.0 cm (1⅜ × 1⅜ × 1⅛ in.)

Photo: Martin Fengel

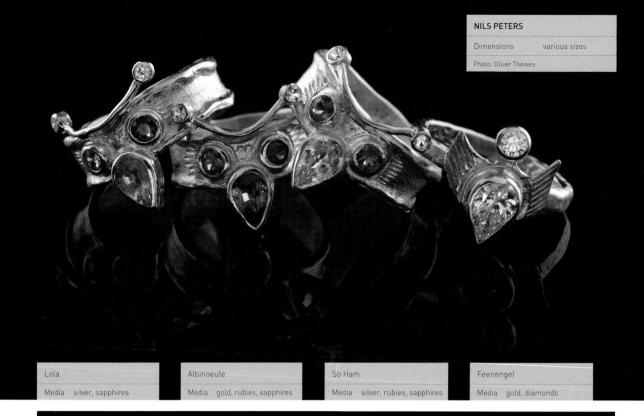

NILS PETERS

Dimensions   various sizes

Photo: Oliver Thewes

Lola

Media   silver, sapphires

Albinoeule

Media   gold, rubies, sapphires

So Ham

Media   silver, rubies, sapphires

Feenengel

Media   gold, diamonds

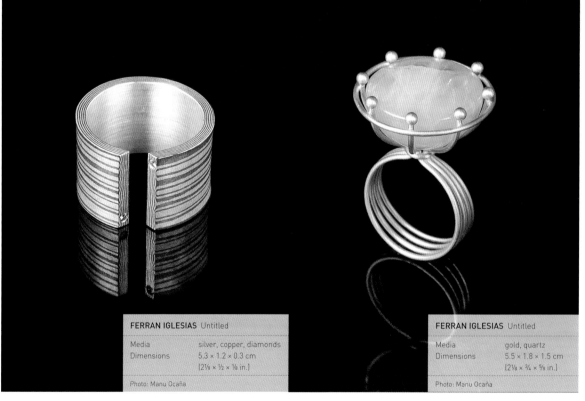

FERRAN IGLESIAS Untitled

Media   silver, copper, diamonds
Dimensions   5.3 × 1.2 × 0.3 cm
               (2⅛ × ½ × ⅛ in.)

Photo: Manu Ocaña

FERRAN IGLESIAS Untitled

Media   gold, quartz
Dimensions   5.5 × 1.8 × 1.5 cm
               (2⅛ × ¾ × ⅝ in.)

Photo: Manu Ocaña

MARÍA GOTI FERNÁNDEZ
Fleur Noire

Media   18ct gold, 925 silver, patina
Dimensions   2.0 × 1.1 cm (¾ × ⅜ in.)

Photo: María Goti Fernández

CYNTHIA DEL GIUDICE
Untitled

Media   925 silver, recycled
             polyethylene
Dimensions   5.0 × 2.0 × 1.0 cm
             (2 × ¾ × ⅜ in.)

Photo: Victor Wolf

ALICIA HANNAH NAOMI
Gneiss Pavé Rings

Media   silver, spinel
Dimensions   each 0.5 cm
               (¼ in.) wide

Photo: Andrew Barcham

RAIMON ALZAMORA
Organic

Media   gold, silver, diamonds, peridot
Dimensions   various sizes

Photo: Quim Roser

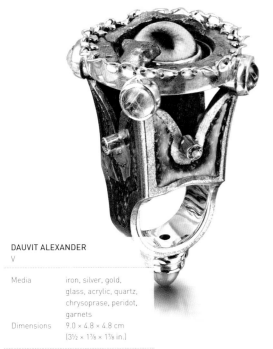

DAUVIT ALEXANDER
V

Media	iron, silver, gold, glass, acrylic, quartz, chrysoprase, peridot, garnets
Dimensions	9.0 × 4.8 × 4.8 cm (3½ × 1⅞ × 1⅞ in.)

Photo: Andrew Neilson

EERO HINTSANEN
Lukit

Media	silver
Dimensions	9.0 × 8.0 × 4.5 cm (3½ × 3⅛ × 1¾ in.)

Photo: Chao-Hsien Kuo

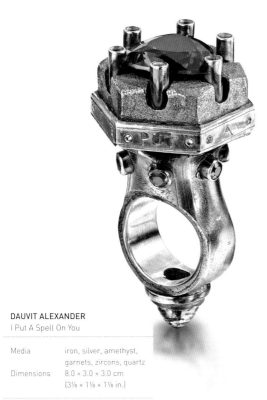

DAUVIT ALEXANDER
I Put A Spell On You

Media	iron, silver, amethyst, garnets, zircons, quartz
Dimensions	8.0 × 3.0 × 3.0 cm (3⅛ × 1⅛ × 1⅛ in.)

Photo: Andrew Neilson

EERO HINTSANEN
Winter Garden

Media	silver
Dimensions	11 × 10.5 × 10.5 cm (4⅜ × 4 × 4 in.)

Photo: Chao-Hsien Kuo

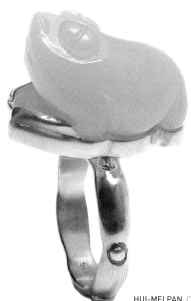

HUI-MEI PAN Miki Ring

Media   925 silver, white jade,
               red jadeite
Dimensions   3.1 × 3.2 × 2.0 cm
               (1¼ × 1¼ × ¾ in.)

Photo: Hui-Mei Pan

HUI-MEI PAN Chinese Toad

Media   925 silver, white jade
Dimensions   3.5 × 2.5 × 2.5 cm
               (1⅜ × 1 × 1 in.)

Photo: Hui-Mei Pan

CHARITY HALL
Bee Ring

Media   silver, copper, peridot,
               yellow sapphire, enamel
Dimensions   2.3 × 2.0 × 2.0 cm
               (⅞ × ¾ × ¾ in.)

Photo: Charity Hall

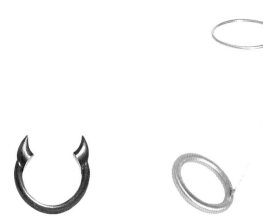

For the Little Devil in You

Media	925 silver, patina
Dimensions	2.3 × 2.5 cm
	(⅞ × 1 in.)

For the Holy Halo Angel in You

Media	18ct gold, 925 silver
Dimensions	6.7 × 2.2 cm
	(2⅝ × ⅞ in.)

For the Lucky Beggar

Media	925 silver, enamel
Dimensions	2.3 × 2.5 cm
	(⅞ × 1 in.)

For the Knotted Thoughts
in Your Head

Media	925 silver, string
Dimensions	3.2 × 3.1 cm
	(1¼ × 1¼ in.)

BEATRIZ PALACIOS
Infinity Amethyst and Infinity Rings

Media   gold, zircons, amethyst
Dimensions   various sizes

Photo: Lourdes Cabrera

BEATRIZ PALACIOS
The Future Eve Ring

Media   gold, zircons
Dimensions   4.2 × 2.0 × 2.0 cm
               (1⅝ × ¾ × ¾ in.)

Photo: Lourdes Cabrera

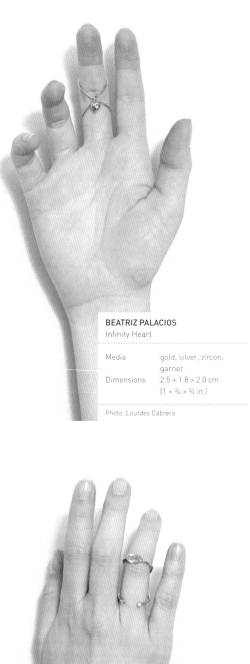

BEATRIZ PALACIOS
Infinity Heart

Media   gold, silver, zircon,
               garnet
Dimensions   2.5 × 1.8 × 2.0 cm
               (1 × ¾ × ¾ in.)

Photo: Lourdes Cabrera

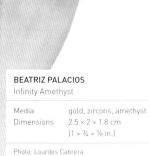

BEATRIZ PALACIOS
Infinity Amethyst

Media   gold, zircons, amethyst
Dimensions   2.5 × 2 × 1.8 cm
               (1 × ¾ × ⅝ in.)

Photo: Lourdes Cabrera

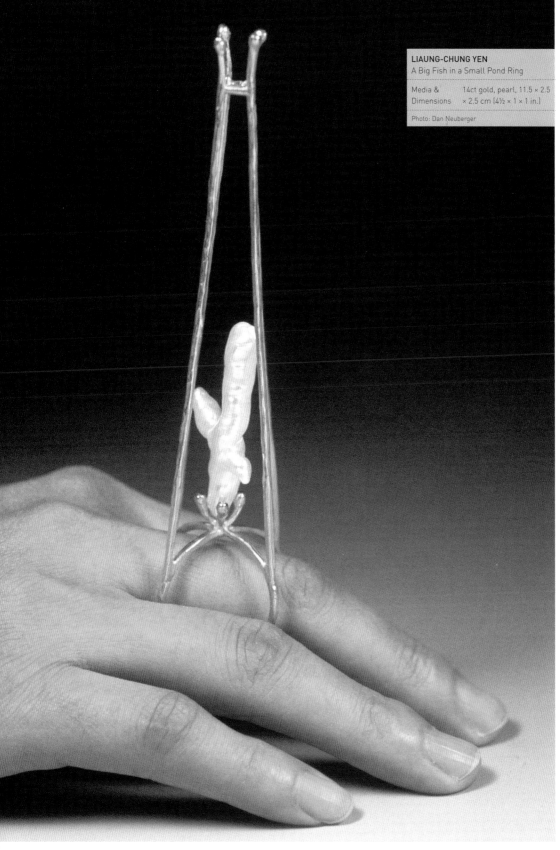

LIAUNG-CHUNG YEN
A Big Fish in a Small Pond Ring

Media &   14ct gold, pearl, 11.5 × 2.5
Dimensions   × 2.5 cm (4½ × 1 × 1 in.)

Photo: Dan Neuberger

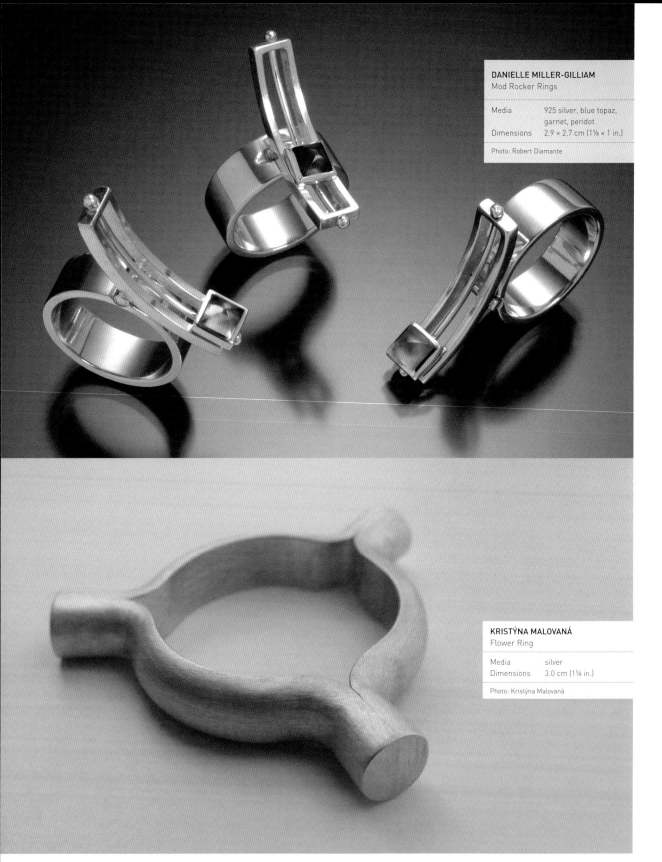

DANIELLE MILLER-GILLIAM
Mod Rocker Rings

Media	925 silver, blue topaz, garnet, peridot
Dimensions	2.9 × 2.7 cm (1⅛ × 1 in.)

Photo: Robert Diamante

KRISTÝNA MALOVANÁ
Flower Ring

Media	silver
Dimensions	3.0 cm (1⅛ in.)

Photo: Kristýna Malovaná

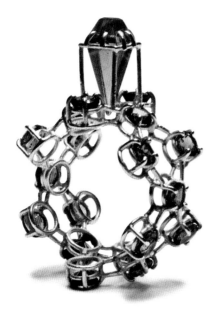

PHILIP SAJET
Purple Ring

Media	amethyst, gold
Dimensions	4.0 × 2.7 × 1.6 cm
	(1⅝ × 1 × ⅝ in.)

Photo: Beate Klockmann

PHILIP SAJET
Pearl Amber Ring

Media	pearl, amber, gold
Dimensions	3.8 × 2.6 × 1.6 cm
	(1½ × 1 × ⅝ in.)

Photo: Beate Klockmann

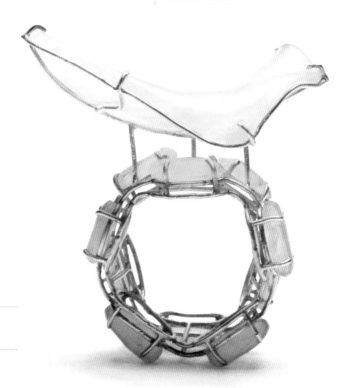

PHILIP SAJET
Potato Chip Ring

Media	amber, gold
Dimensions	4.0 × 2.4 × 1.7 cm
	(1⅝ × 1 × ⅝ in.)

Photo: Beate Klockmann

NIKI ULEHLA
Untitled

Media	18ct gold, raw diamond, plastic
Dimensions	3.1 × 1.9 × 0.7 cm (1¼ × ¾ × ¼ in.)

Photo: Niki Ulehla

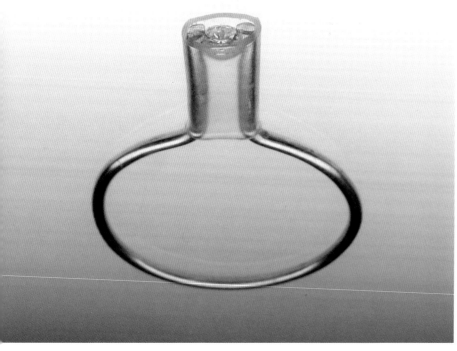

NIKI ULEHLA
Untitled

Media	18ct gold, diamond, plastic
Dimensions	2.9 × 1.9 × 0.3 cm (1⅛ × ¾ × ⅛ in.)

Photo: Niki Ulehla

JULIETA ODIO BERNARDI
Plan Tranquilo

Media   925 silver, beer cap
Dimensions   5.0 × 4.5 × 4.0 cm
             (2 × 1¾ × 1⅝ in.)

Photo: Julieta Odio Bernardi

BEATE KLOCKMANN
Fire on Ice

Media   gold, polymethacrylate
Dimensions   4.0 × 3.5 × 2.5 cm
             (1⅝ × 1⅜ × 1 in.)

Photo: Beate Klockmann

KENNETH C. MACBAIN Ice

Media   925 silver, zircon,
                acrylic magnifier
Dimensions   6.0 × 5.0 × 5.0 cm
                (2⅜ × 2 × 2 in.)

NICOLE DEUSTER
The Elements

Media   gold, silver, stainless
                steel
Dimensions   4.0 × 3.4 cm (1⅝ × 1⅜ in.)

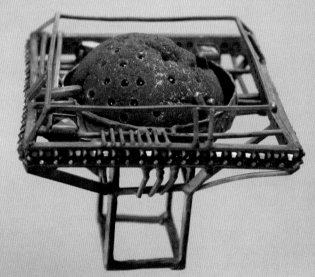

JIŘÍ URBAN Tube

Media	iron, Czech garnets, cold enamel
Dimensions	2.5 × 2.0 cm (1 × ¾ in.)

Photo: Jiří Urban

JIŘÍ URBAN Planet

Media	silver, Czech garnets, golf ball fragment found on a beach, spinel
Dimensions	7.0 × 6.5 cm (2¾ × 2½ in.)

Photo: Jiří Urban

KATHRYN RIECHERT
Regrowth Ring

Media	925 silver, peridot, patina
Dimensions	1.2 cm (½ in.)

Photo: Kathryn Riechert

CATHERINE ALLEN
Thought Bubbles: A Conversation

Media	925 silver, electroformed copper, enamel, polyester
Dimensions	5.0 × 3.0 cm (2 × 1⅛ in.)

Photo: Catherine Allen

FABIANA GADANO
Refugios 1

Media	fine silver, 925 silver, enamel
Dimensions	4.0 cm (1⅝ in.)

Photo: Patricio Gatti

MIGUEL ÂNGELO DURO GROMICHO
Polar Ice

Media	950 silver, quartz, green tourmaline
Dimensions	2.4 × 1.5 cm (1 × ⅝ in.)

Photo: Miguel Ângelo Duro Gromicho

ROBERT W. EBENDORF Bird in Flight

Media   925 silver, copper
Dimensions   5.2 × 3.0 × 3.0 cm
     (2 × 1⅛ × 1⅛ in.)

Photo: Tim Lazure

ROBERT W. EBENDORF Pull-Top Ring

Media   14ct gold, 925 silver,
     silver, pearl, pull tab
     from tin can
Dimensions   3.8 × 3.0 × 2.4 cm
     (1½ × 1⅛ × 1 in.)

Photo: Tim Lazure

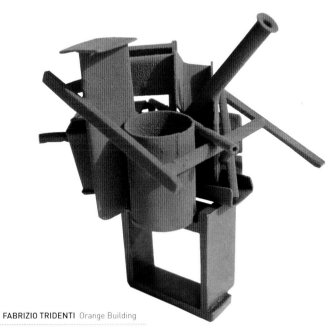

JACKIE ANDERSON Cocktail Ring

Media   925 silver, acrylic
     acetate, Bakelite
Dimensions   8.5 × 4.0 × 3.5 cm
     (3⅜ × 1⅝ × 1⅜ in.)

Photo: Jackie Anderson

FABRIZIO TRIDENTI Orange Building

Media   silver, acrylic paint
Dimensions   6.0 × 5.5 × 3.6 cm
     (2⅜ × 2⅛ × 1⅜ in.)

Photo: Fabrizio Tridenti

HELEN BRITTON
Forest

Media   silver, diamonds, paint
Dimensions   5.0 × 3.5 × 3.0 cm
             (2 × 1⅜ × 1⅛ in.)

Photo: Helen Britton and David Bielander

HELEN BRITTON
Fire Devil

Media   silver, gold, diamonds, paint
Dimensions   3.0 × 2.5 × 2.5 cm
             (1⅛ × 1 × 1 in.)

Photo: Helen Britton and David Bielander

HELEN BRITTON
Sword

Media   silver, diamonds,
             glass, smoky quartz,
             tiger's eye
Dimensions   4.5 × 3.0 × 3.0 cm
             (1¾ × 1⅛ × 1⅛ in.)

Photo: Helen Britton

SAYUMI YOKOUCHI
Ring with a Pearl (Candlestick)

Media &   brass, gold plated, candle, 15
Dimensions   × 15 × 4 cm (5⅞ × 5⅞ × 1⅝ in.)

Photo: D. James Dee

COMMITMENT

KRISTÝNA MALOVANÁ
Organic System

Media	stainless steel
Dimensions	3.0 cm (1⅛ in.)

Photo: Kristýna Malovaná

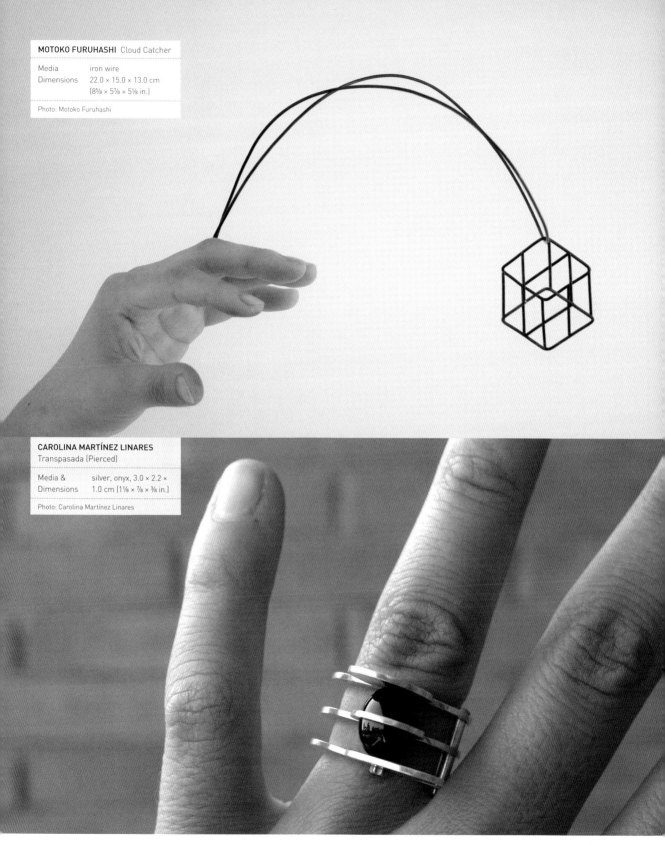

MOTOKO FURUHASHI Cloud Catcher

Media	iron wire
Dimensions	22.0 × 15.0 × 13.0 cm
	(8⅝ × 5⅞ × 5⅛ in.)

Photo: Motoko Furuhashi

CAROLINA MARTÍNEZ LINARES
Transpasada (Pierced)

Media &	silver, onyx, 3.0 × 2.2 ×
Dimensions	1.0 cm (1⅛ × ⅞ × ⅜ in.)

Photo: Carolina Martínez Linares

MARC MONZÓ
Untitled

Media	silver, patina
Dimensions	1.5 × 1.2 cm (⅝ × ½ in.)

Photo: Mikhaela Mikhailova /
Klimt02 Publishers

MARC MONZÓ
Untitled

Media	silver, enamel
Dimensions	1.5 × 1.5 cm (⅝ × ⅝ in.)

Photo: Mikhaela Mikhailova /
Klimt02 Publishers

MARC MONZÓ
Solitaire

Media	white gold, zircon
Dimensions	3.0 × 2.5 cm (1⅛ × 1 in.)

Photo: Mikhaela Mikhailova /
Klimt02 Publishers

MARC MONZÓ
Micro-Rings

Media	18ct gold, synthetic stones
Dimensions	2.5 × 1.7 cm (1 × ⅝ in.)

Photo: Mikhaela Mikhailova /
Klimt02 Publishers

CHRISTA LÜHTJE
Two Rings

Media	22ct gold, haematite
Dimensions	2.1 × 2.1 cm (⅞ × ⅞ in.)

Photo: Eva Jünger

CHRISTA LÜHTJE
Two Rings

Media	22ct gold, onyx
Dimensions	2.3 × 1.4 cm (⅞ × ½ in.)

Photo: Eva Jünger

STEFANIE BAUER
A Hand in the Sewing Box

Media	silver, crystal, nylon, polyester, patina, pearl
Dimensions	2.5 × 2.7 × 1.5 cm (1 × 1 × ⅝ in.)

Photo: Stefanie Bauer

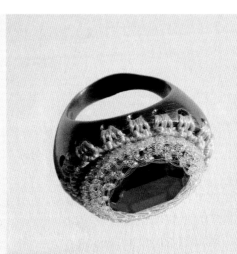

STEFANIE BAUER
A Hand in the Sewing Box

Media	silver, crystal, nylon, polyester, patina
Dimensions	2.5 × 2.7 × 1.8 cm (1 × 1 × ¾ in.)

Photo: Stefanie Bauer

CRISTINA ZANI
My Seoul gold rings

Media	silver, wood, acrylic
	paint, gold leaf
Dimensions	3.0 × 2.5 × 1.0 cm
	(1⅛ × 1 × ⅜ in.)

Photo: Cristina Zani

CRISTINA ZANI
My Seoul blue and yellow rings

Media	silver, wood, acrylic
	paint, gold leaf
Dimensions	1.8 × 1.7 × 1.3 cm
	(¾ × ⅝ × ½ in.)

Photo: Livio Morabito

CRISTINA ZANI
My Seoul oxidized rings

Media	silver, wood, acrylic paint
Dimensions	yellow: 3.0 × 2.0 × 1.0 cm (1⅛ × ¾ × ⅜ in.)
	turquoise: 3.0 × 2.9 × 1.5 cm (1⅛ × 1⅛ × ½ in.)
	pink/yellow: 3.5 × 2.5 × 1.5 cm (1⅜ × 1 × ½ in.)

Photo: Cristina Zani

ADRIANA HENAO
Eclosion

Media	silver, pearls, enamel
Dimensions	3.2 × 2.0 cm (1¼ × ¾ in.)

Photo: Áurea

ADRIANA HENAO
Flora

Media	silver, garnet, jadeite, enamel
Dimensions	3.5 × 2.5 × 1.8 cm (1⅜ × 1 × ¾ in.)

Photo: Áurea

NOEMÍ FOGUET LORCA
R Special UFO

Media	18ct gold, smoky quartz
Dimensions	2.5 × 2.0 × 1.8 cm
	(1 × ¾ × ¾ in.)

Photo: Enric Masdeu Sans

NOEMÍ FOGUET LORCA
R Special Amethyst

Media	18ct gold, silver,
	rhodium plated,
	amethyst
Dimensions	2.2 × 2.0 × 1.7 cm
	(⅞ × ¾ × ⅝ in.)

Photo: Enric Masdeu Sans

NOEMÍ FOGUET LORCA
R Special Smoky Quartz

Media	18ct white gold, 18ct
	yellow gold, smoky quartz
Dimensions	2.2 × 2.0 × 1.3 cm
	(⅞ × ¾ × ½ in.)

Photo: Enric Masdeu Sans

SALIMA THAKKER
Untitled

Media	18ct yellow gold,
	moonstone
Dimensions	2.8 cm (1⅛ in.)

Photo: Salima Thakker

SALIMA THAKKER
Untitled

Media	18ct yellow gold,
	green diamond
Dimensions	3.5 cm (1⅜ in.)

Photo: Salima Thakker

SARAH HOOD
Blue Enamel Ring

Media	fine silver, crystal, enamel
Dimensions	5.0 × 3.8 × 1.5 cm (2 × 1½ × ⅝ in.)

Photo: Doug Yaple

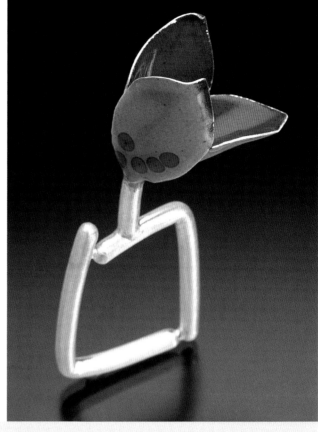

ANDREA VELÁZQUEZ
Little Cushion 1

Media	silver, felt
Dimensions	2.0 × 1.0 cm (¾ × ⅜ in.)

Photo: Fernando Bagué

EMILY WATSON
Single Sip

Media	925 silver, wood
Dimensions	4.5 × 1.5 × 1.5 cm
	(1¾ × ⅝ × ⅝ in.)

Photo: Emily Watson

JUANA ORTIZ
Ears

Media	950 silver, polyester resin
Dimensions	3.5 × 3.3 × 0.5 cm
	(1⅜ × 1¼ × ¼ in.)

Photo: Juana Ortiz

SENAY AKIN The Iron Rose

Media   925 silver, quartz
Dimensions   4.4 × 2.1 × 2.0 cm
               (1¾ × ⅞ × ¾ in.)

Photo: Senay Akin

ÅSA HALLDIN
Ruben

Media   18ct gold, coral
Dimensions   3.5 × 3.0 cm (1⅜ × 1⅛ in.)

Photo: Adrian Nordenborg

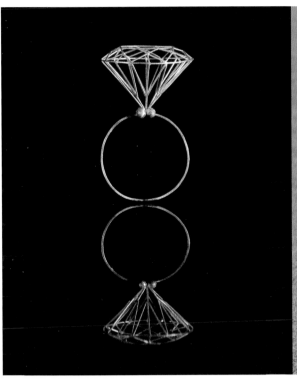

SAMUEL SAAVEDRA
Solitaire

Media	18ct yellow gold,
	18ct white gold
Dimensions	3.5 cm (1⅜ in.)

Photo: Toni Galitó

PILAR GARRIGOSA
Untitled

Media	18ct gold, imperial topaz,
	iolite
Dimensions	3.0 × 2.5 cm (1⅛ × 1 in.)

Photo: Nos & Soto

RAIMON ALZAMORA Es Talaier

Media	18ct gold, silver,
	aquamarine
Dimensions	2.7 × 1.6 cm (1 × ⅝ in.)

Photo: Adrià Estremera

RAIMON ALZAMORA Ses Illetes

Media	18ct gold, silver,
	blue topaz
Dimensions	4.0 × 3.4 cm (1⅝ × 1⅜ in.)

Photo: Adrià Estremera

PAMELA RITCHIE
RememberRing

Media	925 silver, rubber, ribbon
Dimensions	4.0 × 2.3 × 2.1 cm
	(1⅝ × ⅞ × ⅞ in.)

Photo: Perry Jackson

MARTACARMELA SOTELO
Black Sphere

Media	stainless steel wire,
	nylon
Dimensions	4.0 cm (1⅝ in.)

Photo: Martacarmela Sotelo

DAPHNE KRINOS
Pink Ring

Media	18ct yellow gold, tourmaline
Dimensions	2.7 × 1.8 cm (1 × ¾ in.)

Photo: Joel Degen

DAPHNE KRINOS
Yellow Ring

Media	18ct yellow gold, citrine
Dimensions	2.0 × 1.5 cm (¾ × ⅝ in.)

Photo: Joel Degen

BABETTE VON DOHNANYI Ring 127

Media	925 silver, amethyst, lemon quartz
Dimensions	2.6 × 2.5 × 1.3 cm (1 × 1 × ½ in.)

Photo: Federico Cavicchioli

SANNI FALKENBERG Starduster

Media	agate druzy
Dimensions	9.0 × 4.5 × 3.5 cm
	(3½ × 1¾ × 1⅜ in.)

Photo: Manu Ocana

NINA SAJET Birdcage Ring

Media	silver, brass
Dimensions	5.0 × 4.0 × 4.0 cm
	(2 × 1⅝ × 1⅝ in.)

Photo: Nina Sajet

DIANA DUDEK
Iron Rings

Media	iron
Dimensions	2.8 × 2.0 cm (1⅛ × ¾ in.)

Photo: Ralf Stautner

FRANCESCA VITALI Mura Stack

Media	paper
Dimensions	4.0 × 4.0 × 2.1 cm
	(1⅝ × 1⅝ × ⅞ in.)

Photo: Francesca Vitali

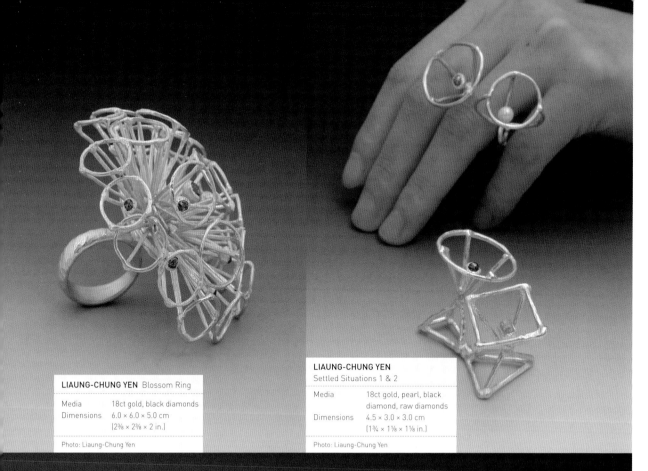

LIAUNG-CHUNG YEN Blossom Ring

Media	18ct gold, black diamonds
Dimensions	6.0 × 6.0 × 5.0 cm
	(2⅜ × 2⅜ × 2 in.)

Photo: Liaung-Chung Yen

LIAUNG-CHUNG YEN
Settled Situations 1 & 2

Media	18ct gold, pearl, black
	diamond, raw diamonds
Dimensions	4.5 × 3.0 × 3.0 cm
	(1¾ × 1⅛ × 1⅛ in.)

Photo: Liaung-Chung Yen

LIAUNG-CHUNG YEN Flourishing Ring

Media	18ct gold, diamonds
Dimensions	5.0 × 2.5 × 0.5 cm
	(2 × 1 × ¼ in.)

Photo: Liaung-Chung Yen

BLANCA SÁNCHEZ Brilliant Collection

Media   gold
Dimensions   2.5 × 2.0 × 1.0 × 0.2 cm
                 (1 × ¾ × ⅜ × ⅛ in.)

Photo: Blanca Sánchez

BLANCA SÁNCHEZ
Flamenco Collection

Media &   gold, 3.5 × 2.0 × 1.0 ×
Dimensions   0.3 cm (1⅜ × ¾ × ⅜ × ⅛ in.)

Photo: Blanca Sánchez

LUZIA VOGT
Coins

Media	antique French and Swiss silver coins
Dimensions	2.0 × 1.9 cm (¾ × ¾ in.)

Photo: Petra Jaschke

CARME FÀBREGAS BARTOK
Leaves

Media	silver, rhodium
Dimensions	3.3 × 2.4 cm (1¼ × 1 in.)

Photo: Carme Fàbregas Bartok

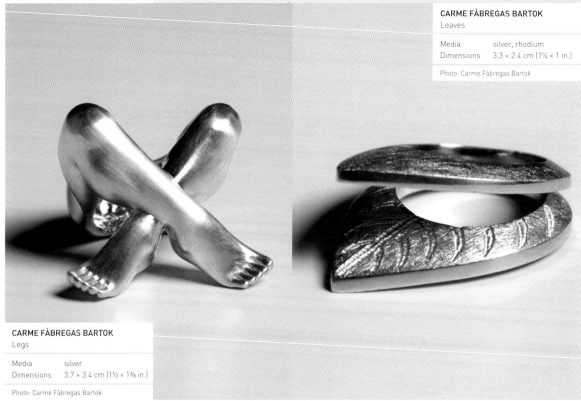

CARME FÀBREGAS BARTOK
Legs

Media	silver
Dimensions	3.7 × 3.4 cm (1½ × 1⅜ in.)

Photo: Carme Fàbregas Bartok

ISABEL ARANGO TISNÉS
Signoria

Media	925 silver, amethyst
Dimensions	3.0 × 2.0 cm (1⅛ × ¾ in.)

Photo: Alejandra Estrada

MANUELA URIBE PIEDRAHÍTA
Leaf with Emerald

Media &	14ct gold, emerald, 2.0 ×
Dimensions	2.0 × 0.6 cm (¾ × ¾ × ¼ in.)

Photo: Manuela Uribe Piedrahíta

SUSAN MAY
Untitled

Media   18ct gold, 925 silver
Dimensions   3.0 × 3.0 × 1.2 cm
             (1⅛ × 1⅛ × ½ in.)

Photo: Joël Degen

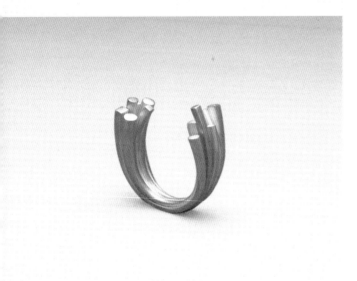

SUSAN MAY
Untitled

Media   18ct gold, 925 silver
Dimensions   3.0 × 3.0 × 1.2 cm
             (1⅛ × 1⅛ × ½ in.)

Photo: Joël Degen

SUSAN MAY
Untitled

Media   925 silver
Dimensions   3.0 × 3.0 × 1.5 cm
             (1⅛ × 1⅛ × ½ in.)

Photo: Joël Degen

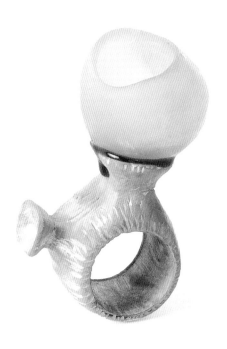

NICOLAS ESTRADA
Fragile & Precious

Media	gold, quartz, wood, pigment
Dimensions	6.5 × 3.5 × 3.0 cm (2½ × 1⅜ × 1⅛ in.)

Photo: Manu Ocaña

NICOLAS ESTRADA
Precious & Fragile

Media	gold, quartz, vegetable ivory, pigment
Dimensions	6.5 × 3.5 × 3.0 cm (2½ × 1⅜ × 1⅛ in.)

Photo: Manu Ocaña

TOVE KNUTS Fold-It 1

Media	silver, patina
Dimensions	3.0 × 2.0 × 2.0 cm
	(1⅛ × ¾ × ¾ in.)

Photo: Tove Knuts

TOVE KNUTS Fold-It 2

Media	silver
Dimensions	3.3 × 2.3 × 1.5 cm
	(1¼ × ⅞ × ⅝ in.)

Photo: Tove Knuts

TOVE KNUTS Fold-It 3

Media	silver, rhodonite
Dimensions	3.5 × 2.4 × 1.0 cm
	(1⅜ × 1 × ⅜ in.)

Photo: Tove Knuts

TOVE KNUTS Fold-It 4

Media	silver
Dimensions	3.0 × 2.4 × 1.0 cm
	(1⅛ × 1 × ⅜ in.)

Photo: Tove Knuts

TOVE KNUTS Fold-It 5

Media	Corian, silver
Dimensions	4.5 × 2.0 × 2.0 cm
	(1¾ × ¾ × ¾ in.)

Photo: Tove Knuts

HEIDEMARIE HERB
Wine

Media	925 silver, star ruby
Dimensions	2.0 cm (¾ in.)

Photo: Silvana Tili

HEIDEMARIE HERB
My Love

Media	925 silver, lemon opal, wood
Dimensions	1.5 × 1.4 × 0.8 cm (⅝ × ½ × ⅜ in.)

Photo: Silvana Tili

HEIDEMARIE HERB
My World

Media	18ct gold, 925 silver, crystal
Dimensions	3.0 cm (1⅛ in.)

Photo: Silvana Tili

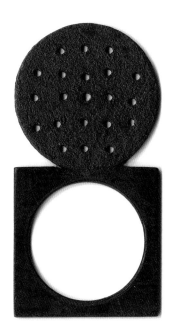

TORE SVENSSON Little Red House

Media	steel, paint
Dimensions	3.8 × 2.0 × 1.7 cm
	(1½ × ¾ × ⅝ in.)

Photo: Anders Jirås

TORE SVENSSON Inside 4 × 4 cm

Media	steel, gilding
Dimensions	4.0 × 2.0 × 0.1 cm
	(1⅝ × ¾ × ⅛ in.)

Photo: Franz Karl

SOYEON KIM Gold i

Media	14ct gold
Dimensions	5.0 × 3.0 × 0.1 cm
	(2 × 1⅛ × ⅛ in.)

Photo: Soyeon Kim

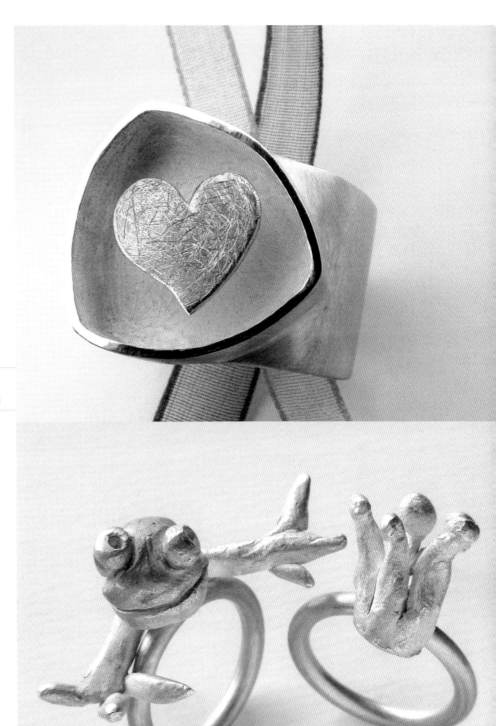

CARMEN PINTOR RODRÍGUEZ
Container of Illusions

| Media | 18ct gold, fine silver, 925 silver |
| Dimensions | 2.5 × 1.5 cm (1 × ⅝ in.) |

Photo: Maglo

JIMENA RÍOS
Frog Prince

| Media | 22ct gold, silver |
| Dimensions | 4.5 × 4.0 cm (1¾ × 1⅝ in.) |

Photo: Negro Karamanian

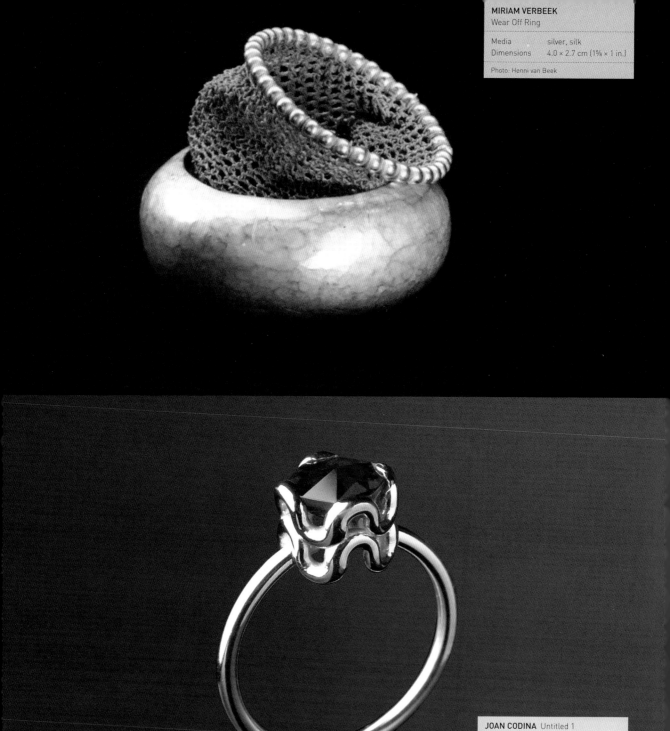

MIRIAM VERBEEK
Wear Off Ring

Media	silver, silk
Dimensions	4.0 × 2.7 cm (1⅝ × 1 in.)

Photo: Henni van Beek

JOAN CODINA Untitled 1

Media	18ct yellow gold, garnet
Dimensions	2.5 × 1.9 × 0.9 cm
	(1 × ¾ × ⅜ in.)

Photo: Federico Szarfer Barenblit

MIA HEBIB
Guggenheim

Media	925 silver, patina
Dimensions	2.6 cm (1 in.)

Photo: Mia Hebib

MIA HEBIB
Folded

Media	925 silver, walnut veneer
Dimensions	2.8 cm (1⅛ in.)

Photo: Mia Hebib

ROOS ARENDS
Small Architecture 1

Media	18ct gold
Dimensions	2.4 × 2.1 cm (1 × ⅞ in.)

Photo: Roos Arends

ROOS ARENDS
Small Architecture 2

Media	18ct gold
Dimensions	2.3 × 2.1 cm (⅞ × ⅞ in.)

Photo: Roos Arends

FRANCE ROY Rose Again

Media	925 silver, garnet, epoxy resin
Dimensions	2.5 × 2.0 cm (1 × ¾ in.)

Photo: Anthony McLean

FRANCE ROY Sky is the Limit

Media	18ct gold, 925 silver, epoxy resin
Dimensions	2.5 × 2.0 cm (1 × ¾ in.)

Photo: Anthony McLean

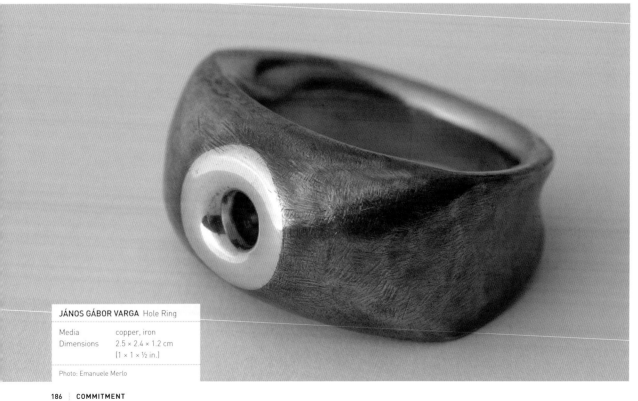

JÁNOS GÁBOR VARGA Hole Ring

Media	copper, iron
Dimensions	2.5 × 2.4 × 1.2 cm (1 × 1 × ½ in.)

Photo: Emanuele Merlo

SEAN O'CONNELL Red Ball Ring

Media   9ct pink gold, stainless
             steel balls
Dimensions   2.9 × 2.9 × 0.8 cm
             (1⅛ × 1⅛ × ⅜ in.)

Photo: Sean O'Connell

SEAN O'CONNELL Ruby Ball Rollers

Media   18ct white gold, 9ct pink
             gold, synthetic ruby beads
Dimensions   2.2 × 2.2 × 0.7 cm
             (⅞ × ⅞ × ¼ in.)

Photo: Sean O'Connell

SEAN O'CONNELL Needle Roller

Media   stainless steel
Dimensions   2.5 × 2.5 × 1.1 cm
             (1 × 1 × ⅜ in.)

Photo: Sean O'Connell

CHAO-HSIEN KUO
Horsma

Media	silver, keum-boo gold foil
Dimensions	8.5 × 5.5 × 2.4 cm
	(3⅜ × 2⅛ × 1 in.)

Photo: Chao-Hsien Kuo

CHAO-HSIEN KUO
Spotty Sunshine

Media	silver, keum-boo gold foil,
	Japanese pearls
Dimensions	7.5 × 4.0 × 4.5 cm
	(3 × 1⅝ × 1¾ in.)

Photo: Chao-Hsien Kuo

CHAO-HSIEN KUO
Spotty Flower with One Flying Seed

Media	silver, keum-boo gold foil,
	Japanese pearl
Dimensions	3.7 × 2.5 × 4.0 cm
	(1½ × 1 × 1⅝ in.)

Photo: Chao-Hsien Kuo

BEATE KLOCKMANN
Butterfly

Media	gold
Dimensions	4.0 × 2.5 × 2.5 cm
	(1⅝ × 1 × 1 in.)

Photo: Beate Klockmann

BARBARA HEINRICH
Tumbling Marquis Diamond Ring

Media	18ct gold, diamonds
Dimensions	2.5 × 0.6 cm
	(1 × ¼ in.)

Photo: Barbara Heinrich Studio

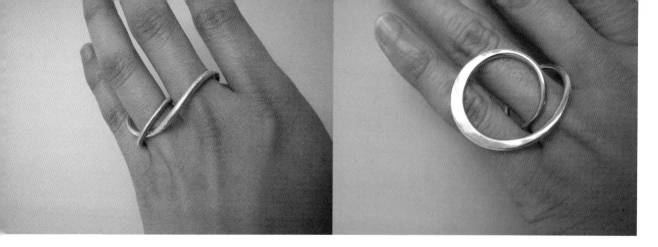

YUKI KAMIYA
Uzu

Media	18ct gold, silver
Dimensions	3.5 × 3.5 × 2.5 cm
	(1⅜ × 1⅜ × 1 in.)

Photo: Yuki Kamiya

YUKI KAMIYA
Ren

Media	silver
Dimensions	4.0 × 3.0 × 1.5 cm
	(1⅝ × 1⅛ × ⅝ in.)

Photo: Yuki Kamiya

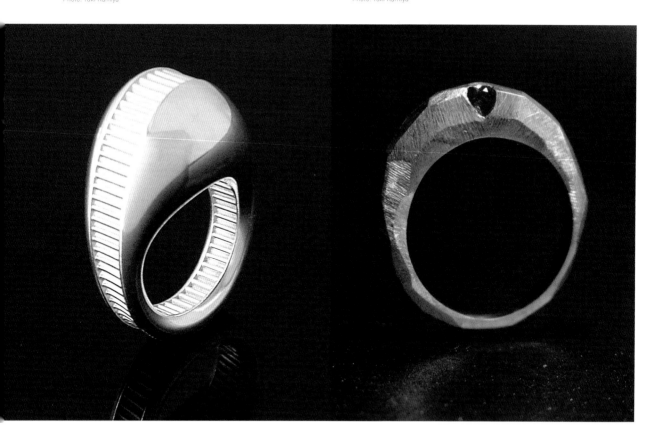

CHRIS IRICK
Junkers Ju

Media	925 silver
Dimensions	3.0 × 2.5 × 1.5 cm
	(1⅛ × 1 × ⅝ in.)

Photo: Chris Irick

LINDA SÁNCHEZ MÉNDEZ
My Love

Media	gold, ruby
Dimensions	2.5 × 1.8 × 0.3 cm
	(1 × ¾ × ⅛ in.)

Photo: Tim Klempay

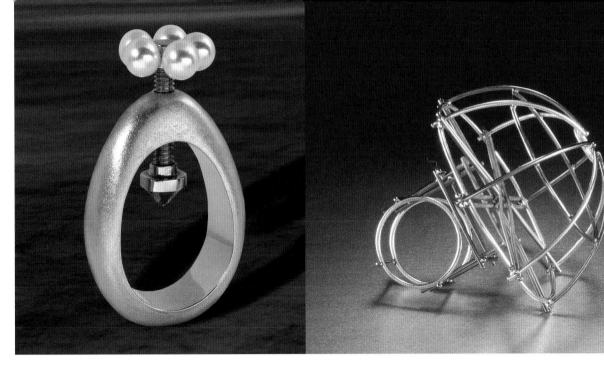

ALAN REVERE

Snug

Media	18ct gold, 925 silver, ruby, pearls
Dimensions	5.1 × 2.9 × 1.8 cm (2 × 1⅛ × ¾ in.)

Photo: Barry Blau

BEN NEUBAUER

Dome Ring

Media	18ct gold, silver, diamond, patina
Dimensions	4.0 × 3.5 × 3.5 cm (1⅝ × 1⅜ × 1⅜ in.)

Photo: Courtney Frisse

MARIA PAOLA BARROTTA

Moon

Media	18ct pink gold, 925 silver
Dimensions	2.6 × 2.4 cm (1 × 1 in.)

Photo: Sergio Stamerra

JURA GOLUB

Miquel Coca Ring

Media	22ct gold, 18ct gold, 14ct gold, titanium, copper
Dimensions	2.3 × 1.1 cm (⅞ × ⅜ in.)

Photo: Jura Golub

THERESA BURGER
Old-Fashioned Romance

Media	platinum, cultured pearls
Dimensions	6.9 × 3.4 × 3.6 cm (2¾ × 1⅜ × 1⅜ in.)

Photo: Theresa Burger

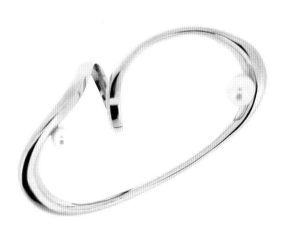

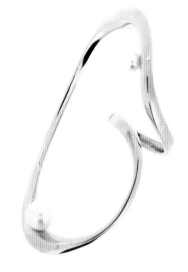

TERRY WARE
Topaz Diamond Finger Ring

Media	14ct white gold, white topaz with iron oxide, diamonds
Dimensions	3.8 × 1.9 × 1.3 cm (1½ × ¾ × ½ in.)

Photo: CarinKrasner.com

NEVIN ARIG
Wave 2

Media	925 silver
Dimensions	3.5 × 2.8 × 2.0 cm (1⅜ × 1⅛ × ¾ in.)

Photo: Eda Celiktin

KIM OANH PHAM
Tender Melancholy

Media	925 silver, spinel, peridot
Dimensions	2.5 × 2.2 × 1.6 cm (1 × ⅞ × ⅝ in.)

Photo: Kim Oanh Pham

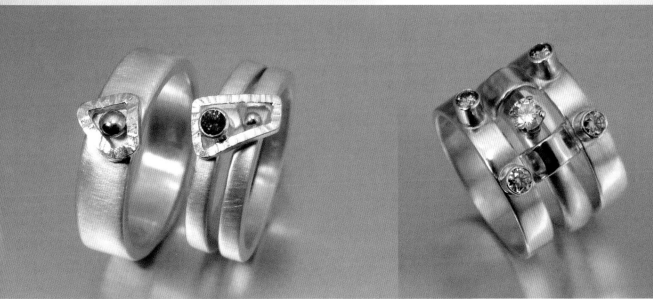

MELODY ARMSTRONG
Frost Ruby Wedding Rings

Media	14ct gold, 925 silver, ruby
Dimensions	2.4 × 2.1 × 1.4 cm (1 × ⅞ × ½ in.)

Photo: Melody Armstrong

MELODY ARMSTRONG
Bridge Wedding Set

Media	925 silver, green and colourless diamonds
Dimensions	2.6 × 2.2 × 1.6 cm (1 × ⅞ × ⅝ in.)

Photo: Melody Armstrong

JORGE CASTAÑON
Colour Ring

Media	wood, lapis lazuli
Dimensions	6.0 × 4.3 × 4.0 cm
	(2⅜ × 1¾ × 1⅝ in.)

Photo: Damián Wasser

JORGE CASTAÑON
Pencil Ring

Media	wood
Dimensions	3.5 × 2.5 × 1.0 cm
	(1⅜ × 1 × ⅜ in.)

Photo: Damián Wasser

JORGE CASTAÑON
Natural Ring

Media	wood
Dimensions	4.6 × 3.2 × 1.5 cm
	(1¾ × 1¼ × ⅝ in.)

Photo: Jorge Castañon

LITO
Untitled

Media	gold, amethyst, tsavorite
Dimensions	3.0 × 2.5 × 1.2 cm (1⅛ × 1 × ½ in.)

Photo: Kostas Satlanis

LITO
Untitled

Media	gold, iolite, diamonds
Dimensions	3.2 × 2.4 × 2.0 cm (1¼ × 1 × ¾ in.)

Photo: Kostas Satlanis

Media   top row: silver, labradorite, amethyst, opal, quartz; centre
row: silver; amazonite, amethyst, carnelian, moonstone;
front row: silver, aquamarine, tourmaline, moonstone,
sunstone, labradorite

Media   top row: silver, opal, amber, sapphire, heliodor; centre
row: silver, gold, tourmaline, amethyst, aquamarine,
opal; front row: silver, amber, tourmaline

CLAIRE WOLFSTIRN
Funambulles

Media   925 silver
Dimensions   2.9 × 2.1 cm (1⅛ × ⅞ in.)

Photo: Gilles Cohen

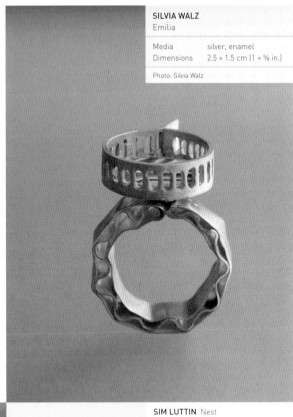

SILVIA WALZ
Emilia

Media   silver, enamel
Dimensions   2.5 × 1.5 cm (1 × ⅝ in.)

Photo: Silvia Walz

SIM LUTTIN Nest

Media   silver, graphite
Dimensions   4.6 × 2.0 × 1.5 cm
               (1¾ × ¾ × ⅝ in.)

Photo: Kevin Montague

CLAIRE WOLFSTIRN
Culbuto

Media   925 silver, moonstone
Dimensions   2.6 × 1.1 cm (1 × ⅜ in.)

Photo: Bruno Colin

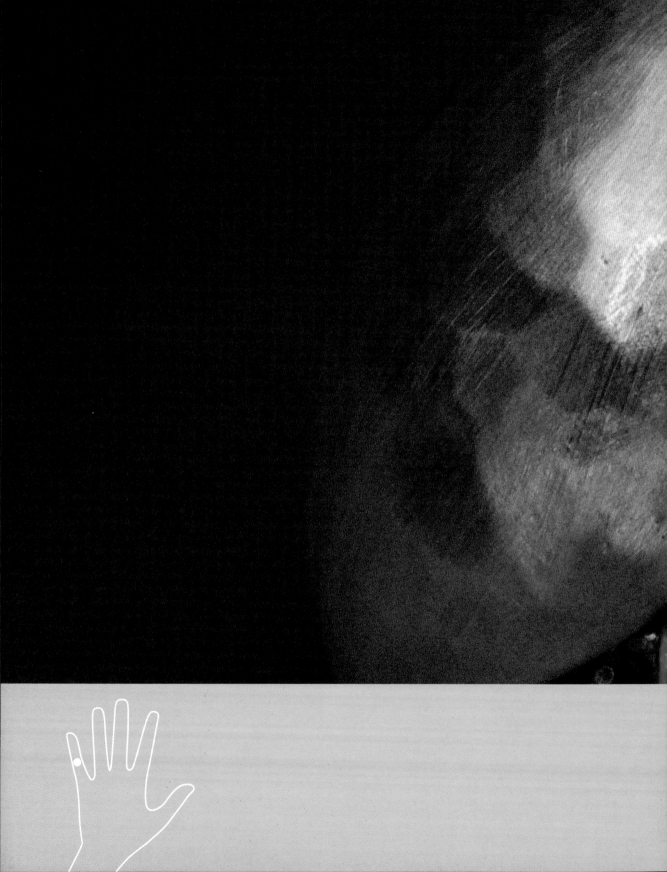

CONNECTION

MARIE PENDARIÈS
Avoir le Coeur sur la Main

Media   porcelain
Dimensions   5.5 × 4.5 cm
               (2⅛ × 1¾ in.)

Photo: Marie Pendariès

ELA BAUER Untitled

Media	yarn, coral, silicone, varnish
Dimensions	3.0 × 1.3 cm (1⅛ × ½ in.)

Photo: Ela Bauer

ELA BAUER Untitled

Media	silver, pearls, coral, yarn, cotton
Dimensions	3.0 × 1.5 cm (1⅛ × ⅝ in.)

Photo: Ela Bauer

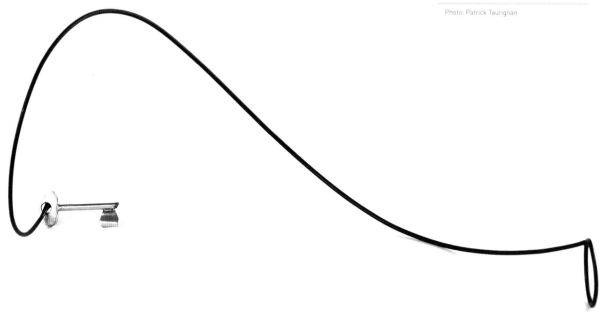

SONIA LEDOS Montrer/Cacher Son
Jeu (Showing/Hiding One's Hand)

Media	gold, silver, brass, steel, patina
Dimensions	2.0 × 1.8 cm (¾ × ¾ in.)

Photo: Patrick Taurignan

SONIA LEDOS
Faux Pli (Crease)

Media	silver, silk thread
Dimensions	1.7 × 14 cm (⅝ × 5½ in.)

Photo: Patrick Taurignan

SARAH HOOD
Landscape Sample Rings

Media	925 silver, model railway landscape materials
Dimensions	5.0 × 3.8 × 1.5 cm (2 × 1½ × ⅝ in.)

Photo: Doug Yaple

SARAH HOOD
Winter Tree Ring

Media	925 silver, plastic
Dimensions	7.5 × 5.0 × 2.5 cm (3 × 2 × 1 in.)

Photo: Doug Yaple

SARAH HOOD Sanibel Island Rings

Media	925 silver, found organic materials
Dimensions	5.0 × 2.5 × 1.5 cm (2 × 1 × ⅝ in.)

Photo: Doug Yaple

SARAH HOOD Three Rings

Media	18ct gold, 925 silver
Dimensions	5.0 × 2.5 × 1.5 cm (2 × 1 × ⅝ in.)

Photo: Doug Yaple

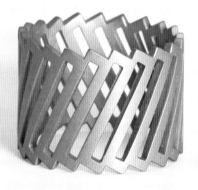

CHRISTA LÜHTJE
Two Rings

Media	22ct gold
Dimensions	2.2 × 1.5 cm (⅞ × ⅝ in.)

Photo: Eva Jünger

CHRISTA LÜHTJE
Ring

Media	22ct gold
Dimensions	1.3 × 1.4 cm (½ × ½ in.)

Photo: Eva Jünger

DANIEL DICAPRIO Orifice Ring 8

Media   wood, gold leaf
Dimensions   5.1 × 3.2 × 2.5 cm
             (2 × 1¼ × 1 in.)

Photo: Daniel DiCaprio

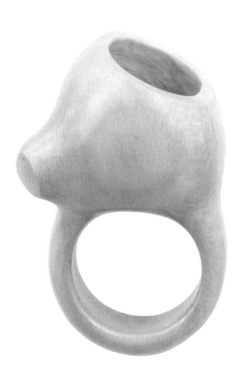

DANIEL DICAPRIO Orifice Ring 16

Media   wood
Dimensions   5.1 × 2.5 × 1.3 cm
             (2 × 1 × ½ in.)

Photo: Daniel DiCaprio

TORE SVENSSON Inside 4 × 4 cm

Media	steel, gilding
Dimensions	4.0 × 4.0 × 0.1 cm
	(1⅝ × 1⅝ × ⅛ in.)

Photo: Franz Karl

TORE SVENSSON Inside 4 × 4 cm

Media	steel, silver plating
Dimensions	4.0 × 3.5 × 0.1 cm
	(1⅝ × 1⅜ × ⅛ in.)

Photo: Franz Karl

TORE SVENSSON Inside 4 × 4 cm

Media	steel, gilding
Dimensions	4.0 × 4.0 × 0.1 cm
	(1⅝ × 1⅝ × ⅛ in.)

Photo: Franz Karl

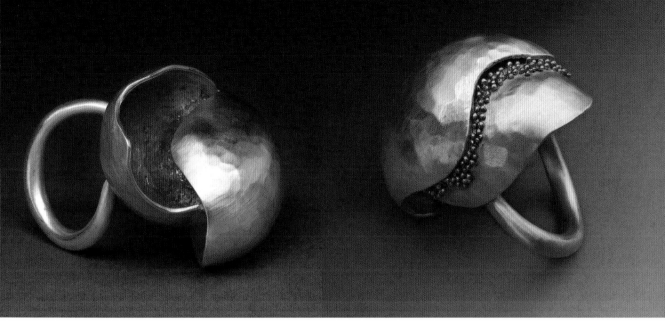

DAVINA ROMANSKY Bestowed #2

Media   silver, keum-boo
Dimensions   6.4 × 3.8 × 3.8 cm
     (2½ × 1½ × 1½ in.)

Photo: Elizabeth Lemark

DAVINA ROMANSKY Bestowed #1

Media   18ct pink gold, silver
Dimensions   6.4 × 3.8 × 3.8 cm
     (2½ × 1½ × 1½ in.)

Photo: Elizabeth Lemark

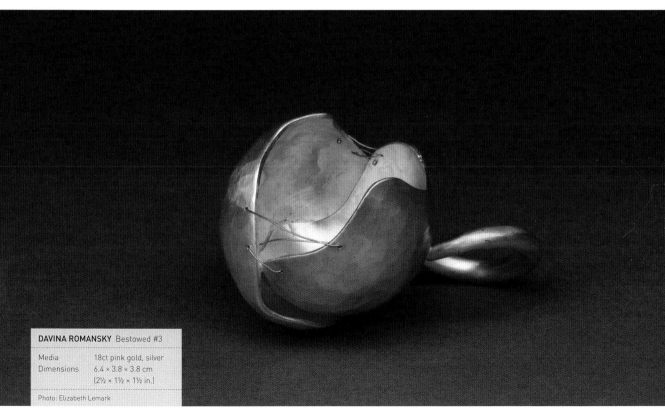

DAVINA ROMANSKY Bestowed #3

Media   18ct pink gold, silver
Dimensions   6.4 × 3.8 × 3.8 cm
     (2½ × 1½ × 1½ in.)

Photo: Elizabeth Lemark

SELDA OKUTAN
Angel Ring

Media   gold-plated silver, amethyst
Dimensions   6.6 × 3.1 × 2.5 cm
               (2⅝ × 1⅛ × 1 in.)

Photo: Mehmet Arda

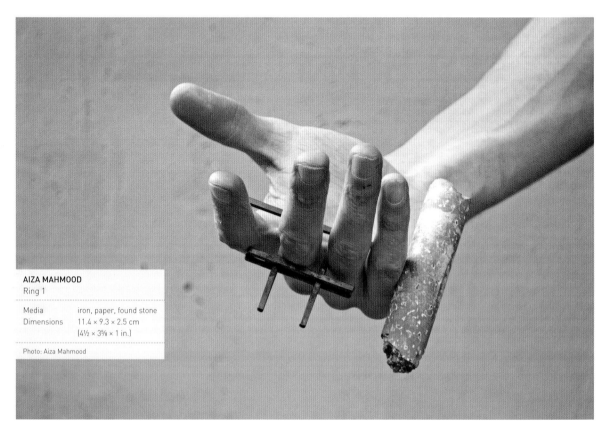

AIZA MAHMOOD
Ring 1

Media   iron, paper, found stone
Dimensions   11.4 × 9.3 × 2.5 cm
               (4½ × 3⅝ × 1 in.)

Photo: Aiza Mahmood

KARIN SEUFERT
Untitled

Media   silver, Colorit
Dimensions   3.0 × 2.0 cm (1⅛ × ¾ in.)

Photo: Karin Seufert

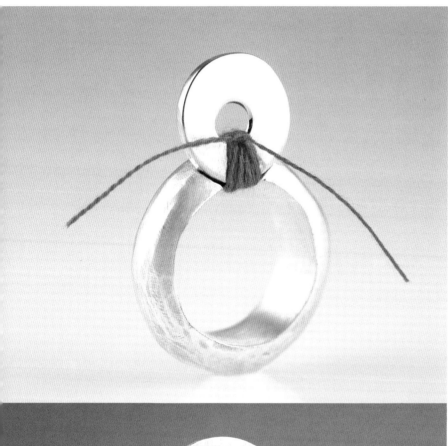

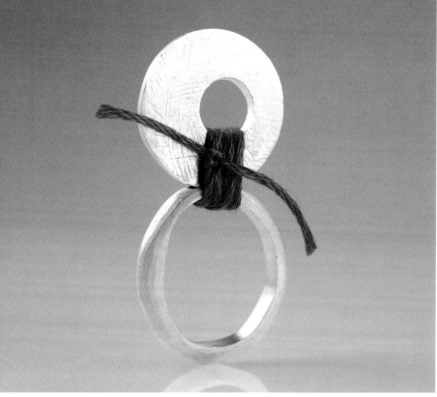

STEPHANIE JENDIS Matterhorn

Media	18ct gold, synthetic stone, ebony
Dimensions	6.0 × 3.5 × 2.0 cm (2⅜ × 1⅜ × ¾ in.)

Photo: Eric Knoote

BABETTE VON DOHNANYI Rocks

Media	gold-plated bronze, acrylic paint
Dimensions	4.3 × 3.2 × 2.6 cm (1⅝ × 1⅛ × 1 in.)

Photo: Federico Cavicchioli

STEPHANIE JENDIS Rock

Media	stainless steel
Dimensions	3.5 × 2.5 × 1.0 cm (1⅜ × 1 × ⅜ in.)

Photo: Eric Knoote

BIBA SCHUTZ Floral Ring

Media   925 silver, patina
Dimensions   1.7 × 1.7 × 2.0 cm
             (⅝ × ⅝ × ¾ in.)

Photo: Ron Boszko

ARATA FUCHI
The Time of One's Nativity

Media   24ct gold, silver,
             silver dust, patina
Dimensions   7.2 × 3.2 × 2.8 cm
             (2⅞ × 1¼ × 1⅛ in.)

Photo: Ichiro Usuda

ALINA LÓPEZ
Temple

Media	silver
Dimensions	3.2 × 2.2 cm (1¼ × ⅞ in.)

Photo: Julio César Gómez

ALINA LÓPEZ
Clover Mandala

Media	silver
Dimensions	3.2 × 2.2 cm (1¼ × ⅞ in.)

Photo: Gabriel Pintado

ANN JENKINS
Cup Garden Ring Stack

Media	fine silver, 925 silver, enamel
Dimensions	3.0 cm (1⅛ in.)

Photo: Ann Jenkins

JENNACA LEIGH DAVIES
Alphabet Rings

Media 925 silver
Dimensions 2.0 × 2.0 × 0.5 cm
(¾ × ¾ × ¼ in.)

Photo: Steffen Knudsen Allen

NICOLAS ESTRADA
Little Bird 3

Media silver, enamel
Dimensions 1.2 × 0.8 cm (½ × ⅜ in.)

Photo: Pancho Tolchinsky

SENAY AKIN
Mosaic Ring II

Media	gold, silver
Dimensions	3.2 × 2.6 × 2.2 cm
	(1¼ × 1 × ⅞ in.)

Photo: Mikail Cebeci

SENAY AKIN
Autumn Ring

Media	gold, silver, agate
Dimensions	2.9 × 2.8 × 2.6 cm
	(1⅛ × 1⅛ × 1 in.)

Photo: Mikail Cebeci

IGNASI CAVALLER
Tramuntana 2

Media	wood, fossilized wood, silver
Dimensions	7.6 × 4.0 × 1.6 cm
	(3 × 1⅝ × ⅝ in.)

Photo: Manu Ocaña

IGNASI CAVALLER
Tramuntana 1

Media	amber, limestone, fossilized wood, gold
Dimensions	6.0 × 4.3 × 3.5 cm
	(2⅜ × 1⅝ × 1⅜ in.)

Photo: Manu Ocaña

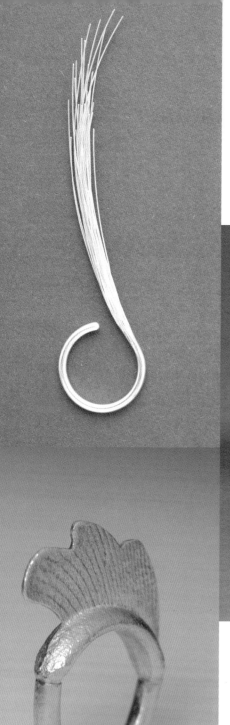

LULU TEHILA FEINSILVER
Valley

Media	925 silver
Dimensions	8.8 × 2.0 × 2.0 cm
	(3½ × ¾ × ¾ in.)

Photo: Lulu Tehila Feinsilver

SUSAN MAY Untitled

Media &	18ct gold, 925 silver, 2.8 ×
Dimensions	1.8 / 2.5 × 2.0 / 2.3 × 2.2 cm
	(1⅛ × ¾ / 1 × ¾ / ⅞ × ⅞ in.)

Photo: Susan May

MAREEN ALBURG DUNCKER
Cockscomb

Media	silver
Dimensions	3.5 × 2.0 cm (1⅜ × ¾ in.)

Photo: Mareen Alburg Duncker

TITHI KUTCHAMUCH
A Secret Friend

Media	silver, bronze
Dimensions	5.5 × 5 × 2.5 cm
	(2¼ × 2 × 1 in.)

Photo: Seng Jakoon

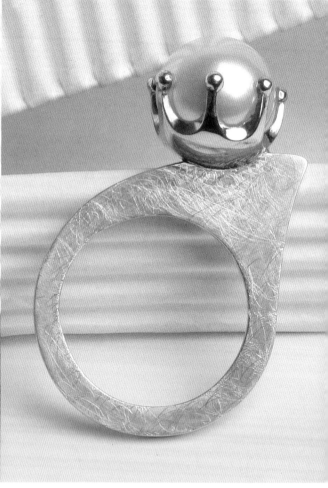

SENAY AKIN The Knight Ring

Media	18ct gold, 925 silver, amethyst
Dimensions	4.2 × 2.6 × 1.7 cm [1⅝ × 1 × ⅝ in.]

Photo: Senay Akin

SENAY AKIN The Princess Ring

Media	18ct gold, freshwater pearl, sterling silver
Dimensions	3.1 × 2.2 × 1.1 cm [1¼ × ⅞ × ⅜ in.]

Photo: Senay Akin

NICOLAS ESTRADA
Repaired

Media	gold, silver, iron, emerald, quartz, wood, natural fibre
Dimensions	8.0 × 3.5 × 2.5 cm (3⅛ × 1¼ × 1 in.)

Photo: Manu Ocaña

NICOLAS ESTRADA
Sinner Inside

Media	gold, silver, pearl, opal, vegetable ivory, pigment
Dimensions	9.5 × 6.5 × 6.0 cm (3¾ × 2¼ × 2⅜ in.)

Photo: Manu Ocaña

NATALIA MILOSZ-PIEKARSKA
Zoe's Ring

Media	yellow gold, Australian sapphire
Dimensions	2.0 × 2.0 × 0.3 cm (¾ × ¾ × ⅛ in.)

Photo: Natalia Milosz-Piekarska

NATALIA MILOSZ-PIEKARSKA
Hidey Hole Ring

Media	silver, copper, wood
Dimensions	5.0 × 5.0 × 4.0 cm (2 × 2 × 1⅝ in.)

Photo: Natalia Milosz-Piekarska

NATALIA MILOSZ-PIEKARSKA
Grandmother Rings

Media	silver, copper, found objects, resin
Dimensions	5.0 × 5.0 × 4.0 cm (2 × 2 × 1⅝ in.)

Photo: Terence Bogue

ALAN REVERE
Implosion

Media	18ct gold, diamonds
Dimensions	2.8 × 2.8 × 1.5 cm
	(1⅛ × 1⅛ × ⅝ in.)

Photo: Barry Blau

CECILIA RICHARD
Reversible

Media	18ct gold, silver, patina
Dimensions	diameter 3.0 cm (1⅛ in.)

Photo: Juan Der Hairabedian

FABRICE SCHAEFER
Immortelle

Media	24ct gold, titanium,
	yellow sapphire
Dimensions	2.8 cm (1⅛ in.)

Photo: Fabrice Schaefer

DJURDJICA KESIC Transformations

Media &   18ct gold, 925 silver,
Dimensions patina, 2.5 × 1.8 × 1.6 cm
            (1 × ¾ × ⅝ in.)

Photo: Djurdjica Kesic

DJURDJICA KESIC Transformations

Media   18ct gold, 925 silver,
            patina
Dimensions 2.5 × 1.8 × 1.6 cm
            (1 × ¾ × ⅝ in.)

Photo: Djurdjica Kesic

IRENE BEATRIZ PALOMAR
Ring for Looking At

Media   925 silver, leather
Dimensions   8.0 × 2.7 cm (3⅛ × 1 in.)

Photo: Marianela Depetro

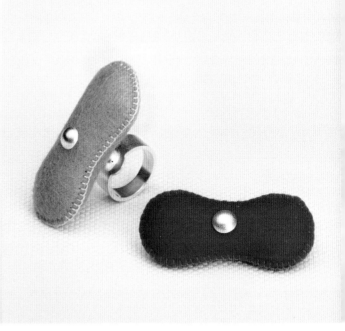

AUGOUSTA THEMISTOCLEOUS
Untitled 2

Media &   925 silver, red-thread
Dimensions   temari ball, 3.0 × 3.0 ×
              5.0 cm (1⅛ × 1⅛ × 2 in.)

Photo: Michalis Theocharides

ANDREA VELÁZQUEZ
Little Cushion 2

Media   silver, felt
Dimensions   2.5 × 1.0 cm (1 × ⅜ in.)

Photo: Fernando Bagué

MOTOKO FURUHASHI Growth

Media	iron wire
Dimensions	from 3.0 × 2.5 × 0.3 (1⅛ × 1 × ⅛ in.) to 14.0 × 7.0 × 3.0 cm (5½ × 2¾ × 1⅛ in.)

Photo: Motoko Furuhashi

ALEXANDRA DE SERPA PIMENTEL
Greenfingers series   Photos: the designer

We Hold the World in Our Hands		Watch It Grow		Water Wisely		Sow the Seed		Till the Soil	
Media & Dimensions	silver, crystal, 5.1 × 2.5 × 2.2 cm (2 × 1 × ⅞ in.)	Media & Dimensions	gold, silver, 4.8 × 4.2 × 4.0 cm (1⅞ × 1⅝ × 1⅝ in.)	Media & Dimensions	gold, silver, 5.2 × 4.8 × 1.9 cm (2 × 1⅞ × ¾ in.)	Media & Dimensions	gold, silver, 5.3 × 2.3 × 2.1 cm (2⅛ × ⅞ × ⅞ in.)	Media & Dimensions	gold, silver, 5.8 × 2.8 × 2.5 cm (2¼ × 1⅛ × 1 in.)

TOMOYO HIRAIWA Japanese Beauty

Media	silver, acrylic paint
Dimensions	6.0 × 6.0 × 4.0 cm
	(2⅜ × 2⅜ × 1⅝ in.)

Photo: Shinichi Ichikawa

TOMOYO HIRAIWA Japanese Beauty

Media	silver, acrylic paint
Dimensions	7.0 × 7.0 × 3.0 cm
	(2¾ × 2¾ × 1⅛ in.)

Photo: Shinichi Ichikawa

BEATE KLOCKMANN
Green Glasshouse Ring

Media	gold, silver, enamel
Dimensions	3.7 × 2.5 × 2.2 cm
	(1½ × 1 × ⅞ in.)

Photo: Beate Klockmann

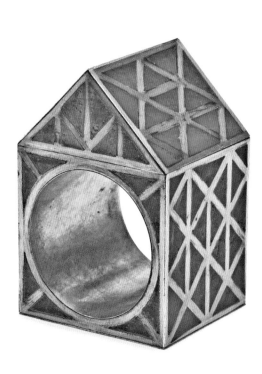

JUDY McCAIG
Amanecer (Dawn)

Media	gold, silver
Dimensions	3.8 × 3.6 cm (1½ × 1⅜ in.)

Photo: Gonzalo Cáceres

JUDY McCAIG
Crepúsculo (Twilight)

Media	gold, silver
Dimensions	4.1 × 4.0 cm (1⅝ × 1⅝ in.)

Photo: Gonzalo Cáceres

JUDY McCAIG
Noche Oscura (Dark Night)

Media	silver, methacrylate, paint, rock crystal
Dimensions	3.8 × 3.8 cm (1½ × 1½ in.)

Photo: Gonzalo Cáceres

TERESA KLEINEIDAM
Aus dem Nähkästchen (The Inside Story)

Media   925 silver, enamel
Dimensions   3.9 × 1.6 cm (1½ × ⅝ in.)

Photo: Teresa Kleineidam

ANNIE TUNG
Hold On, rings with hand-held
lockets/mementoes

Media   silver, brass, stainless
             steel, methacrylate, hair
Dimensions   2.5 × 3.0 × 21 cm
             (1 × 1⅛ × 8¼ in.)

Photo: Saad Qattan

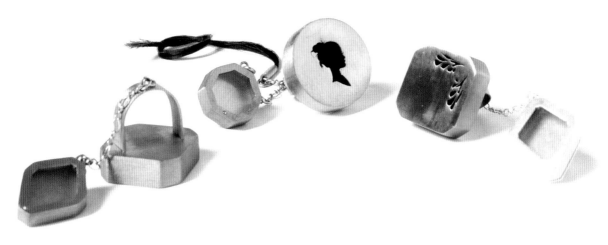

JÁNOS GÁBOR VARGA
Black Bone Ring

Media	gold, bone
Dimensions	4.5 × 2.9 × 2.3 cm
	(1¾ × 1⅛ × 1 in.)

Photo: Luca Orlandini

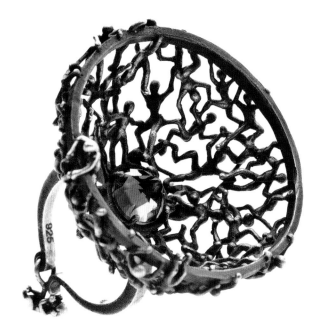

GREGORY LARIN
Heart Ring

Media	gold, garnet
Dimensions	4.3 × 1.5 × 1.5 cm
	(1⅝ × ⅝ × ⅝ in.)

Photo: Yoav Reinshtein

SELDA OKUTAN
Araf Ring

Media	gold, silver, amethyst
Dimensions	4.9 × 4.9 × 3.7 cm
	(2 × 2 × 1½ in.)

Photo: Serhat Ozsen

ALICIA HANNAH NAOMI
Somni Ring, Umbra Ring, Molt Ring, Hush Ring, Muir Ring, Cinder Ring,
Ember Ring, Ash Ring, Ruins Ring, Atlas Ring, Murmur Ring

Media   silver, spinel
Dimensions   various sizes

Photo: Andrew Barcham

ALICIA HANNAH NAOMI
Somni Ring

Media   silver
Dimensions   1.9 × 1.5 × 0.7 cm
               (¾ × ⅝ × ¼ in.)

Photo: Andrew Barcham

ALICIA HANNAH NAOMI
Atlas Ring

Media   silver, spinel
Dimensions   1.4 × 0.7 × 0.3 cm
               (⅝ × ¼ × ⅛ in.)

Photo: Andrew Barcham

NORA PATRICIA SOLARTE Ring 2

Media	silver, quartz
Dimensions	5.5 × 2.0 × 0.2 cm
	(2⅛ × ¾ × ⅛ in.)

Photo: Daniel Bueno

NORA PATRICIA SOLARTE Ring 3

Media	silver, quartz
Dimensions	5.5 × 2.0 × 0.2 cm
	(2⅛ × ¾ × ⅛ in.)

Photo: Daniel Bueno

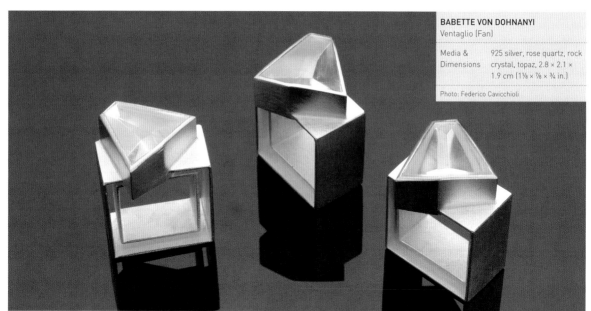

BABETTE VON DOHNANYI
Ventaglio (Fan)

Media &   925 silver, rose quartz, rock
Dimensions   crystal, topaz, 2.8 × 2.1 ×
               1.9 cm (1⅛ × ⅞ × ¾ in.)

Photo: Federico Cavicchioli

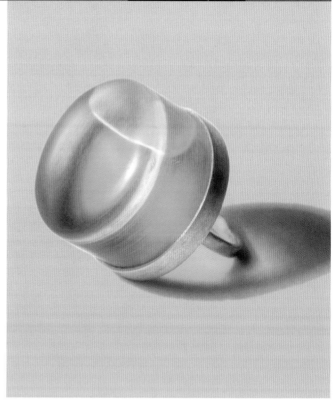

CARACTÈRE (GEMA BARRERA &
PASCAL CRETIN) Illusion

Media &   silver, polymethacrylate
Dimensions   beads, 3.8 × 3.4 × 1.9 cm
               (1½ × 1⅜ × ¾ in.)

Photo: Caractère

IACOV AZUBEL
Water

Media &   925 silver, polymethacrylate,
Dimensions   water, 4.5 × 3.7 × 3.7 cm
               (1¾ × 1½ × 1½ in.)

Photo: Iacov Azubel

SELDA OKUTAN
Gossip Ring

Media	gold, silver, diamond
Dimensions	2.8 × 2.1 × 0.5 cm
	(1⅛ × ⅞ × ¼ in.)

Photo: Mehmet Arda

EMILY WATSON
Birdie Ring

Media	Formica, silver
Dimensions	3.8 × 3.8 × 1.9 cm
	(1½ × 1½ × ¾ in.)

Photo: Emily Watson

EMILY WATSON
LavenderHotFlint

Media	Corian
Dimensions	5.7 × 4.5 × 0.7 cm
	(2¼ × 1¾ × ¼ in.)

Photo: Emily Watson

MICHAL OREN
4 Paper Loops

Media	silver, patina
Dimensions	2.7 × 2.2 × 0.5 cm
	(1 × ⅞ × ¼ in.)

Photo: Michal Oren

MICHAL OREN
Tear-Loops

Media	silver, patina
Dimensions	2.7 × 2.2 × 0.5 cm
	(1 × ⅞ × ¼ in.)

Photo: Ilit Azoulay

MICHAL OREN
Tear #2

Media	silver, patina
Dimensions	2.6 × 2.4 × 0.4 cm
	(1 × 1 × ⅛ in.)

Photo: Uri Gershuni

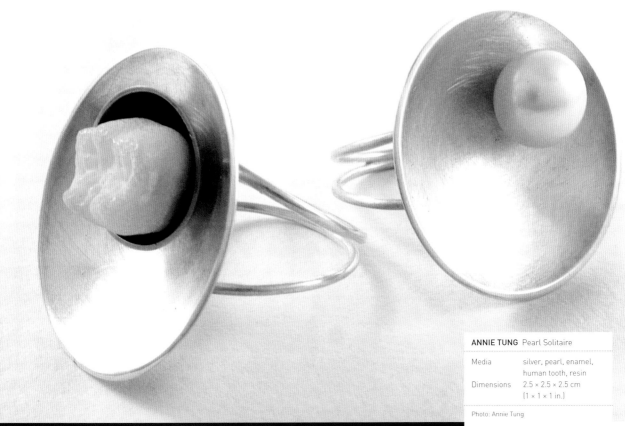

ANNIE TUNG Pearl Solitaire

Media	silver, pearl, enamel, human tooth, resin
Dimensions	2.5 × 2.5 × 2.5 cm (1 × 1 × 1 in.)

Photo: Annie Tung

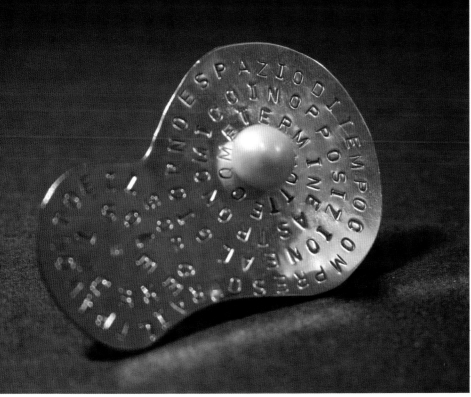

FLAVIA BRÜHLMANN
White Night

Media	silver, pearl
Dimensions	6.0 × 5.5 × 3.0 cm (2⅜ × 2⅛ × 1⅛ in.)

Photo: Flavia Brühlmann

ISABEL ARANGO TISNÉS
Spiders

Media	925 silver, white topaz, blue topaz
Dimensions	2.6 × 1.8 cm (1 × ¾ in.)

Photo: Alejandra Estrada

PILAR GARRIGOSA
Untitled

Media	18ct gold, rock crystal
Dimensions	3.0 × 2.5 cm (1⅛ × 1 in.)

Photo: Nos & Soto

ANALYA CÉSPEDES
Floral

Media	gold, 925 silver
Dimensions	3.5 × 3.0 cm (1⅜ × 1⅛ in.)

Photo: Anything Photographic

TING-CHUN ARA KUO Brush

Media	brass, wool brush, pearls
Dimensions	5.0 × 4.0 × 4.0 cm (2 × 1⅝ × 1⅝ in.)

Photo: Federico Cavicchioli

KATJA PRINS Ring/Objects

Media	silver, porcelain
Dimensions	6.5 × 2.5 × 2.5 cm (2½ × 1 × 1 in.)

Photo: Eddo Hartmann

SAMUEL SAAVEDRA
ABAC Ring

Media   gold, pearls
Dimensions   1.7 × 1.7 × 1.5 cm
             [¾ × ¾ × ⅝ in.]

Photo: Montse Poch Giró

SIM LUTTIN
Varieties of Things

Media	silver, porcelain, patina
Dimensions	5.0 × 2.5 × 1.0 cm
	(2 × 1 × ³⁄₈ in.)

Photo: Kevin Montague

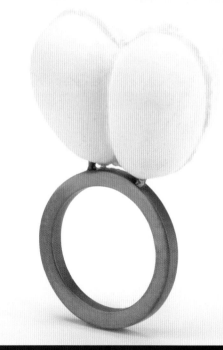

SIM LUTTIN
Cupping My Hands to Catch
My Thoughts

Media	silver, plastic, patina
Dimensions	4.5 × 2.5 × 0.4 cm
	(1³⁄₄ × 1 × ¹⁄₈ in.)

Photo: Kevin Montague

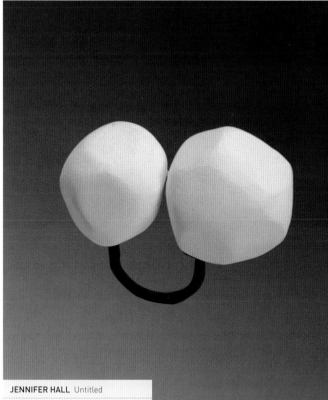

JENNIFER HALL Untitled

Media	copper, paper, paint,
	epoxy resin
Dimensions	5.1 × 5.1 × 2.5 cm
	(2 × 2 × 1 in.)

Photo: Doug Yaple

HISANO SHEPHERD
Tahitian Point Ring

Media	gold, pearls, rubies
Dimensions	2.7 × 1.9 × 0.9 cm
	(1 × ¾ × ⅜ in.)

Photo: Katja Bresch

HISANO SHEPHERD
Seed Pearl Finestrino Ring

Media	gold, pearls
Dimensions	2.5 × 1.9 × 1.2 cm
	(1 × ¾ × ⅜ in.)

Photo: Angela Peterman

HISANO SHEPHERD
Triplicity Ring II

Media	gold, pearls
Dimensions	2.3 × 2.2 × 1.3 cm
	(1 × ⅞ × ½ in.)

Photo: Katja Bresch

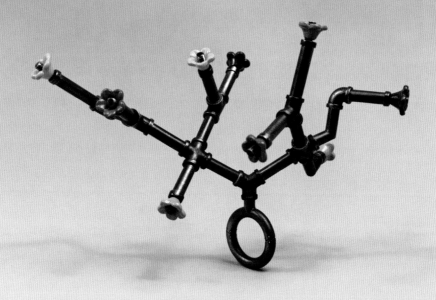

JINA SEO Flower Tree

Media	silver, bronze
Dimensions	12.7 × 11.4 × 10 cm
	(5 × 4½ × 3⅞ in.)

Photo: Jung-soo Park

CATALINA GÓMEZ AYARZA
Black Zigzag Ring

| Media | 950 silver, patina |
| Dimensions | 3.0 × 3.0 cm (1⅛ × 1⅛ in.) |

Photo: Andrés Gómez

MARINA MOLINELLI WELLS
Pura Vida: interchangeable rings

| Media | fine silver, 925 silver, gold leaf |
| Dimensions | 2.0 × 2.0 × 0.4 cm (¾ × ¾ × ⅛ in.) |

Photo: Pablo Mehanna

ANA SÁNCHEZ Mousse

Media	18ct gold, 925 silver
Dimensions	2.0 × 2.0 × 1.2 cm
	(¾ × ¾ × ½ in.)

Photo: Víctor Sánchez

REBECCA HANNON Trapped Bird

Media	gold, silver
Dimensions	2.5 × 2.0 × 2.0 cm
	(1 × ¾ × ¾ in.)

Photo: Jeremy Tressler

REBECCA HANNON Cigar Band

Media	silver
Dimensions	1.5 × 1.5 × 1.0 cm
	(⅝ × ⅝ × ⅜ in.)

Photo: Rebecca Hannon

PATRICIA LEMAIRE
Enchanted Fruit

Media	18ct gold, 925 silver
Dimensions	3.0 × 3.0 cm (1⅛ × 1⅛ in.)

Photo: Patricia Lemaire

SARAH ROBINSON Pod

Media	925 silver
Dimensions	4.5 × 3.0 × 1.5 cm
	(1¾ × 1⅛ × ⅝ in.)

Photo: Sarah Robinson

PILAR RESTREPO Eucalyptus

Media	925 silver
Dimensions	3.0 × 3.0 × 2.0 cm
	(1⅛ × 1⅛ × ¾ in.)

Photo: María Elisa Duque

MARTA FERNÁNDEZ CABALLERO
Daisies

Media	silver, cultured pearls
Dimensions	5.0 × 4.0 cm (2 × 1⅝ in.)

Photo: Ibai Zubizarreta

ADRIANA HENAO | Colombian
aurea@aureajoyas.com / www.aureajoyas.com
Adriana Henao Mejía began her jewelry training by experimenting and letting her curiosity reign in her father's industrial machine shop. After plunging herself into self-study, she decided to found her own jewelry workshop, Áurea, and has since designed collections inspired by the observation of nature and the study of ethnic American iconography. She also creates unique personalized pieces that reflect the personalities of their wearers. Adriana's work has been exhibited at the Modern Art Museum in Medellín and in galleries in Bogotá, Medellín, Cali and Cartagena. She has participated in events including 'Green Jewels: Eco Friendly Expo' and 'Latin American Cultural Week' in New York City, and her work has featured in shows in London, New York, Mexico City, Lima and Bogotá. > p. 163

AIZA MAHMOOD | Pakistani
aiza.mahmood@hotmail.com /
www.behance.net/AizaMahmud
Aiza Mahmood's jewelry describes social issues and explores possible ways of coping with them. She questions the way that society functions and analyses her own perception of the system as it is presented to us as members of that society. The use of rigid structures in her work echoes the dominating nature of society, while the hard and unyielding nature of the pieces reflects the aggression and physical power of rapidly growing social restrictions. The inclusion of other materials represents her own defiant stance against these cultural norms. > p. 208

ALAN REVERE | American
alan@revereacademy.com / www.revereacademy.com
Alan Revere holds a unique position in the jewelry community, with one foot firmly planted as an award-winning designer and the other as one of the country's foremost jewelry educators. Revere teaches primarily at the school he founded and directs, the Revere Academy of Jewelry Arts (est. 1979), in San Francisco, California. He has created instructional books, articles and videos for goldsmiths and jewelers, including *Professional Jewelry Making*, *The Art of Jewelry* and *Revere on Goldsmithing*. Revere is a founder of the Contemporary Jewelry Design Group, past president of the American Jewelry Design Council, and recipient of the German Kontraste Prize and Jewelers of America Jewel Award. He has been inducted into the National Metalsmiths Hall of Fame.
> pp. 21, 191, 221

ALEJANDRA SOLAR | Mexican
joyeriasolar@gmail.com
Alejandra is currently based in Luxembourg. Born in Mexico City and with degrees from the US, Spain

and Germany, she holds a Master in Fine Arts from Trier University of Applied Sciences in Idar-Oberstein. Her work has been published in various books, magazines and catalogues and exhibited worldwide. In 2006, Alejandra won a contest to design the JORGC Award for the Jewelers, Gold and Silversmiths, Watchmakers and Gemmologists Association of Catalonia, and in 2014 she was awarded the New Traditional Jewellery prize at SIERAAD Art Fair in Amsterdam. Her work is part of the permanent collection of the Schmuckmuseum Pforzheim. > pp. 21, 47

ALEXANDRA DE SERPA PIMENTEL | Portuguese
alexspimentel@gmail.com
After majoring in jewelry design at the Central School of Art and Design in London, Alexandra de Serpa Pimentel became a design pioneer in Portugal, opening Lisbon's first jewelry gallery, Artefacto 3, in 1984, and founding and teaching in the jewelry department of Ar.Co, the Centre of Art and Visual Communication in Lisbon. Alexandra's work has been published in *1000 Rings*, *500 Silver Jewelry Designs* and *Art Jewelry Today 2* and *3*, and shown internationally in locations including Goldsmiths' Hall in London, Velvet da Vinci in San Francisco, and the National Museum of History in Rio de Janeiro. Strongly influenced by her love of nature, Alexandra uses simple shapes to create complex pieces that flow and move with the body when worn. > p. 224

ALICIA HANNAH NAOMI | Australian
www.aliciahannahnaomi.com
Alicia Hannah Naomi's body of work is made using both classic and contemporary gold- and silversmithing techniques. This approach forges a delicate balance between the traditional cues of craftsmanship and the way inspiration is articulated through fabrication. Her work explores the poetry found in natural objects and processes that possess a dark beauty. Jewelry becomes an intimate manifestation of its wearer, with surface textures that are meticulously hand-carved and adorned with precious gems to echo the subversiveness that is the essence of Alicia's post-luxury philosophy.
> pp. 138, 230

ALIDRA ALI | Danish
info@alidraalic.com / www.alidraalic.com
Copenhagen-based jewelry artist Alidra Alić created quite a stir when she first invited the world into her fairytale garden of fine jewelry. She studied art history and jewelry-making in Italy and Denmark and her work has been been exhibited at galleries and museums in Denmark, Sweden, the Netherlands, Italy, Russia, Germany and the US. She also received a Special Mention at Preziosa Young 2009, a jewelry

event in Lucca, Italy, and has been awarded grants from Danish Crafts and the Danish Arts Foundation among others. Alidra's exploration of the theme of flowers and ability to combine her own techniques with traditional goldsmithing merge to produce mesmerizing and covetable modern jewelry. There is a sense of delicate light and transience in her blooming orchids, irises and hyacinths in sumptuous colours and luxuriously fluttering shapes. Working with the intricate and fragile forms of nature and the simple expression of different surfaces, precious metals and stones, Alidra creates every piece by hand. Her jewelry may stand alone or interlock with other pieces for a more elaborate effect. Her range of ready-to-wear jewelry is created with the same sense of detail and craftsmanship. > p. 84

ALINA LÓPEZ | Colombian
alinalopez@yahoo.es
Alina López studied fashion design, metal art, and jewelry in Medellín, New York and Barcelona. A two-time recipient of Colombia's prestigious Steel Pencil Award for her designs, Alina shapes silver, copper and enamel into innovative pieces using forging and fold-forming techniques. Alina's work has been published in *The Compendium Finale of Contemporary Jewellers* and *Think Twice: New Latin American Jewellery* and shown in Medellín, Bogotá, New York, Mexico and Estonia. Joy in creation and a love of intricate detail mark Alina's oeuvre, which is based on the observation of external forces, particularly those found in nature, including leaves, flowers, stones and metals. She is interested in finding meaning through encounters with nature and in the idea of combining the present moment with action.
> pp. 84, 213

AMY TAVERN | American
atavern@gmail.com / www.amytavern.com
Amy Tavern's work is based on memory and, although autobiographical, refers to shared experience and universal themes. Amy has exhibited nationally and internationally with solo shows in the US, Belgium, Sweden and Iceland. She has taught and lectured across the US and in Europe and her work as a metalsmith has been included in numerous publications, most notably on the cover of *Metalsmith* magazine. Through the creation of objects and spaces, Amy strives to make the fleeting more permanent, preserving her memories and connecting with her audience. > p. 30

ANA CHECA | Mexican
anacheca@anacheca.com / www.anacheca.com
Ana Checa trained in Mexico, Italy and the US at Universidad Iberoamericana, Universidad del Centro, Art Studio FUJI, Perseo Jewelry School, Le Arti Orafe and Parsons. The winner of the 'Mexico Tercer

INDEX OF ARTISTS

Milenio' jewelry contest sponsored by Swarovski, Ana has exhibited at Expo Joya in Guadalajara and Bisutex in Madrid and has been featured in numerous specialized publications. Seeking inspiration in the architecture, customs, and culture of every place she visits, Ana attempts to transmit her essence and love of architecture in each of her pieces. She also argues that jewelry should be seen and worn as art and sculpture, as a statement. > p. 85

ANA SÁNCHEZ | Spanish
aina_st@msn.com / www.ana-creaciones.com
Ana Sánchez has completed several workshops in applied jewelry techniques and studied jewelry-making at the Higher School of Design in Palma de Mallorca. In addition to using silver, gold and precious stones in her creations, Ana also utilizes Murano glass, porcelain and enamel. Ana's work is inspired partly by the organic forms of nature, leading her to design complex structures that reflect movement, and partly by simple geometric shapes, which she turns into pieces that are minimalist, austere and elegant. > p. 243

ANALYA CÉSPEDES | Chilean, lives in the US
analya@mac.com / www.analyacespedes.com
Analya Céspedes is a studio jeweler based in Washington, DC. She started creating jewelry 15 years ago in Santiago de Chile, and after moving to the US, continued her education in the jewelry department of MICA (Maryland College Institute of Arts). Austerity, repetition and symmetry characterize Analya's pieces, which reflect her attraction to an aesthetic rooted in nature. Much more than adornments, they serve as a diary, documenting meaningful events and an obsession with shapes, materials or colours that linger in time. > p. 237

ANDREA VELÁZQUEZ | Spanish
andreavelazquez@tiny-lab.com / www.tiny-lab.com
Andrea Velázquez Calleja trained at the Massana School, the Industrial School of Barcelona, and the Chamber of Skilled Crafts of Munich and Upper Bavaria in a variety of techniques including art jewelry, primitive casting, lost-wax casting, enamels on metals, keum-boo and Berber jewelry. A finalist in the Swarovski Awards, she has been featured in the magazines *Actitudes* and *Casa Viva*. Since childhood, Andrea has delighted in creating jewelry. She draws inspiration from objects and artifacts, antique jewelry, city life, and her travels, forging pieces that transcend feelings yet allow for individual style and philosophy. > pp. 166, 223

ANGELO VERGA | Italian
info@angeloverga.com / www.angeloverga.com
Angelo Verga studied at the State Arts School in Brera, Milan. He now lives and works in Münster, Germany. His recent exhibitions include the Cominelli Foundation Award 2015 in Cremona, 'Gioielli in Fermento' in Piacenza, and FiloRosso Bijoux in Madrid. His work has also been featured in *Art Aurea* (autumn 2015), *New Earrings* (2013) and *La cultura pavese* (2010). Working with steel, mokume gane, wood and various precious metals, Angelo aims to combine cold metals with warm materials (e.g. steel with wood), creating a synthesis between the two contrasting parts. The result is an aesthetically balanced, harmonious work of art, in which shapes, colours and materials meld together in a communicative symbiosis. > p. 78

ANN JENKINS | American
jenkinskeith@yahoo.com / www.annjenkinsjewelry.com
Since finishing her studies at the University of Louisville and the Memphis Academy of Art, Ann Jenkins has enjoyed a successful jewelry-making career. She was a featured artist in *Ornament* magazine in 2002 and her work was showcased in the book *500 Brooches* in 2005. Ann has exhibited at the Facèrè Jewelry Art Gallery in Seattle, Aaron Faber Gallery in New York, and Velvet da Vinci in San Francisco. Ann Jenkins's recent studies explore colour, texture and simplicity, demonstrating a fascination with the visual relationship between timeworn and modern. Formed from enamel, fine silver and sterling, Ann's adornments seem to move with a life of their own. > p. 213

ANNIE TUNG | Chinese Canadian
she.smiled.and.ran@gmail.com / www.shesmiledandran.com
A native of Toronto, Annie Tung graduated from Ontario College of Art and Design with a Bachelor of Design degree. Upon graduation, she participated in a three-year artist-residency programme at Harbourfront Centre's Craft Studio, one of Canada's leading cultural institutions in the heart of Toronto. Following her passion for finely detailed objects with a poetic perspective, Tung pursued a Master's in Design for Luxury and Craftsmanship at the École Cantonale d'Arts de Lausanne (ÉCAL). Tung's practice is process- and research-based, coupled with a sensitivity for materials. Through her craft objects and drawings, she is interested in making the intangible tangible. Annie has been the recipient of 15 industry awards and grants for her work and has exhibited in Canada, the US, the UK, South Korea, Germany and Italy. > pp. 227, 235

ARATA FUCHI | Japanese
mail@arata-fuchi.com / www.arata-fuchi.com
Arata Fuchi studied industrial design at Tokyo Zokei University and jewelry-making at Le Arti Orafe in Florence. His work has been exhibited in Germany, Japan and Italy and published in *Vogue Gioiello*, *Contemporary Craft in Japan* and *Dreaming Jewelry*. Arata is the winner of several prestigious international awards, including the Design Podium, the Young Lucca Preziosa Award, and the Cominelli Foundation Award. Arata draws inspiration from the beauty and pulse of life in nature. Combining silver, silver powder, fine gold, fine silver, and niello, his work is imbued with emotions which cannot be expressed through words alone. His work has been exhibited in countries including the US and Canada, and has featured in publications including *Metalsmith* magazine and *The Contemporary Jewellery Yearbook*. > pp. 73, 111, 212

ÅSA HALLDIN | Swedish
asahalldin@hotmail.se / www.asahalldin.com / www.wurma.nu
Åsa Halldin first studied blacksmithing, metalsmithing and silversmithing at Sweden's Steneby School and later received her MFA from the School of Design and Crafts of the University of Gothenburg. Since then, she has dedicated most of her time to jewelry-making, travelling to Palermo to experiment with jewelry and to Bombay to develop painting and illustrating skills. Åsa's work has been featured in the books *1000 Rings*, *500 Bracelets*, *500 Brooches* and *Artistar Jewels 2015*. She has shown her pieces both locally and internationally,

including at Velvet da Vinci in San Francisco, Platina in Stockholm, and Out of the Blue in Bombay. She has recently begun a collaboration with Helle Rasmussen Theliander, under the name Wurma Jewellery. > p. 168

AUGOUSTA THEMISTOCLEOUS | Cypriot
augousta.th@gmail.com
Augousta Themistocleous studied jewelry design at the Mokume School in Greece. Her pieces combine silver, plastic and industrially compressed paper into playfully intertwined and overlapped geometric forms. In 2008, Augousta was commissioned to design and create a collection of jewelry that was later featured on the runways in a Cypriot fashion design show. Her pieces have been exhibited at the XI Athens Biennial for Young Artists from Europe and the Mediterranean and at the Gallery Argo in Cyprus. > pp. 50, 223

BABETTE VON DOHNANYI | German
info@bd-jewellery.com / www.bd-jewellery.com
Babette von Dohnanyi received her degree from the State College for Glass and Jewelry in Neuglabonz, Germany. Featured in Lark Books' *500* series and other publications, she was awarded First Prize at the International Craft Fair in Florence in 2000 and received a special mention at the Cominelli Foundation Awards in 2014. She has also taken part in several workshops, including Ruudt Peters's Face Now (2014) and Ground Now (2015) and Philip Sajet's No Diamonds Please (2015). Babette works with precious metals such as silver and gold, which she occasionally embellishes with semi-precious stones. For the last few years, her research has centred around pentagons, which have appeared in much of her jewelry, as an expression of architectural form in balance. She sees the core of her work as a quest for the optimal technical solution needed to attain the aesthetic goal of each piece > pp. 84, 132, 171, 211, 232

BANDADA (ANA MARÍA RAMÍREZ & ADRIANA DÍAZ) | Colombian
www.cuadernobandada.blogspot.com / bandada2008@yahoo.es
Adriana Díaz and Ana María Ramírez formed Bandada seven years ago to merge their experiences and interests in jewelry and design, blending handcrafted work with industrial methods of production. Previously, Adriana studied industrial and product design, silversmithing and jewelry, and Ana María studied fine arts, jewelry and graphic design at schools including the Bogotá School of Arts and Trades, the Massana School, La Industrial and Elisava. Both members of the Bandada team view jewelry as a means of expression and experimentation that must constantly bear its wearer in mind. They therefore seek to balance expression and functionality in each piece. > p. 108

BARBARA CHRISTIE | British
Barbara Christie studied at the Sir John Cass Polytechnic (now part of London Metropolitan University) and was a regular exhibitor at the Goldsmiths' Fair in London, Art in Action in Oxford and SOFA in New York. Her work featured in *Made to Wear*, *The Earrings Book* and *The Australian Craft Magazine*. She also won the De Beers Diamond Competition and designed catwalk pieces for Valentino and Tivoli. In her pieces, she strove to unite a sculptural quality with maximal wearability.

Construction, colour, tactile surfaces and movement created a common narrative that ran through her work, yet each piece remained individual. Barbara Christie died in January 2013, but her creative contribution to contemporary British jewelry remains greatly admired and much missed. > p. 73

BARBARA HEINRICH | German
info@barbaraheinrichstudio.com /
www.barbaraheinrichstudio.com
A graduate of Pforzheim College of Design and Rochester Institute of Technology, Barbara Heinrich has run her own jewelry studio in upstate New York for over 25 years. She has been featured in numerous books, including *Profiting by Design: A Jewelry Maker's Guide to Business Success*; *Masters: Gold*; and *Brilliance! Masterpieces from the American Jewelry Design Council*. Since 2001, Barbara has participated in 'Pearls', the American Museum of Natural History's touring exhibition, won the Couture Design Award for Best of Gold in 2009, and received the 2011 Luster Award and Fashion Award in the Cultured Pearl Association of America's International Pearl Design Contest. Barbara brings her animated designs – inspired by art, nature, architecture, and music – to life as wearable pieces. Predominantly using traditional goldsmith's techniques, she creates 18-carat gold pieces that display her trademark multi-textured finishes. > pp. 29, 80, 189

BARBARA STUTMAN | Canadian
mail@barbarastutman.com / www.barbarastutman.com
Born in Montreal, Barbara Stutman studied Fine Arts and Art History at the Montreal Museum of Fine Arts, the Saidye Bronfman Center and Concordia University. She specializes in working with metal wire using textile techniques such as weaving, knitting and crochet. A frequent participant at SOFA exhibitions with Charon Kransen Arts, she has held solo exhibitions at the Jocelyne Gobeil and Noel Guyomarc'h galleries in Montreal and the Joanne Rapp Gallery in Scottsdale, Arizona. Barbara's work has been exhibited in galleries and museums throughout Canada, the US, Europe and Asia and has featured in publications including *Metalsmith* magazine and *Adorn: New Jewellery*. Her pieces are in the permanent collections of the Musée National des Beaux-Arts in Quebec City, the Montreal Museum of Fine Arts, the Alice and Louis Koch Collection in Switzerland, the Racine Art Museum in Wisconsin, and the Museum of Arts and Design in New York City. > p. 74

BEATE KLOCKMANN | German
klockmann@gmx.de / www.beateklockmann.de
Beate Klockmann began creating jewelry after training as a goldsmith and went on to receive her degree in jewelry from the Burg Giebichenstein University of Art and Design in Halle, Germany. She held her first solo exhibition at the Marzee Gallery in the Netherlands in 2003, and since then has shown regularly there and at the Slavik Gallery in Vienna, Tactile Gallery in Geneva, Caroline Van Hoek Gallery in Brussels, and Ornamentum Gallery in Hudson, New York. Beate sees classic jewelry as a form of three-dimensional painting that happens to be wearable. She has shared this approach as a guest instructor in the Gemstone and Jewelry Design Department of the University of Applied Arts in Idar-Oberstein, Germany. Since 2012, she has taught design at Hanau Design Academy. > pp. 147, 189, 225

BEATRIZ PALACIOS | Spanish
info@beatrizpalacios.es / www.beatrizpalacios.com
Beatriz Palacios Jiménez is the designer and director behind the Beatriz Palacios jewelry brand. The sources of inspiration behind her collections range from the European art and design movements of the last century to animal and plant forms. The brand launches two collections every year. Each one is different in its ideas, techniques and materials, but all of them are united by the distinctive style that Beatriz has developed over her lifetime. The aim of the brand is to maintain a consistently high focus on quality, craftsmanship and design, making use of the traditional techniques of fine jewelry. All of the pieces are designed and handcrafted in Beatriz's workshop in Madrid. > p. 142

BEN NEUBAUER | American
ben@benneubauer.com / benneubauer.com
Since graduating from Oregon College of Art and Craft in 2000, Ben Neubauer has contributed to many exhibitions in the US and abroad. Highlights include the Smithsonian Craft Show and SOFA Chicago as well as a 2008 trip to South Korea to lecture on trends in American art jewelry. The winner of the American Craft Council's Award of Achievement, he has been featured in articles in *American Craft*, *Ornament* magazine and *Lapidary Journal*. Ben's work creates intimate spaces by building transparent geometric architectural forms using gold and silver wire. > pp. 50, 96, 132, 191

BIBA SCHUTZ | American
biba@bibaschutz.com / www.bibaschutz.com
Biba Schutz's storied career includes over 75 exhibitions; including a notable solo show at Sienna Patti Gallery in Lenox, Massachusetts. She has been featured in multiple publications including *Metalsmith* magazine, *The Compendium Finale of Contemporary Jewellers* and the Lark Books' *500* series. Schutz has been an award winner at the Smithsonian Craft Show, American Craft Council and Philadelphia Museum of Art Craft Fair. Her pieces are included in the permanent collections of the Corning Museum, Corning, NY; Museum of Fine Arts, Boston; the Newark Museum, Newark, NJ; the Rotassa Foundation, Mill Valley, CA; and the Renwick Gallery, Washington, DC. Space, form and repetitive processes characterize her body of work, which is stimulated by her urban environment. Often drawn to the idea of 'a place to hide', she aims to use her sculptural pieces to create a dialogue that engages emotions and memories. > pp. 37, 102, 212

BLANCA SÁNCHEZ | Spanish
blancasanchez13@gmail.com / www.blancasanchez.com
Blanca Sánchez studied jewelry-making at the School of Arts and Crafts in Madrid, followed by jewelry and sculpture at the Massana School in Barcelona. In 2001 she became a founder member of the contemporary jewelry group Peu de Reina. Her work has been shown internationally in many group exhibitions and her first solo show, 'Quiero tenerte junto a mí', was held at the Alea Gallery in Barcelona in 2005. The Françoise van den Bosch Foundation has selected pieces from her work to be part of their Young Talents Collection. She currently designs jewelry at the Can Brillant workshop in Poble Espanyol, Barcelona, which she co-founded with her colleague Christine Harwart. Her goal is to alter the conventional forms of jewelry, turning each piece into an object that provokes curiosity. > p. 175

BLANDINE LUCE | French
contact@blandine-luce.com / www.blandine-luce.com
Blandine Luce pursued her undergraduate studies in contemporary jewelry crafts in Brussels and received her master's degree in Art History and Archaeology from the University of Lille. Her striking pieces incorporate silver, plastics, Corian, wood, and found objects, and have been shown in Belgium, France and the UK. Captivated by the architectural 'in-between' that is sometimes considered too ordinary even to justify a glance, Blandine explores urban reality in her work. For her, creation is a conscious dialogue with the material, forms, and ideas, the opportunity to invent a portable architectural gem. > p. 96

BORIS BALLY | American
boris@borisbally.com / www.borisbally.com
After receiving a BFA in Metals from Carnegie Mellon University in Pennsylvania, Boris completed an intensive goldsmith apprenticeship in Basel, Switzerland. The recipient of fellowships from the Council on the Arts in both Rhode Island and Pennsylvania, Boris placed second in the Fortunoff Silver Competition in 1990. His pieces have been featured in more than 25 publications, at the Museum of Arts and Design in New York, and in solo shows at sites including the Patina Gallery and Velvet da Vinci. His jewelry has also been added to the permanent collections of Boston's Museum of Fine Arts and the RISD Museum in Providence, Rhode Island. Boris's work is a disciplined body of objects that vary from eccentric through formal to humorous, provoking thought and reflecting some of the distortions of our ordered world. > p. 37

BRONWYNN LUSTED | Australian
bronwynn@conkerberry.com.au
Although she studied at the Sydney College of the Arts in the 1980s, Bronwynn Lusted first began making wooden jewelry as a hobby in 2005 in collaboration with her husband. Since then, her pieces have been featured at Velvet da Vinci in San Francisco and in the books *500 Pendants & Lockets*, *Bead Love*, *The Art of Jewelry: Wood*, *1000 Beads* and *Showcase 500: Beaded Jewelry*. From tiny flowers to towering gum trees, gnarled and weathered wood to swirling streams, Bronwynn's art is influenced by the natural forms of her youth, which surround her in the present day at her lovely sandstone and bush property. > p. 79

CARACTÈRE (GEMA BARRERA & PASCAL CRETIN) | Swiss
info@galeriecaractere.com / www.galeriecaractere.com
Gema Barrera and Pascal Cretin studied jewelry design and watchmaking at the Higher School of Applied Arts in La Chaux-de-Fonds and Geneva, Switzerland. The pair co-founded the Caractère Gallery in Neuchâtel in 2000, and have been featured in more than 50 exhibitions in Switzerland, Spain, France and the US, including 'Function-Fiction' at Neuchâtel's Art and History Museum in 2002. Caractère's creations, constructed of silver interspersed with resin, silicone, wood, lacquer, PVC and glass, generate an intimate and sensual relationship with the jewels set into them. Expressing dreams, desires, emotions and questions about the contemporary world, they aspire to perfection, creativity and innovation. > pp. 88, 232

CARLES CODINA ARMENGOL | Spanish
codinaarmengol@gmail.com / www.codina.co.uk
A graduate of the Massana School, Carles Codina Armengol is a prominent Spanish jewelry designer and instructor. He has exhibited locally and worldwide. At Fostering Arts and Design (FAD) and the Museum of Decorative Arts in Barcelona, SOFA New York and Chicago, the Velvet da Vinci Gallery in San Francisco, and the Beeld & Aambeeld Gallery in the Netherlands. Carles has also served on the jury for various jewelry exhibitions and authored the books *Orfebrería*, *Nueva Joyería*, *Técnicas Básicas* and *Color, Textura y Acabados*. At present, Carles splits his time between working in his own atelier, teaching at the Massana School and giving courses all around the world. > p. 114

•

CARME FÀBREGAS BARTOK | Spanish
carmefabre@hotmail.com
Carme Fàbregas Bartok pursued her undergraduate degree at the Hungarian University of Arts and Design in Budapest before undertaking graduate studies at Barcelona's Massana School. She also spent a year taking courses at the Goldsmithing and Watchmaking School in Pforzheim, Germany, then studied gemmology at the University of Barcelona. She holds the European Gemmologist Certification from the Federation for European Education in Gemmology and taught jewelry workshops at the Arsenal Municipal Art School in Vilafranca del Penedès from 2007 to 2014. She now teaches stonecutting at the Massana School, and has worked as a freelance for Joid'art since 2006. Using metals and unusual minerals, Carme's pieces take personal themes or materials that speak to her as their starting point and are inspired by travel, culture, nature, people and sensations. > pp. 53, 176

•

CARMEN PINTOR RODRÍGUEZ | Spanish
info@galeriameko.com / www.galeriameko.com
Born in Santiago de Compostela, Spain, in 1962, Carmen Pintor Rodríguez is a key figure in Barcelona's new generation of designer goldsmiths. Certified in metalworking, enamel firing, industrial jewelry design, wax modelling and gemmology, she established her own showroom and workshop in Barcelona in 1990, under the name Galeria Meko. In 2004, Carmen was named a Master Artisan by the Government of Catalonia, the highest prize awarded to Catalan goldsmiths. Her work has been exhibited at many national and international jewelry fairs. Carmen uses the colours, textures, materials and organic shapes present in nature as sources of inspiration for her delicate jewelry. > p. 183

•

CAROLINA HORNAUER | Chilean
carohornauer@gmail.com / joyasdelaodisea.blogspot.com
Carolina graduated in architecture in her native Chile after which she moved to Barcelona to study jewelry-making at the Massana School. She now lives and works in Viña del Mar, Chile. Carolina is fascinated by handicrafts and detail and often uses objects from flea markets and family mementoes in her creations. Inspired by the idea of curiosity cabinets, her stories often revolve around the Mapuche worldview and mythology. She works with materials collected from the shore on her travels, such as pieces of larch wood, fragments of buoys, knotted ropes and pieces of fishing nets.

CAROLINA MARTÍNEZ LINARES | Colombian
panapitok@hotmail.com
Carolina Martínez Linares studied industrial design at the European Institute of Design and art jewelry at the Massana School. In 2010, Carolina exhibited her work at the Galerie Noel Guyomarc'h in Montreal, the Museum of Arts and Design in New York, and the Marzee Gallery in the Netherlands, and was honoured as a recipient of the Marzee Graduate Prize. For as long as she can remember, Carolina has been fascinated by anatomy and the human body, seeking to understand its many facets. Her jewels are prosthetics that adorn our most precious possessions, our bodies, even when they are incomplete. In 2010 she became a founder member of the Bórax08001 collective, working on its creative direction and graphic design. The aim of this project is to create a closer relationship between contemporary jewelry and society by means of street interventions and personalized events. > p. 157

•

CATALINA BRENES | Costa Rican
catalina.brenes@gmail.com / www.catalinabrenes.com
Born in Costa Rica, Catalina Brenes now lives and works in Berlin. She is obsessed with the natural world, and particularly the way that growth, death and rebirth are constant presences within it. Her aim is to create forms that are remarkable for their purity and balance, treating the ceaseless flow of nature as her guiding light. She is influenced by the world around her, but always seeks to evoke a sense of timelessness in her work. > p. 19

•

CATALINA GÓMEZ AYARZA | Colombian
info@catalinagomez.com.co / www.catalinagomez.com.co
After winning the Carolina Oramas Scholarship to pursue a BA in Visual Arts at the University of Los Andes in Bogotá, Catalina Gómez Ayarza went on to study art jewelry at the Massana School in Barcelona, and product design and marketing at the Pontifical Xavierian University in Bogotá, before gaining a master's degree in Cultural Management from the Bogotá School of Management and Business, and a master's in Art Marketing from Nebrija University in Madrid. A regular participant in the Gilberto Alzate Avendaño Foundation's 'Salón del Fuego' and the Club El Nogal's contemporary jewelry exhibitions, Catalina has been featured in the magazines *Carrusel* and *Fucsia*, and has exhibited her work at the Pôle Bijou gallery in Baccarat, France. Catalina's jewels capture contemporary concepts while reflecting the artisanal and ancestral identity of her native Colombia. Applying textile techniques to jewelry, she creates 100% hand-made pieces that are both unique and modern. > p. 242

•

CATHERINE ALLEN | Canadian
info@catherineallen.ca / www.catherineallen.ca
Catherine Allen holds a Bachelor of Science from Dalhousie University and a Master of Fine Arts from NSCAD University in Nova Scotia. After completing the jewelry arts programme at George Brown College, she was awarded a residency at the Harbourfront Centre Craft Studios in Toronto. In addition to her professional practice, she has taught at both the Ontario College of Art and Design and NSCAD University. Catherine's studies of psychology, architecture and metal provide her with a unique foundation for jewelry design. Her academic background inspires pieces that are a marriage

between art and science, using the human body as both the site and context for her jewelry. > p. 150

•

CECILIA RICHARD | Argentinian
richardceci@gmail.com / www.ceciliarichard.com.ar
Cecilia Richard received her BA in sculpture from the National University of Córdoba in Argentina. She has had solo exhibitions at the Martorelli-Gasser Art Gallery (2001) and the Centre for Contemporary Art (2011) in Córdoba, Argentina, and her work has been featured in the international touring exhibition 'Think Twice: New Latin American Jewelry' (2010–15), at Schmuck 2008 in Munich, and in *The Compendium Finale of Contemporary Jewellers*. Cecilia's work also won first prizes in the Museo Castagnino's 6th Contemporary Design Competition and the 17th FERIAR in Córdoba, Argentina. Cecilia's jewelry investigates the relationships between subject and object – usable vs. portable, portable vs. non-portable, portable vs. manipulable, and static vs. transformable – probing the limits, interests, and implications therein. > pp. 77, 221

•

CÉDRIC CHEVALLEY | Swiss
cedric@cbijoux.com / www.cbijoux.com
Cédric Chevalley studied glass working in the Czech Republic and jewelry-making at the Technical School of the Vallée de Joux in Switzerland, where he won the Golay Prize, the highest award for young Swiss jewelers. In 15 years as a designer, he has exhibited at many international jewelry fairs, including 100% Design Tokyo; Éclat de Mode-Bijorhca in Paris; Blickfang International Design Fair in Zurich, Stuttgart and Basel; Autor in Bucharest; and JOYA in Barcelona. Cédric's pieces draw on a broad palette of materials such as tantalum, titanium, platinum, ceramics, exotic woods, diamonds, enamels, plastics and even upcycled skateboards. His jewelry brands include Mood, Cbijoux and Diirt. > p. 85

•

CHAO-HSIEN KUO | Taiwanese, lives in Finland
chao@chaoeero.com / www.chao-hsienkuo.com
Born in Taiwan, Chao-Hsien Kuo now lives in Finland, a country that has had a profound influence on her jewelry. Its natural surroundings and four distinct seasons fill her with inspiration. Her works are designed to make us focus on the beauty and wonder around us, which might be easily missed unless we take time to appreciate them. Her jewelry has a stylish elegance and is very sculptural. > p. 188

•

CHARITY HALL | American
charityhall@yahoo.com / www.charityhall.com
Charity Hall studied metalwork at Colorado College and the Penland School of Crafts. She received her MFA in Metal Design from East Carolina University. Her work has been featured in *Behind the Brooch*, *Humor in Craft* and *500 Enameled Objects*, and she is a contributing author for *Art Jewelry* magazine. Her work has been featured in a variety of solo and juried exhibitions and she was a 2012 NICHE Award finalist. Charity is a former botanist and interested in the intricate relationships between art and science. Using copper, silver, enamel and precious stones, she explores metalworking and jewelry, showcasing a diverse range of insects and investigating our own anthropomorphic biases towards them. > pp. 21, 140

CHRIS IRICK | American
cirick@roadrunner.com / www.chrisirick.com
Chris Irick received a BFA from Texas Tech University and an MFA from University of Massachusetts

Dartmouth. Her work has recently been exhibited at Velvet da Vinci in San Francisco, Facéré Jewelry Art Gallery in Seattle, and the National Ornamental Metal Museum in Memphis. Chris has been featured in over 40 publications, including the books *21st Century Jewelry* and *Behind the Brooch*. Her work is in several public and private collections, including the Smithsonian Museum of American Art. Chris is keenly interested in our earliest attempts at aviation. Much of her Flight series combines aspects of these historical contraptions with forms from contemporary aeronautics. > pp. 62, 190

CHRISTA LÜHTJE | German
c.luehtje@t-online.de / www.christaluehtje.com
Christa Lühtje apprenticed in Hamburg and studied at the Academy of Fine Arts in Munich. The winner of the Bavarian State Prize, Edwin Scharff Prize and Hamburg State Prize, she has been featured in Lark Books' *Masters: Gold* and in the monograph *Christa Lühtje: Schmuck/Jewellery* (2002) Her creations have been exhibited at the Saatchi Gallery, London, the Museum für Kunst und Gewerbe in Hamburg, the Handwerksmesse in Munich and in many other galleries all over the world. Passionate about jewelry-making, Christa endeavours to capture traces of life in all of its forms and expressions in her pieces. Her aim is for her jewels to not only adorn the wearer but also grace him or her in the truest sense of the word. > pp. 160, 204

CINNAMON LEE | Australian
cinnamon@cinnamonlee.com / www.cinnamonlee.com
Cinnamon Lee is an Australian artist and designer who makes contemporary jewelry and lighting. A keen interest in new technologies and their ability to offer new ways of seeing continues to inform her practice. She specializes in using computer technology and additive manufacturing in conjunction with traditional gold- and silversmithing techniques to produce objects that extend perceptions of what is physically possible. Through her studio practice over the past decade, Cinnamon has established a reputation as an innovator in her field. She holds a Bachelor of Visual Arts and a Master of Philosophy Degree (both majoring in gold- and silversmithing) from the Australian National University School of Art. In her 20 years of experience as a maker, Cinnamon has lectured at a number of institutions, received numerous awards, and exhibited internationally. Examples of both her jewelry and lighting are held in public collections including the National Gallery of Australia and the Art Gallery of Western Australia. > pp. 31, 124

CLAIRE WOLFSTIRN | French
claire.wolfstirn@free.fr / clairewolfstirn.com
Claire trained as an industrial and graphic designer before falling under the spell of jewelry-making, drawn by the physical contact with materials and the body/object relationship. Inspired by the consistency and strength of geometric forms and nature, she presents sober, refined pieces. Passionate about materials, she pushes metal to its physical limits. Her designs testify to her deep insight into form and graphic dynamism. Claire teaches at AFEDAP and is a member of the jewelers' association D'un Bijou à l'Autre. Many of her works were shown at the Musée des Arts Décoratifs in Paris as part of the exhibition 'Dans la ligne de mire, scènes du bijou contemporain en France' (2013–14). She is represented by Galerie Elsa Vanier in Paris. > p. 197

CLARA SALDARRIAGA | Colombian
clarasol@une.net.co / clarasoljoyas.blogspot.com
Self-taught sculptor and jewelry designer Clara Saldarriaga was nominated for *Veranda* magazine's Art of Design Awards 2010 and has been featured in books such as *Colour: Details and Design* and *La Decoración en Colombia*. One of her works was acquired for the permanent collection at the National Museum of Women in the Arts in Washington, DC. Clara's work is fuelled by a passion for forms, textures and volumes. She reaches beyond, attempting to reveal the magic in the commonplace. Her pieces seek inspiration in nature, evolving organically out of studies of insects, leaves and flowers and paying homage to Colombia's biodiversity. This background ensures that her jewels become part of the wearer's history. > p. 28

CLAUDIO PINO | Canadian
claudio@pinodesign.net / www.pinodesign.net
Claudio Pino is renowned for his one-of-a-kind sculptural and kinetic rings. Since 1995, Pino's collections have been exhibited at many prestigious museums, international fairs and galleries, including Aaron Faber Gallery, New York; Velvet da Vinci, San Francisco; Reinhold Jewelers, Puerto Rico; Museum of Decorative Arts, Santiago de Chile; Museum of Vancouver, Vancouver; Elegance Gallery, Taipei; Carnegie Museum of Natural History, Pittsburgh; Forbes Galleries, New York; Mobilia, Cambridge, MA; Galerie Noel Guyomarc'h, Montreal; Armelle Bertin-Toublanc, Paris; and Meister und Margarita, Frankfurt. His work has received awards including the 2005 Special Prize from the Cheongju International Craft Biennale in South Korea, the 2009 Steel Trophy from the Metal Arts Guild of Canada, and second prize in the 2013 Unity Pearl Design Contest; he was also a 2015 NICHE Award finalist. In 2013, his first monograph was published and several of his rings appeared in the Hollywood film *The Hunger Games: Catching Fire*. Pino's highly distinctive pieces are remarkable for their sculptural quality and their ability to harness colour. His work is recognized for the fascinating and innovative ways in which he transforms raw materials into unique and extraordinary works of art. > p. 83

COLLEEN BARAN | Canadian
info@colleenbaran.com / SeeSeeBe.blogspot.com
Colleen Baran is a multidisciplinary artist working in Vancouver. She has exhibited in galleries and museums in eleven countries and has been widely published. Exhibitions include 'The Ring Show' at the Georgia Museum of Art, 'Repeat, Repeat' at the Harbourfront Centre, Toronto, and 'The Northern Lights' at the Design Exchange, Toronto. Recent publications include the books *Humor in Craft* by Brigitte Martin and *Behind the Brooch* by Lorena Angelo, along with articles in *Metalsmith*, *Art Jewelry* and *Vogue Gioiello*. Colleen's pieces are inspired by a love of language, pattern and form. Notable examples include the 'Like Wearing a Love Letter' ring series, which was the subject of a solo exhibition in Vancouver. Some of her elegant, versatile creations can be worn across several fingers. > pp. 91, 106

CRISTINA ZANI | Italian
info@cristinazani.com / www.cristinazani.com
After a career in corporate communication, Italian-born artist Cristina Zani completed her MFA in Jewelry at Edinburgh College of Art in 2012. In 2011 she was awarded a bursary that enabled her to study jewelry in Seoul for four months. After living and working in several countries, Cristina set up her workshop in the Lake District where she is currently based. Inspired by Italo Calvino's *Invisible Cities*, her work is a reflection on the urban environment. Her series My Seoul is influenced by the contrast between antique and contemporary architecture in Korea. Her work explores the vulnerability of materials that transform with passing time – simple in form yet rich in stories. The necklaces of her Infinite Maps collection stem from aerial views of cities and the patterns drawn by roads. By taking sections of maps out of context, she makes the city become invisible. > p. 162

CUCÚ RUIZ | Spanish
cucu.ruiz@gmail.com / www.cucujoyas.com
Cucú Ruiz has been a jewelry-maker since 2007. She earned a degree in history of art at the University of Seville before travelling to Italy, where she studied at Florence's Le Arti Orafe School. Her pieces have been displayed at Aura in York in 2009, Palterman & Thomas in Swansea in 2010, and at London Jewellery Week 2010. Aiming to forge bonds between jewel and wearer, Cucú dips into her day-to-day life and thoughts to find the ideas and forms that underlie her work. She handles a wide range of materials, from silver and gold to acrylic paint, stones, horn and thread. > pp. 37, 228

CYNTHIA DEL GIUDICE | Argentinian
cynthiadelgiudice@hotmail.com / CynthiaDelGiudice.blogspot.com
Cynthia del Giudice is a self-taught eco-friendly jewelry-maker from Argentina. She has exhibited at the Casa de la Provincia de Buenos Aires and the Yrurtia House Museum, both in Argentina, and at the Luke and Eloy Gallery in Pittsburgh. Her work is featured in Lark Books' *30 Minute Rings*. Cynthia's strikingly original work is born from the artist's dedication to recycling, giving used materials a second life. In her Fused Plastic collection, she produces rings made out of a combination of metals such as sterling silver, copper and brass with recycled plastic bags. Though they appear delicate, these pieces are actually extremely durable. > p. 137

DANIEL DICAPRIO | American
dandicaprio@gmail.com / www.dandicaprio.com
Daniel DiCaprio has participated in fairs and exhibitions in the US, Italy, Spain, Germany, South Korea and Japan. He is currently the Assistant Professor of Metalwork and Jewelry at the University of Louisiana at Lafayette. Sponsored by the Society of North American Goldsmiths, he appeared as a guest lecturer at SOFA Chicago in 2008 and presented at SNAG Boston in 2015. He has been published in *Metalsmith* magazine, *American Craft*, *Ornament* and the Norwegian arts and crafts journal *Kunsthåndverk*. Daniel is inspired by unusual creatures and the evolution of organisms in their environment. Using ebony, holly, maple, paint, silver and gold, his jewels are shaped by an attempt to make these beautiful changes and transformations relevant to the processes of adaptation undergone by the viewer. > pp. 76, 205

DANIELLE MILLER-GILLIAM | American
danielle@daniellemillerjewelry.com / www.daniellemillerjewelry.com
Danielle Miller-Gilliam completed a BFA at Temple

University in Philadelphia. The recipient of an honourable mention at the American Jewelry Design Council's New Talent 2010 Awards, she is also a nine-time NICHE Award finalist. Her work has been exhibited internationally and featured in publications including *1000 Rings*, *Art Jewelry Today 3*, *Creative Chains*, *Jewelry Design Challenge* and *Ring a Day*. Danielle draws inspiration from the juxtaposition of rolling hills and architectural elements that comprised her native landscape. Clean, simple geometric forms are the cornerstones of her playful designs, which combine the influences of architecture, machines and toys. Many of her pieces boast kinetic elements, translating the gestures of the wearer into movements of gems and metals. > p. 144

●

DAPHNE KRINOS | Greek
daphnekrinos@aol.com / *www.daphnekrinos.com*
A jewelry design graduate from Middlesex University, London, Daphne Krinos has shown her work across the globe, including at COLLECT London at the Saatchi Gallery in 2014 and Goldsmiths' Hall in 2015. Her work has appeared in books including *500 Gemstone Jewels*, *The Jeweller's Directory of Gemstones* and *Masters: Gemstones*, and can be seen in the public collections of the Victoria and Albert Museum, the Goldsmiths' Company and the Crafts Council. Daphne is influenced by buildings and constructions in London where she lives, street art, hand-drawn cartoons and early animation, her homeland of Greece, and objects she comes across in her daily life. > pp. 18, 171

●

DAUVIT ALEXANDER | British
justified.sinner@gmail.com / *www.justified-sinner.com*
Dauvit Alexander, also known as the Justified Sinner, makes jewelry primarily aimed at men, made from scrap metal salvaged from derelict factories and the sides of the road, corroded, battered and damaged. He treats this material with the same respect and value that would be given to the more traditionally 'precious' metals; he sets iron with gemstones, enamels it, engraves its surface or inlays it with gold. His work harks back to the Renaissance – the last time that men could freely wear elaborate jewelry – but also owes something to contemporary hip-hop and rap culture. His work has been featured in many books and magazines on contemporary jewelry and he has exhibited widely in Europe and the US. Perhaps surprisingly for a man with permanently filthy fingers, he was recently nominated as 'Most Stylish Man in Scotland' at the Scottish Style Awards. > pp. 16, 139

●

DAVID FOWKES | British
info@djfewellery.co.uk / *www.dfjewellery.co.uk*
In his atelier, David Fowkes and his team make elegant and timeless jewelry that displays exquisite craftsmanship, with a strong focus on high-quality artisan-cut coloured gemstones. > p. 51

●

DAVINA ROMANSKY | American
davina.romansky@gmail.com /
www.davinaromansky.com
Davina studied metal techniques in Italy, earned a BFA in Metals/Jewelry from Rochester Institute of Technology and a graduate diploma from the Gemological Institute of America. Her pieces have been featured in over 22 publications and several exhibitions and have won numerous awards, including the Saul Bell Design Award, a NICHE

Award, the Louis Comfort Tiffany Foundation Award and the MJSA Future of the Industry Award. Aiming to excite the imagination, capture emotions and challenge viewers to appreciate original art, Davina uses her aesthetic understanding of form and expression, conceptual depth, classical metalsmithing techniques and technical proficiency to explore natural tension, movements and textures found in nature, creating ornamental abstract designs that embody fluidity while imparting artistic identity to each handcrafted piece. > p. 207

●

DIAN YU | Chinese, lives in the US
yudian430@126.com / *www.dianyujewelry.com*
Dian Yu was born in Shanghai and now lives and works in New Jersey. By utilizing different materials in unexpected ways, her body of work questions the concept of value. The value of jewelry is often related to the dollar sign, but beyond precious materials and luxury brands, there are many intangible components that can also be converted into value. As the most intimate art form, jewelry relates to the human body. Dian believes that the aesthetic pleasures of touch and the wearing experience should be the focus when determining value. Her creative approach to art jewelry forces viewers to rethink how they might value these pieces that are not traditionally viewed as precious. > pp. 52, 102

●

DIANA DUDEK | German
dianadudek@yahoo.com
Diana attended classes at the Massana School in Barcelona before continuing her studies at the Higher School of Applied Arts in Geneva. She was honoured by Munich's Prince Regent Luitpold Foundation in 2008 and by the Munich Department of Culture in 2010. Her work has been displayed in a several exhibitions, including 'Near and Far' at the Museum of Cultures in Helsinki. Rome-based Alternatives Gallery recently presented her pieces at COLLECT London at the Saatchi Gallery. She is also featured in the collections *500 Necklaces* and *The Compendium Finale of Contemporary Jewellers*. > p. 173

●

DJURDJICA KESIC | Australian
mail@djurdjicakesic.com / *www.djurdjicakesic.com*
Djurdjica Kesic studied for an Advanced Diploma of Engineering Technology and Metalsmithing at the Box Hill Institute in Melbourne, Australia, where she received an award for design. She was also a finalist for the Filippo Raphael Fresh! Award. Djurdjica is currently pursuing a MFA from RMIT University, Melbourne. Her solo exhibition 'Nomad' opened at Melbourne's Pieces of Eight Gallery before travelling to Sydney's Metalab Gallery. Djurdjica's work has been exhibited in Australia and internationally at locations including Velvet da Vinci in San Francisco, Galeria Tereza Seabra in Lisbon and Lopdell House Gallery in New Zealand. Djurdjica uses an abundant palette of materials, from the very precious to the often forgotten or overlooked. Her creative process is nourished by the challenge of looking for novel ways of expressing and exploring motifs such as home, place, change and migration. > p. 222

●

DRILLING LAB | Taiwanese
info@drillinglab.com / *www.drillinglab.com*
Drilling Lab and its products follow a philosophy of revealing one's true self. Stripped of all superfluous embellishments, the jewelry takes a playful approach to the aesthetics of industrial manufacturing. Factory-made in Taiwan, the Clamp

collection consists of a range of rings in the shape of mechanical clamps. Each ring can be taken apart and reassembled using the hex key provided. Screws are supplied with each ring in three different colours, adding the perfect finishing touch to the piece and expressing the user's individuality. After the success of the ring series, the Clamp collection has been expanded to include bracelets and earrings. Fascinated by the sturdy and unadorned quality of things made with traditional machining processes, the designer gives the pieces no extra surface treatment, retaining a casual and rugged feel. The intention is to create something genuine and unpretentious, which simply lasts. > p. 99

●

EDGAR MOSA | Portuguese, lives in the US
www.edgarmosa.com
Turning unclaimed trash into unique treasure, Edgar Mosa makes bold pieces designed to stir curiosity at first sight. He lives in New York. > p. 100

●

EDITH BRABATA | Mexican
edith@edithbrabata.com / *www.edithbrabata.com*
Edith Brabata studied industrial design before receiving a degree in jewelry-making from the European Institute of Design in Rome. She has won awards at the competitions Mexico Tercer Milenio, Gold Virtuosi 2 and the International Pearl Contest, and in 2003 was an invited up-and-coming designer at the 'Talents' exhibition at Ambiente in Frankfurt. Her designs have been featured in over 45 publications including the books *Vida y Diseño* and *Diseño Industrial Mexicano e Internacional: Memoria y Futuro*. Edith's pieces are accurate, simple, and pure. Her vibrant and at times symbolic colours highlight the contrast between natural forms and geometric shapes, which is expressed with great freedom and balance. Every year she launches a new collection, using a range of materials including gold, silver and alloys, producing both unique pieces and series. Her work extends across the jewelry sector and she designs collections for other businesses in the field. She is also a qualified university lecturer. > p. 85

●

EERO HINTSANEN | Finish
eero@chaoeero.com / *www.eerohintsanen.com*
Eero Hintsanen has been working professionally in the field of jewelry since 1999. Applying his traditional skills as a Master Goldsmith, Hintsanen works mainly with gold and silver and is influenced by his surroundings, from his childhood in the Finnish countryside to urban cultures seen on his travels. All his unique pieces for private clientele are created in his studio in Lahti, Finland. > p. 139

●

ELA BAUER | Polish
ela@elabauer.com / *www.elabauer.com*
After training in Jerusalem, Ela Bauer studied at Amsterdam's Rietveld Academy and at the European Ceramic Centre in Den Bosch. She has displayed her work in galleries and museums across the world, including the Textile Museum, CODA Museum and Gorcums Museum in the Netherlands, Eretz Israel Museum in Tel Aviv and the Museum of Fine Arts in Montreal. She participated in and co-curated the touring show 'First We Quake, Now We Shake', which visited many countries and venues, and she has been awarded grants by the BKVB Foundation, Prince Bernhardt Fund and Mondriaan Foundation. Ela's organic designs reveal an awareness that things are incomplete and subject to ongoing processes. Many of her recent pieces involve cell

and root-like particles made of silicone, porcelain, minerals and fabric, often sutured together. Sewing has evolved into a vital component of her work, serving to create meaning and construct form. Colour is the starting point for Ela's latest works, particularly its meanings and effects when worn. In parallel with this, she explores basic forms, contemplating the metamorphoses that form can undergo and the ways in which it may evolve into an evocative, meaningful symbol. > p. 201

•
ELENA GORBUNOVA | Russian/ Spain
lena.connect@gmail.com / www.elenagorbunova.com
Elena Gorbunova is fascinated by observing other people and by the mysteries of human understanding and communication. The cognitive processes inside our heads mean that each of us has a unique reality. The ring illustrated here was inspired by the complex network that lies within the human brain, with its countless number of connections; it creates its own space, becoming an individual. Elena views jewelry as a pure example of transition from the non-material to the material, a way of sharing our thoughts and feelings. > p. 30

•
ELIZABETH SHYPERTT | American
Elizabeth began studying metalsmithing in high school in San Francisco. She graduated in literature from the University of Navarra in Pamplona, Spain, in 1975. Upon returning to San Francisco in the early 80s, Elizabeth found herself working in international banking, and taking night courses in jewelry-making at the de Young Museum School. In 1991 she founded the contemporary art jewelry gallery Velvet da Vinci and ran it for 22 years. In 2013 she decided it was time to do something new. She is currently working with San Francisco clothing designer Babette, who has eight boutiques around the US. Elizabeth curates jewelry for the boutiques and for the e-commerce site. Elizabeth recently curated a jewelry exhibition, 'All That Glitters', at the Petaluma Arts Center in Petaluma, California.

•
ELS VANSTEELANDT | Belgian
els.vansteelandt@skynet.be / www.elsvansteelandt.be
Els Vansteelandt's work has been recognized by Design Flanders and acquired by museums and galleries at home and abroad. She has presented her designs internationally and throughout Belgium, including at the Design Museum in Ghent and the European Parliament in Brussels. In 2007 her work was taken to the World Best Design Exchange in Seoul, and she has twice been selected for the Silver Triennial. She is featured in *The Compendium Finale of Contemporary Jewellers*, among other publications. In 2010 Els decided to open a gallery and workshop in the centre of Brussels and create her own place: a meeting point and creative lab all in one. Els's creative process draws on the objects and events around her. She allows her imagination free rein to flow and connect shapes, feeding on emotional impulses which inform her choice of metals. > pp. 14, 94

•
ELVIRA GOLOMBOSI | Ukrainian, lives in Germany
elviragolombosi@gmail.com / www.elviragolombosi.com
Elvira Golombosi follows the ancient belief that objects are not merely empty matter but they are endowed with magical powers. Her pieces are amulets, companions that support and empower the wearer. She has always felt the necessity of rituals and magic and has admired them in various tribal cultures and ancient societies. But despite this fascination with indigenous cultures, she realized that she could not appropriate their symbols and so began to build her own personal mythology, filled with her own versions of gods, totemic figures, demons and fantastic creatures. > pp. 32, 33

•
ELVIRA H. MATEU | Spanish
elvirahmateu@gmail.com / www.elvirahmateu.com
Elvira Hernández Mateu pursued a BFA at the Polytechnic University of Valencia in Spain, where she specialized in casting and microfusion. In 2004 she co-founded the Rara Avis Nidus studio, and in 2008 she began studies in art jewelry at Valencia's Higher School of Art and Design. Currently, she combines making jewelry in her own workshop with teaching. Elvira's work is influenced by nature and humanity's attempt to apprehend it through anatomy, botany and entomology. Constructed of silver and bronze, metals that change as time goes by, and found objects – each with a story of its own – her pieces aim to instil curiosity, respect and wonder about these little things in the eyes of user and beholder. > p. 63

•
EMILY CULVER | American
emilyculverstudio@gmail.com / www.emily-culver.com
Emily Culver grew up in a small rural town in Pennsylvania, surrounded by the natural world that so much inspires her work. She attended Tyler School of Art, Temple University, where she received a BFA in Metals/Jewelry/Computer Aided Design and Manufacture in 2012. Currently she lives and works in Bloomfield Hills, MI, where she is pursuing an MFA in Metalsmithing at Cranbrook Academy of Art. Her works have been shown in numerous exhibitions throughout the US. Reminiscent of microscopic forms in its structure and opalescence, her Membrane ring's unique setting means that its top caps are interchangeable. When worn on the finger, the large bulging shell shields the space between the knuckles, changing and manipulating the landscape of the hand. While the form resembles a barrier, its decorative pattern makes it permeable and delicate as if it were a thin membrane. > p. 95

•
EMILY WATSON | American
mail1@metalemily.com / www.metalemily.com
Emily Watson creates vividly coloured tableaux by hand-carving a wide array of materials. The directness of this work allows her to create organic shapes out of commercial or synthetic products such as industrial plastics, often mimicking natural materials. She combines these with enamel, metal, wood, horn, bone, rubber, reconstituted stone and found objects. Removing the element of material recognition makes it easier to focus on subtler aspects of a piece such as colour, texture, pattern, and to see the relationships between different elements. > pp. 30, 58, 167, 233

•
ENRIC MAJORAL | Spanish
info@majoral.com / www.majoral.com
Enric Majoral took up jewelry-making in 1974. The co-founder of La Mola Art and Crafts Fair in Formentera, Spain, Enric is a member of Barcelona-based FAD (Fostering Arts and Design). He was honoured by the Catalan Government in 2004, and received the National Craftwork Award in 2007. Two pieces from his Sand Jewels series were acquired by the Museum of Arts and Design in New York. Enric's work is personal and boundless, never confined to any one technique or material. The products of intuition and experimentation, his pieces are striking, daring and essentially modern. His creations are grounded in his roots, experiences and memories, making his life and work indistinguishable. > p. 119

•
EUN YEONG JEONG | Korean, lives in the US
ejeong5@gmail.com / www.eunyeongjeong.com
The holder of a BFA from Konkuk University in Korea and a MFA in Jewelry and Metals from the University of Illinois at Urbana-Champaign, Eun Yeong Jeong also trained in Italy at the Alchimia and Le Arti Orafe Schools. She was selected as one of the 2010 Emerging Artists of the Year by the Society of North American Goldsmiths and her work was represented by Charon Kransen Arts at SOFA Chicago. She was also selected for Talente, an international handicraft fair in Munich in 2009. A winner in the 2009 NICHE Awards, she has been featured in *Metalsmith* magazine and the books *500 Plastic Jewelry Designs* and *500 Vessels*. Eun Yeong's pieces, inspired by natural forms, processes and movement, investigate the mystery of creation and seek to capture the moment in which both void and fragment become substance. Eun Yeong Jeong resides in Virginia with her husband and three daughters. > p. 107

•
EWA DOERENKAMP | German
edoerenkamp@web.de / ewadoerenkamp.de
Ewa Doerenkamp graduated from the Salzburg Summer Academy. Goldsmithing apprenticeships followed in Milan and Frankfurt and at Hanau Design Academy. The recipient of three awards in her native Germany, including the prestigious Hessische Design Prize, Ewa was also granted a scholarship to study silversmithing at the Canberra School of Art, Australia. Canberra was the setting for Ewa's first major exhibition, 'Suddenly the Lake', in 1999. She has subsequently exhibited in Munich, Berlin and London. Her most recent work was showcased in 'Poetry in Silver' in Schoonhoven, the Netherlands, which also hosted her exhibition 'Silver as Water' in 2002. > p. 54

•
FABIANA GADANO | Argentinian
info@fabianagadano.com.ar / www.fabianagadano.com.ar
Fabiana Gadano studied fine arts and industrial design in Argentina. Her initiation into the world of metalsmithing came at the New York School of Visual Arts in 1990, and she later attended several workshops in her native Buenos Aires. Fabiana's work has been featured in the books *Éclat: The Masters of New Jewellery Design*, *I Love You: Design, Jewelry & Accessories* and *500 Silver Jewelry Designs*. She has exhibited in Argentina, Germany and Italy, where she was won a special mention at the Cominelli Foundation Awards 2015. She was also invited to take part in 'LOOT: MAD About Jewelry 2015' at the New York Museum of Arts and Design. Fabiana's ongoing creative quest has recently been fuelled by a desire to experiment with non-traditional materials such as recycled plastics. Her work is informed by natural textures, reading and her travels. > p. 150

•
FABRICE SCHAEFER | Swiss
info@tactile.ch / www.fabriceschaefer.ch
Fabrice Schaefer attended the University of Art

and Design in Geneva. A multiple prizewinner in Switzerland, he has had work exhibited in several European museums, including the V&A in London, Die Neue Sammlung in Munich, the Musée des Arts Décoratifs in Paris and MUDAC in Lausanne. Schaefer believes that a jewel's soft and sensual surface is only revealed in all its captivating splendour when in contact with the skin. An alchemist extraordinaire, he handles mysterious combinations of metals, seeking to distil the perfect contrast between materials such as gold and rust, titanium and pure silver, white gold and niello, and zinc and garnet powder. > pp. 126, 221

FABRIZIO TRIDENTI | Italian
fabriziotridenti@alice.it
Fabrizio Tridenti was educated at the State School of Art in Penne, Italy. In 2008, he was awarded a silver medal at the Amberif Design Awards, while in 2010 he garnered second prize at the Cominelli Foundation Awards in Cisano di San Felice del Benaco, Italy. As well as contributing to the book *Éclat: The Masters of New Jewellery Design*, he is also the author of *Hard Wear Beauty*. Fabrizio's work stands out for its use of industrial waste, recycled materials and industrial paint. He offers reinterpretations of these materials by embedding them within jewels, creating chaotic structures that simultaneously boast an aesthetic function and submerge the viewer in architectural chaos. > pp. 38, 151

FEDERICA PALLAVER | Italian
federica@pallaver.it / www.federicapallaver.com
After studying goldsmithing in Florence, Federica Pallaver spent several summers at the Salzburg Summer Academy. She opened her own workshop in Bolzano, Italy in 1996. Her works have been displayed in solo and group exhibitions across Italy, in locations including the Prisma Gallery in Bolzano, Cristiani Gallery in Turin, Ugo Carà Museum of Modern Art in Trieste, Fioretto Gallery in Padua, Fondazione Heller in Brescia and Alchimia in Florence. Beyond her homeland, her jewelry has also been shown at Galerie Oko and Schmuckfrage in Berlin, the Roundhouse in London, AV17 Gallery in Vilnius and the Orpheus Institute in Ghent. In 2010 she was invited to the 13th Erfurt Jewelry Symposium. She has also been honoured at the International Biennial Art Awards at the Amber Museum in Kaliningrad, Russia, and at the Wurst und Schmuck Awards in Weiden, Germany. Federica's pieces probe the intrinsic tension between movement, change and stability. Her highly mobile rings demonstrate an acute awareness of the relationship between art and architecture. > p. 103

FERRAN IGLESIAS | Spanish
atelieriglesias@telefonica.net / www.atelierferraniglesias.com
Ferran Iglesias was born in Barcelona and undertook a goldsmithing apprenticeship in Santiago de Chile, building on this experience with studies at Barcelona's Massana School and School of Arts and Trades. His pieces are inspired by rhythmic elements that recur in nature. In 2014 he won the 3rd Award of the Mayor of the City at the 23rd Legnica International Jewellery Competition, in Poland. His works have been exhibited worldwide and have appeared in many publications. His pieces arise from a state of mind, as he allows the creative process

to flow freely through him. Logic, precision and articulation are the key ingredients for the creation of his volumetric shapes. > p. 136

FLAVIA BRÜHLMANN | Swiss
voilagioielli@gmail.com
Swiss-born Flavia Brühlmann attended jewelry-making courses in Florence after graduating from the European Institute of Design in Milan. Her creations have been shown at the Spazio-Tempo Gallery in Minusio, Switzerland, among others. Working primarily with silver, Flavia also regularly experiments with materials such as copper, brass and her favourite stones: pearls and volcanic rock. She takes her inspiration from anything and everything, although she particularly admires the use of colour and clear-cut shapes in Hundertwasser's work. In 2009 she opened her own workshop in Bellinzona where she designs and makes bespoke creations in silver. > pp. 39, 235

FLORA BHATTACHARY | British
flora@florabhattachary.com / www.florabhattachary.com
Flora Bhattachary is an award-winning jeweler based in London. She creates dramatic fine jewelry with an opulent and seductive edge. Inspired by her family's links with India since the 18th century, Flora brings together Asian influences and an interest in pattern to create her bold designs. Drawing on a rich tradition of hand stone-carving in India, Flora mixes historic artifacts, family history and Islamic and Hindu art to inspire her designs. Mixing new technology with ancient tradition, Flora is, in the words of Maria Doulton, 'devoted to telling a story not in words, or on canvas, but in gold and precious stone'. > p. 112

FLORENCIA PIERANTONELLI | Argentinian
pierflori@yahoo.com.ar / www.fpierantonelli.com.ar
Florencia Pierantonelli was born in Córdoba, Argentina, where she gained a degree in sculpture before going on to teach at the National University of Córdoba. She has been a finalist for two years running at the Contemporary Object Design Exhibition in Rosario and won first prize in the Clothing and Accessories category at the 2009 Design Exhibition at the Virla Cultural Centre in Tucumán. Florencia works towards deconstructing and reconsidering issues related to the meaning, use and inherent connotations of the term 'jewel'. She endeavours to divert the viewer's attention, doing away with the orthodox, strictly functional understanding of the piece's relationship with the body. > p. 228

FLORIAN WAGNER | German
info@floschmuck.at / www.floschmuck.at
Born in Berlin in 1948, Florian Wagner served as a jewelry apprentice until 1969. He set up his first studio in Johannesburg in 1971, subsequently moving to Vienna to study at the Academy of Fine Arts. He later founded the Mana Fine Art Gallery in 1983 and was shortlisted for the Austrian State Award for Jewelry Design in 1993. Florian's pieces have been showcased at the 10th Silver Triennial in 1992, at Expo '92 in Seville and at the Sixth International Biennial of Amber Art Works 'Alatyr 2015'. Florian works primarily with fine metals and precious stones. His goal is to inspire the women who wear his creations to embrace their own beauty. > p. 134

FRANCE ROY | Canadian
fr-roy@videotron.ca / www.franceroyjewelrydesign.com
France Roy is a graduate from the Montreal Jewelry School (1996), and has taught jewelry techniques and studio organization there since 2001. Her artworks have featured in prestigious publications and been awarded several grants, while a major exhibition of her work was held at the Galerie Noel Guyomarc'h in Montreal in 2008. An exceedingly imaginative designer, France combines silver and gold with alternative materials such as coloured resins. Viewing jewelry as both ornament and artform, she sees the wearers of her pieces as playing a part in defining their meaning. Most importantly, France strives to create jewelry that is relevant to our times. > p. 186

FRANCESC OLIVERAS | Spanish
foorfebre@gmail.com / www.argejoies.com
The work of Francesc Oliveras Ballús is based on an ongoing search for the perfect harmony between purity of line and texture, between minimalism and baroque: the natural balance of life. > p. 31

FRANCESCA VITALI | American
fruccidesign@gmail.com
Francesca Vitali was a practising chemist before commencing her jewelry design studies at the Revere Academy of Jewelry Arts in San Francisco, California. In her pieces, art and chemistry find an point of intersection in the alchemy of paper jewelry. Her unique work has been featured in exhibitions at the Society of Arts and Crafts in Boston, Aaron Faber Gallery in New York, and Miami University Art Museum in Oxford, Ohio. Francesca's pieces transform paper, a humble and ordinary material, into precious objects that incorporate fragments of everyday lives, reflecting her love for this material and for eco-friendly living. > pp. 74, 173

GABI VEIT | Italian
gv@gabiveit.it / www.gabiveit.it
Gabi Veit studied graphic design in Innsbruck and Venice, and jewelry design at Florence's Alchimia School. Gabi currently directs a graphic design studio and works in her jewelry workshop in Bolzano, Italy. Her interests are diverse – she founded the Carambolage Theatre in Bolzano, acting as its artistic director until 2008; she loves spoons and nature is always a major source of inspiration. Influenced by her native Italian Alps, the Dolomites, and her love of hiking, Gabi often incorporates images of stones, mountains, rocks and glaciers into her striking pieces. > p. 55

GERTI MACHACEK | Austrian
gerti.machacek@atelier-machacek.at / www.atelier-machacek.at
Born in Vienna in 1955, Gerti Machacek served her goldsmith's apprenticeship with Hans Muliar and studied history of art at the University of Vienna. Since 1981 she has worked as a freelance artist and has participated in many national and international exhibitions, in locations including Belgium, Italy, Germany and Spain. Her work has appeared in publications including *The Compendium Finale of Contemporary Jewellers*, *Art Meets Jewellery: 20 Years of Galerie Slavik Vienna*, *New Earrings* and *Art Jewelry Today: Europe*. In 1992 Gerti Machacek received a Recognition Award from the Austrian State Prize for Craft. Her jewelry has been acquired by several public and private collections and she is a founding

member of the jewelry group ANIMAVIENNA. Gerti's work is marked by the playful manner in which body and form are treated, with an emphasis on sculptural pieces that can also serve as mementoes or means of self-identification. > p. 35

GIOVANNI CORVAJA | Italian
info.corvaja@me.com / www.giovanni-corvaja.com
Giovanni Corvaja studied art in Padua before pursuing an MA in Goldsmithing, Silversmithing, Metalwork and Jewelry at the Royal College of Art in London. His work is regularly showcased at TEFAF in Maastricht, COLLECT London and the PAD London Art Fair. In 2009, Giovanni presented his Golden Fleece collection – the subject of a special report in the *New York Times* – at the International Trade Fair in Munich. Giovanni was honoured at the 1997 International Jewelry Art Competition in Tokyo, and won the 1997 Bavarian State Prize and the 1992 Herbert Hofmann Prize in Munich. In 2013, he was the subject of a solo show at the Moretti Gallery in London, called 'Gold: Status and Glory, Masterpieces from the Middle Ages and Today'. Giovanni is a passionate alchemist, delighting in transforming gold – which he sees as the pinnacle of nature and creation – into new combinations. > p. 15

GLORIA GASTALDI | Argentinian
gloriagastaldi@gmail.com / gloriagastaldi.blogspot.com
Gloria Daniela Gastaldi has completed goldsmithing workshops in Buenos Aires and Barcelona, including at the Massana School. Her work was displayed at the 'Sintesi' exhibition held by A-FAD in Barcelona. In Argentina, she participated in the 2009 exhibition 'Puro diseño' in Rosario, and a selection of her work was exhibited under the title 'BUE BOG BCN, Gestos en el cuerpo' at the Spanish Cultural Centre in Buenos Aires. Fusing materials, Gloria crafts playful jewels that encourage interaction between wearer and object. She espouses the notion that jewelry should not be static in its relationship with the body, but rather active and dynamic. > p. 42

GREGORY LARIN | Israeli
gritzel@gmail.com / gregorylarin.tumblr.com/
Gregory studied jewelry at Shenkar College of Engineering, Design and Art in Tel Aviv. He is currently a lecturer in the jewelry department at Tel Hai College. He has given lectures and workshops in Israel and Russia and his work has been shown in numerous exhibitions worldwide. In his extreme and radical jewelry, he is drawn to the dark side, to the forbidden worlds from which we are made. He combines traditional materials such as sterling silver with innovative ones such as epoxy and synthetic hair in a way that is unique to him. He sees art as a filter through which he can express aspects of himself. > p. 229

HEIDEMARIE HERB | German
heidemarie.herb@gmail.com / www.heidemarieherb.com
After qualifying as a goldsmith in Germany in 1991, Heidemarie Herb received a certificate in precious gems at the German Diamond Institute (DDI). She attended various courses, conferences and workshops. Attendance at a DuPont powder-coating workshop in 2008 and the International Amber Researcher Symposium in 2013 were milestones in her development. Her works has been displayed in exhibitions in more than 15 countries including 'Amber Chamber' at Velvet da Vinci in San Francisco. She has also been honoured by awards from Poland,

Russia and Italy. Her works are in the permanent collections of the Amber Museum in Gdansk and the Malbork Castle Museum in Poland, and the Cominelli Foundation in Italy. > p. 181

HELEN BRITTON | Australian, lives in Germany
helenbritton@mac.com
Helen Britton lives and works in Munich. Her work tackles themes from popular culture: violence, love, riches, humour, wisdom, exotica. Her pieces may be a friendly companion or a lucky charm. While the rings themselves often reference classical forms, the sentiment they convey reaches into the deepest abyss. Her stimulus to make rings comes from an interest in the historical uses of jewelry. Now her rings drift around the planet, collecting along the tidelines of human activity and becoming parts of a longer story. Who knows where they will end up, out there in the world, and what meanings they will convey? > pp. 48, 152

HISANO SHEPHERD | Japan, lives in the US
hisano@littlehjewelry.com / www.littlehjewelry.com
Hisano Shepherd's Geode and Finestrino collections use pearls and gemstones in an unprecedented way. Pearls are sliced or bored into, their interiors removed, polished and then lined with colourful gemstones, creating a look very similar to natural geodes. Among the pearls Hisano uses are hollow freshwater soufflé pearls, tissue-graft freshwater pearls, cultured Tahitian pearls and South Sea pearls. For the pieces in the Finestrino collection, she wanted to create an opening that viewers can peek into, revealing the colourful gem-studded interior of the pearl. The word *finestrino* means 'little window' in Italian. > p. 240

HUI-MEI PAN | Taiwanese
panhm@yahoo.com / www.panstyle.com
Born in Taiwan, Hui-Mei Pan studied Metals and Jewelry and Graphic Design at the Savannah College of Art and Design, where she received the Presidential Scholarship. Her work has been shown in London, Denver and Chicago, and she has been featured in the books *500 Gemstone Jewels* and *500 Wedding Rings*. In addition to being an acclaimed designer, Hui-Mei is an award-winning children's book illustrator, and her work in this field was recognized at the Fifth Chen Gwo-Jeng Children's Literature Awards. Hui-Mei's organic, intricate creations are influenced by her background and culture. She uses materials including sterling silver, white jade and red jadeite. > p. 140

IACOV AZUBEL | Argentinian
iazubel@fibertel.com.ar / www.iacov.com.ar
Iacov Azubel completed a degree in Physical Education in 1989 at the Wingate Institute in Israel. His artistic training comes mainly from childhood. In 1990 he began working as a swimwear designer. From 2001 onwards, he studied jewelry-making with Antonio Pujá, María Medici, Francine Shloeth, Charon Kransen, Jorge Castañon and Silvana Chiavetti, among others. He often works with non-traditional materials and likes to decontextualize their use, experimenting with new techniques and concepts to turn them into jewelry. He has participated in many exhibitions, both in Argentina and abroad, and was selected for Schmuck 2012 in Munich, the most prestigious event in contemporary jewelry. His pieces have appeared in publications including *Jewelbook: International Annual of*

Contemporary Jewel Art and several editions of *The Contemporary Jewellery Yearbook*. > p. 232

IGNASI CAVALLER | Spanish
ignasicavaller@gmail.com
Ignasi Cavaller Triay is fascinated by the idea of memory. Whenever he spends long periods away from Menorca, the island where he was born, he feels that he is carrying his memories, experiences and roots with him. He feeds this obsession in two ways: firstly by working with old materials that once had a specific function but have now been set aside, thereby committing them to memory; secondly by trying to reproduce the atmosphere of Menorca with materials from other places. > p. 215

IRENE BEATRIZ PALOMAR | Argentinian
irenepalomar@gmail.com / www.joyeriadeautor.com.ar
Irene Beatriz Palomar took her first steps in art jewelry in 2007. In Buenos Aires, she studied engraving at the Sindicato de Joyería, then trained at the Jewelry Education Complex. She has attended jewelry workshops in Buenos Aires with Mabel Pena, Antonio Pujía (lost wax), Francine Schloeth (Japanese lacquer) and Luis Acosta (paper jewelry), and in Barcelona with the jeweler Eugen Steier. Her work has been exhibited in Italy, the US, Greece and Spain, and she participated in JOYA Barcelona in 2012, 2013, 2014 and 2015. She is a member of Klimt02 and Joyeros Argentinos. Irene is interested in the contrast between inner and outer worlds, and deploys a variety of materials, techniques and textures. Each piece lays bare her emotions, interacting with the viewer through creativity, playfulness and art. > p. 223

ISABEL ARANGO TISNÉS | Colombian
isarango@gmail.com
After pursuing studies in international business at EAFIT University in Medellín, Colombia, Isabel Arango Tisnés went on to study jewelry at the Perseo Training Institute in Florence, Italy. Her exhibitions in Medellín include '15 Propuestas de Joyería' and 'Biodiversidad, Joyería de diseñador' at the Naranjo and Velilla Gallery as well as a permanent exhibition at the Noi Jewelry Gallery. Isabel experiments with tools and materials, allowing her pieces to evolve spontaneously during the process of creation. Inspired by organic elements, her travels, figures from various cultures, and events engraved upon her memory, she strives for each finished piece to glow with its own unique magic. > pp. 177, 236

ISABEL MIR | Spanish
joies@isabelmir.com / www.isabelmir.com
Isabel Mir studied jewelry design at the Massana School in Barcelona and at the Menorca School of Art; she also has a degree in fine arts from the University of Barcelona, specializing in sculpture. She won the Young Designers prize at the 8th Menorca Craft Festival, an honourable mention at EuroBijoux, the SEBIME International Fair of Fashion Jewelry Manufacturers, first prize at the 1st Córdoba Jewelry Fair, and second prize at the 1st Talayótica de Menorca Jewelry Fair. Isabel's jewelry is organic, imperfect, even somewhat primitive, and takes its inspiration from the island of Menorca, where she lives. Her pieces, which she describes as small sculptures for the body, are characterized by the combination of gold and oxidized silver, which creates striking volumes and contrasts. She wants her jewelry to transmit sensations and reflect

elements of nature such as the wind, the stars, water and the passing of time. > pp. 53, 89

JACKIE ANDERSON | Canadian
juell1@shaw.ca
A recipient of an Alumni Award of Excellence from the Alberta College of Art and Design (ACAD) in Calgary, Jackie Anderson is also a Platinum Level member of the Metal Arts Guild of Canada, and a member of the Royal Canadian Academy of Arts. Her explorations of concept, line, colours and materials result in evocative and whimsical works inspired by the ever-evolving visual language of our natural, cultural and urban landscapes. In a studio and exhibition career that has lasted more than 40 years, Jackie has taught, mentored, lectured and has had her award-winning work exhibited in solo and group exhibitions in galleries and publications in Canada, the US, Germany, Spain and Australia. > p. 151

JACQUELINE CULLEN | British
info@jacquelinecullen.com / www.jacquelinecullen.com
Jacqueline Cullen received a first-class BA in Jewelry Design from Central Saint Martins College of Art and Design in London. Jacqueline's Whitby jet collections have been featured in *Vogue, Vogue Gioiello, Harper's Bazaar, ELLE, The New York Times, Tatler, The Financial Times, The Times, The Telegraph, The Sunday Telegraph, The Independent, Wallpaper** and on BBC TV and radio amongst others. Jacqueline has also been commissioned to make bespoke items for a number of major Hollywood films, most recently for Tom Cruise in *Mission: Impossible – Rogue Nation*. Jacqueline has developed innovative processes that celebrate rather than disguise the inherent flaws of Whitby jet, allowing the natural beauty of the material to speak for itself. She is inspired by dramatic acts of nature: placid skies ripped open by lightning, erupting volcanoes, or cliff edges left jagged from erosion. Hiatuses inform her aesthetics and the interruption or breaking up of a bold, fluid form is central to her work where fractures, fissures and crevices release a luxurious cascade of textured gold or glittering diamonds. > p. 77

JAN ARTHUR HARRELL | American
jannyh@swbell.net / www.janharrell.com
A holder of a BFA in Studio Art from Texas Tech University and an MFA in Sculpture from the University of Houston, Jan Arthur Harrell is an active jewelry designer and sculptor. Her one-woman installation show 'Vanitas: The Muse in her Boudoir' opened in Houston, Texas, in 2010, while her exhibit 'Offerings: Gifts for the Muse' showed at the Mesa Art Center in Arizona in 2012. Jan participates regularly in the International Enamel Exhibitions and is featured in numerous books, including five titles in Lark's *500* series. She is also the author of a chapter on etching in *Enameling for Professionals*. > p. 128

JAN KERKSTRA & MARION PANNEKOEK | Dutch
atelier@thejewelrystory.com / www.thejewelrystory.com
Jan Kerkstra and Marion Pannekoek trained at the Vakschool Edelsmeden in Amsterdam and the University of Georgia. Their work has won a variety of awards and has been placed in the collection of the Fries Museum in Leeuwarden in the Netherlands and the Columbia Museum of Art in Columbia, South Carolina. The duo runs The Jewelry Story atelier and boutique. Jan and Marion create one-of-a-kind

designs that are as unique as their wearers. They take their inspiration from architecture, fashion and their love of ballet and dance. > p. 45

JANICE PEREZ | Brazil
www.aneisruda.com.br
Janice Perez is the designer behind the brand Rudá, a range of contemporary rings made from Brazilwood and Brazilian hardwood – sourced from old furniture and salvaged houses – and raw stones from all around the world. Production is a handcrafted process, like carving a small sculpture. Each ring is unique and takes from two to five days to be finished. The limited output reflects the brand's eco-friendly values and also the way the rings are produced, one by one. Every piece produced is registered with a reference number. > p. 112

JÁNOS GÁBOR VARGA | Hungarian
janosvarga9@yahoo.co.uk / blindspotjewellery.com
János Gábor Varga first studied agriculture in his native Hungary, where he carried out ethno-veterinary research for 10 years. He started making jewelry after moving to England and, aside from a basic-level course, is largely self-taught. Now living in Italy, he runs his own workshop in a village near Genoa. János is inspired by metal tools and the natural textures created by their use. He constantly experiments with all sorts of materials, although his favourite media are iron and silver. > pp. 30, 186, 229

JEFFREY LLOYD DEVER | American
*info@jeffreylloyddever.com /
www.jeffreylloyddever.com*
All of Jeffrey Lloyd Dever's works are miniature sculptural studies. The fact that they are wearable at all is almost incidental to the poetic qualities he seeks. Each piece is born through a series of sketches, exploring a concept, a notion, or merely a whim. The sketches mature into fabricated forms of polymer clay built over reinforced armatures. Through repeated cycles of fabrication, veneering and oven-curing, a piece grows slowly layer by layer. Each visible colour gradient is the actual colour of the clay, and an individual piece can easily go through between ten and twenty fabrication/curing cycles and take weeks to complete. > p. 46

JENNACA LEIGH DAVIES | American
contact@jennaca.com / www.jennaca.com
Jennaca received her master's degree from the Rhode Island School of Design in 2007 and continues to explore design work focusing on combining ancient jewelry-making techniques paired with new technologies such as laser cutting, waterjet cutting, and CAD/CAM. She currently teaches part time at the Rhode Island School of Design, the Massachusetts College of Art and Design, and the school of Museum of Fine Arts in Boston. Jennaca has exhibited her work at international fairs such as the SIERAAD Art Fair 2015 in Amsterdam and at the Talente exhibition as part of the Internationale Handwerksmesse in Munich; she has also shown at the Model Citizens show during New York Design Week. In 2007, she received the Hayward Prize for Fine Arts from the American Austrian Foundation and in 2010, she was a Faces of Design award winner. She received Bachelor of Architecture and Bachelor of Building Science degrees from Rensselaer Polytechnic Institute and continues to practise architecture part-time. > pp. 103, 214

JENNIFER HALL | American
jennifer.hall.artist@gmail.com
Jennifer Hall attended the Pratt Fine Arts Center in Seattle and the Oregon College of Art and Craft in Portland before working as a studio assistant at the Penland School of Crafts in North Carolina. Exhibition highlights include 'The Pendant Show' at San Francisco's Velvet da Vinci Gallery, 'Touching Warms the Art' at the Portland-based Museum of Contemporary Craft and Seattle's Facèré Jewelry Art Gallery's 'Amuse, Amaze, Amend: Jewelry for the Uninhibited'. She appears in the books *500 Pendants & Lockets, The Art and Craft of Making Jewelry* and *500 Bracelets*. Jennifer reaches into the natural world for her inspiration, reflecting on structural forms, their interrelations and growth, and the processes of maturation and adaptation. > p. 239

JENNY WINDLER | American
jennywindler@gmail.com / www.jennywindler.com
Jenny Windler is a jewelry-maker based in the San Francisco Bay area. She earned her MFA from Colorado State University in 2007. Her love for functional objects, industrial design and architecture, blended with daily observations of chaos, decay and the natural world play a major role in informing her jewelry designs. > p. 89

JILLIAN MOORE | American
jillian.a.j.moore@gmail.com / www.jillianmoore.net
Jillian Moore pursued a BFA at Western Illinois University and an MFA in Jewelry and Metal Arts at the University of Iowa. She presented a solo show, 'Fruits of My Labor', at Beyond Fashion in Antwerp in 2014. Her work is represented by Velvet da Vinci in San Francisco and Friends of Carlotta in Zurich, Switzerland. Jillian utilizes composite and epoxy resins, polymer clay, copper and paint to fashion jewels that explore the themes of biological structures, diseases, vivisection and taxonomy. > p. 71

JIM COTTER | American
studio@jcottergallery.com / www.jcottergallery.com
Jim Cotter attended Wayne State College in Nebraska where he obtained a bachelor's degree in Fine Arts Education. He owns two contemporary jewelry and art galleries in Vail and Beaver Creek, Colorado, as well as a full-time jewelry studio. His pieces are displayed in museums and collections across the US and worldwide, including the Samuel Dorsky Museum of Art at the State University of New York at New Paltz, the Wustum Museum of Fine Arts in Racine, Wisconsin, the McDonald's Corporation Collection, and Cheongju National Museum in Korea. Jim's pieces often utilize concrete, capitalizing on its association with industrial processes and its power to surprise, given that it is a material not normally used in jewelry-making. > pp. 108, 128

JIMENA BOLAÑOS | Costa Rican
jimicricket@gmail.com
Jimena Bolaños Durman studied advertising design at Veritas University and metalsmithing at the Crisol School, both in her native Costa Rica. After moving to New York, she attended the Jewelry Arts Institute and trained in gemmology and jewelry design at the Gemological Institute of America. Jimena's pieces convey sensations and impressions that are germane to her wider convictions. These include an appreciation of forms, the importance of colour and an awareness of how jewels can influence

our frame of mind and enable us to express our feelings. > p. 40

JIMENA RÍOS | Argentinian
hola@jimenarios.com / www.jimenarios.com
After moving to Barcelona in 2000, Jimena Ríos studied art history at the University of Barcelona and jewelry design at the Massana School. She spent the last semester of her degree in Florence, where she completed her final project at the Alchimia School. As well as exhibiting, she has contributed to the books *Jewellery Using Textile Techniques* and *Jewellery, Schiedam's Choice*, the latter published by the Marzee Gallery in the Netherlands. Jimena is attracted to the notion of jewelry-making as a form of heritage passed down from generation to generation – a gift serving as a symbol of love and unity, which both reveals and conceals. She works with textiles and found objects. > pp. 36, 183

JINA SEO (1) | South Korean, lives in Illinois
zina336@gmail.com / jinaseo.com
Working at the intersections of sexuality and art, humour and craft, and fetish and fashion, Jina Seo uses vintage gloves to explore the intimate and sensual energy of the human body. Dress gloves have long functioned as a device for expressing the desire for beauty, power and wealth in Western culture. This focus on the hidden power beneath the skin of gloves is intended to reveal the truth of human nature that reaches beyond the social expectations of race and gender. > p. 23

JINA SEO (2) | South Korean, lives in New York
j@byjinaseo.com / www.byjinaseo.com
Jina Seo's Pipeworks collection combines the beauty of flowers with the functionality of connecting pipes. The rings in the collection are playful, incorporating modular and interchangeable components that allow the designs to be customized. Wearers become an integral part of the design process, incorporating their own personal tastes. The customizable pipe systems are complemented with a valve handle, the most interactive part of the system, which has been abstracted into an appealing floral shape. These flower handles serve as interactive elements, forming a bond between pipes and people. > pp. 87, 241

JIŘÍ URBAN | Czech
galerie-u@seznam.cz / www.cisarskakoruna.cz
Boasting over 35 years of jewelry experience, Jiří Urban initially trained as a goldsmith in Turnov, Czech Republic before pursuing a master's in Arts and Crafts in Prague in 1986. He designed and produced a cross for Pope John Paul II in 1990 and a Czech garnet jewelry collection for Queen Elizabeth II in 1996. In 2009 he completed a replica of the Imperial Crown of the Holy Roman Empire. Jiří's work has also been showcased at the Peters Valley Craft Center in New Jersey, the Seoul Art Festival in South Korea and the China Art Festival. Jiří draws inspiration from nature, space, calligraphy and the culture of ancient civilizations. > p. 149

JOAN CODINA | Spanish
joancodinarebull@gmail.com / www.codina.co.uk
Joan Codina A.J.P. studied jewelry at the Massana School in Barcelona, Birmingham City University and GIA in London. He currently works in London as a high-end CAD jewelry designer while running Codina Barcelona alongside with his father, the internationally renowned jeweler Carles Codina Armengol. He also teaches jewelry design in Spain and the UK. > p. 184

JOANNE HAYWOOD | British
joannehaywood51@hotmail.com / www.joannehaywood.co.uk
Leading studio jeweler, writer and educator Joanne Haywood has worked and exhibited in the UK and internationally. She holds a BA from Central Saint Martins College of Art and Design and is recognized for her individual voice and skill in mixed media making. Her book *Mixed Media Jewellery* was published by A&C Black in 2009. She has also been commissioned to write articles for a number of contemporary jewelry books, such as the design chapter in Vannetta Seecherran's *Contemporary Jewellery Making Techniques: A Comprehensive Guide for Jewellers and Metalsmiths* and a project chapter for *Jewellery Using Textile Techniques* by Sarah Keay. > p. 55

JORGE CASTAÑÓN | Argentinian
info@jorgecastanon.com.ar / www.jorgecastanon.com.ar
Jorge Castañón graduated in biology from Buenos Aires University, but started training as a jeweler in his early twenties. His works has been exhibited all over Europe, the US and Argentina and some of his pieces are part of private collections such as the Helen Duft Gallery in New York. His work focuses on natural elements and on the concepts of the past, disappearance, oblivion and how to rescue materials and stories from the past in order to make them speak to us in the here and now. > p. 194

JOSÉE DESJARDINS | Canadian
jd.bijoux@hotmail.com / www.joseedesjardins.co
Josée Desjardins graduated from the Montreal Art Jewelry and Metalsmithing School (EJMAM) in Quebec. In 2010, Montreal's Galerie Noël Guyomarc'h housed her solo show 'Bijoux d'une voyageuse et son cabinet de curiosités', later exhibited as 'A Jeweller's Travel Memorabilia' at the Harbinger Gallery in Waterloo, Canada. She is featured in the books *Ornament and Object*, *500 Wedding Rings* and *500 Bracelets*, and also designed Quebec's prestigious medal for cultural and scientific achievements, the Médaille du Québec. For Josée, jewels are distinctive objects in which she turns her life experiences into material forms. She never designs from the abstract, always embedding organic life, dreams, reality and social issues into her pieces. > p. 120

JUANA ORTIZ | Colombian
juana.camila.ortiz@gmail.com / www.jos.com.co
Juana Camila Ortiz completed a degree in anthropology in 2007 and went on to study jewelry design, fold-forming, and digital photography. She has exhibited at the Gilberto Alzate Avendaño Foundation in 2008 as well as at design fairs sponsored by *Cartel Urbano* magazine in Bogotá. Urban culture, romance, video games, and postmodern thought have all helped to shape Juana's artistic vision. Using resin and silver, she brings these images to life in pieces designed to evoke childhood dreams. > pp. 89, 167

JUDY McCAIG | British
judymccaig@gmail.com
After studying jewelry and silversmithing at the Duncan of Jordanstone College of Art in Scotland,

Judy McCaig received a master's degree from London's Royal College of Art. Her many exhibitions include solo shows at Amaranto, Barcelona; Villa Bengel, Idar-Oberstein; Hipòtesi and the Dterra Gallery, Barcelona; the Queen's Hall Arts Centre in Northumberland; and the Scottish Gallery in Edinburgh. She also won the Greater London Arts Grant, the Alatyr 2005 Competition, and first prize at the 19th Legnica International Jewellery Competition. Judy's pieces employ silver, gold, paint, mixed media and perspex, and tackle the contrasts between light and dark as well as past, present and future. They have been featured in the books *New Earrings*, *Jewellery Design and Development*, *Jewelbook*, *Behind The Brooch*, *Adorn: New Jewellery*, *500 Brooches* and *Jewellery Moves*. > p. 226

JULIA DEVILLE | New Zealander, lives in Australia
julia@discemori.com / www.discemori.com / www.juliadeville.com
Julia deVille studied jewelry-making at Northern Melbourne Institute of TAFE (NMIT). She is represented by Sophie Gannon Gallery and e.g.etal in Melbourne and Jan Murphy Gallery in Brisbane. She has exhibited at Schmuck 2009 in Munich, MONA in Hobart, the National Gallery of Victoria, the Art Gallery of South Australia and the Museum of Contemporary Art in Sydney, and has been featured in *New Directions in Jewellery 2*, *Handmade in Melbourne*, and *Bijoux, illustration et design*. Julia works in traditional gold and silversmithing techniques, combined with materials that were once living such as jet, human hair and most importantly, taxidermy. These materials serve as a memento mori, a reminder of mortality. Her work ranges from one-off jewelry pieces using taxidermy animals, to taxidermy animal sculptures that are adorned with jewelry materials and techniques. > p. 125

JULIETA ODIO BERNARDI | Costa Rican
julietaodio@gmail.com
Julieta Odio Bernardi trained at the University of Costa Rica and the Perseo and Alchimia Schools in Florence, Italy. Recent exhibitions of her work have included 'Think Twice: New Latin American Jewelry' at the Museum of Arts and Design (MAD), New York and the Gray Area Symposium in Mexico City. She has also contributed to exhibitions and magazines in her homeland, including the publications *Estilo y Casas* and *Revista Perfil*. Julieta's jewels utilize sterling silver and found objects to explore notions of being and having been, penetrating into our collective consciousness. Her pieces demand something from the wearer, whether it be interaction, continuation, conclusion or simply participation in a process. > p. 147

JURA GOLUB | Russian
juragolub@gmail.com / juragolub.hautetfort.com
Jura Golub's first exhibitions were in the Soviet Union in places such as Moscow, Volgograd and Kostroma. On moving to Austria in 1990, he continued to show his work abroad, in Germany, the US and Spain. Since 2012 he has lived and worked in Spain. Articles on his work have appeared in *Kunsthandwerk* (2002), while examples of his work have featured in *Art Jewelry Today: Europe* (2014), as well as in a book for teachers entitled *Maker Magic* (2014). Russian art has been a major influence on his work, along with world cultural heritage in its many different forms as experienced through travel, literature and visits to museums. He seeks

to present his concept of beauty and aesthetics, while maintaining his own specific artistic identity. > p. 191

•

KARIM OUKID | Algerian
arteyanibis@yahoo.es
Karim attended the Berber Decorative Art School in Tizi Ouzou, Algeria. He has exhibited at the Ethnology Museum of Barcelona, La Pedrera in Barcelona, the US Embassy in Algiers and the Folk Art Alliance in Santa Fe. As well as teaching at the Massana School in Barcelona, Karim has participated in several conferences, including 'Filigree in Berber Jewelry' in Póvoa de Lanhoso, Portugal and 'The Aesthetics of the Body in North Africa' at the Egyptian Museum in Barcelona. His work has been featured in the books *Aula de Joyería: Técnicas Básicas*, *New Earrings* and *The Work of Art: Folk Artists in the 21st Century*, and in the magazine *Arte y Joya*. In 2014 he was awarded the title of Master Craftsman of Catalonia. Karim uses silver, wood, enamel, Mediterranean coral and other stones in his pieces, which strive to revive the memory and methods of ancient jewelers. More than decorative objects, they represent poems, histories, rivers, mountains, tastes, colours, flowers and the artist's love for his homeland. > p. 75

•

KARIN SEUFERT | German
kgseufert@gmx.de / *www.karinseufert.de*
Karin Seufert trained in the Netherlands, first in Schoonhoven and then at Amsterdam's Gerrit Rietveld Academy. Soon after graduating, she contributed to the exhibition 'Jewelryquake', shown in Tokyo, Munich and Amsterdam. Her work has been showcased in solo exhibitions at the Marzee Gallery in Nijmegen and the Museum of Applied Art in Frankfurt. She obtained first prize at the 2004 International Jewelry Competition in Frankfurt, and in 2003 received an award from the Legnica Gallery of Art in Poland. Fashioned from PVC, plastic, porcelain and Colorit, Karin's most recent pieces explore our consumer society, examining daily trends and re-contextualizing used materials, well-known figures and familiar stories. > pp. 90, 209

•

KATHRYN RIECHERT | American
kjr@kathrynriechert.com / *www.kathrynriechert.com*
Kathryn Riechert studied metalsmithing at the Savannah College of Art and Design, graduating with honours in 2002. Her work has been featured in publications such as *Jewelry Artist* and *Art Jewelry* magazines. Kathryn is fascinated by the personal connection that can be established and transmitted by a piece of jewelry as it is passed from hand to hand. Her playful works explore the themes of nature, family and humour, incorporating sterling silver and gemstones, other metals, glass enamel and found objects into her designs. > p. 149

•

KATJA PRINS | Dutch
info@katjaprins.com / *www.katjaprins.com*
Katja Prins graduated from the Gerrit Rietveld Academy in Amsterdam. Her solo and group exhibitions have taken place across Europe, the US, Asia and Russia, and her work can be found in public collections such as the Rijksmuseum in Amsterdam; the Museum of Arts and Design, New York; the Mint Museum of Craft and Design in Charlotte, North Carolina; and the Schmuck-museum in Pforzheim, Germany. She has also lectured at institutions including the Rhode Island

School of Design, Massachusetts College of Art, Tainan National University of the Arts in Taiwan, Konstfack in Stockholm, the Academy of Fine Arts in Maastricht, Savannah College of Art and Design and Montreal Jewelry School. In 2009 she published her monograph *The Uncanny Valley*, which gives an overview of her work. Katja's pieces tell stories about the intimate relationships between human bodies and mechanic devices, medical technology and industry. > p. 237

•

KENNETH C. MACBAIN | American
kmacbain@gmail.com
Jeweler and metalsmith Kenneth C. MacBain has been published in 30 books, including *Humor in Craft* and *On Body and Soul*, as well as periodicals such as *The New York Times* and *American Craft*. He holds a BFA in Gold and Silversmithing from the State University of New York, New Paltz, and an MFA in Metals from the Tyler School of Art in Philadelphia. Currently an associate professor of art at New Jersey City University, he has participated in over 80 exhibitions, and was granted a fellowship from the New Jersey State Council on the Arts. His work is included in many permanent collections including the Museum of Arts and Design in New York and the Newark Museum. Kenneth's latest conceptual jewelry – rendered using metal, plastics and found objects – addresses issues of social status, preciousness and human relationships. > pp. 103, 148

•

KEPA KARMONA | Spanish
kepakarmona@gmail.com / *kepakarmona.blogspot.com*
Kepa Karmona attended the Basque Country's School of Jewelry and Watchmaking before graduating with honours from Barcelona's Massana School. He boasts a degree in fine arts from the University of the Basque Country and in 2008 he wrote the thesis 'Project Homeless: Jewels for People in Transit' as part of his master's in Artistic Production at the Polytechnic University of Valencia. He has been featured in contemporary jewelry symposiums and exhibitions worldwide, with many pieces being acquired by museums and private collections. Kepa's work hinges on the use of materials discarded by consumer society, often utilizing the assemblage technique. Beyond mere adornments, his pieces are bolstered by a political message about identity and group belonging. > p. 123

•

KIM OANH PHAM | Canadian
yunako@live.ca
Kim Oanh Pham has spent more than half a decade teaching jewelry-making at the Montreal Jewelry School, whose prize, the EJM Award, she received in 2010. Jewelry is an artform that allows Kim Oanh to express her state of mind and feelings in ways that far outstrip the power of words – an art through which parts of her fantasy world are revealed. Her inspiration derives from nature, architecture, and the people she encounters on her travels. She largely works with sterling silver, gems and pearls and aims to create jewelry that carries a deep significance. > p. 193

•

KRISTÝNA MALOVANÁ | Czech
kristynamalovana@gmail.com / *www.morphe.cz* / *www.kristynamalovana.com*
Kristýna Malovaná graduated from the Academy of Arts, Architecture and Design (AAAD) in Prague

in 2012. She is co-founder of MORPHE design studio, based in Prague. They specialize in product, furniture and interior design, exhibition stands and installations, consultancy and art direction. She has received several awards for her work and has participated in group exhibitions including the Salone del Mobile in Milan, DMY International Design Festival in Berlin and Czech Designblok in Prague. She has also taken part in workshops with Makkink & Bey, Estern and Raumlabor Berlin. Kristýna has a very close relationship with jewelry, which she sees as a personal form of expression. All of her items are made in limited editions, often working with different materials. She generally takes a bright and minimalist approach, with a focus on attention to detail and user-friendliness. > pp. 144, 156

•

LEE HYE RAN | Korean
yurial0419@hanmail.net / *www.hyeranlee.com*
A graduate of the Metal Art and Design Department at Hongik University, Lee Hye Ran was selected for the 2009 exhibition 'Destination' at the Museum of Modern Art Design Store in New York and for the Seoul Design Olympiad of the same year. Lee Hye's most notable work is her Farfalle series, whose title refers to the famous bow-tie pasta. This collection aims to create new roles for certain products, by reviving the characteristics of an everyday item, pasta, and boosting the formative and material attractiveness of its design. Her metal pasta pieces are designed to show the difference between solid, delicate handiwork and the cookie-cutter products manufactured en masse in factories. > p. 90

•

LENKA TRUBAČOVÁ | Czech
info@lenkatrubacova.com / *www.lenkatrubacova.com*
Lenka Trubačová trained in Prague at the Academy of Arts, Architecture and Design and the Vocational School of Goldsmiths. Her works have appeared at the Designblok Gallery in Prague and in 'Czech Republic – Crossing of Europe', a contemporary jewelry exhibition held at the Imperial Art Gallery in Beijing. She was a finalist in The Next Episode Lapponia International Jewelry Design Competition in Finland, and her pieces from the competition were later exhibited in Munich. Lenka uses a combination of materials, often mixing non-precious and precious metals with perspex. Contrasting materials create a special tension in her work, and she is not afraid of unorthodox solutions – an example being the interchangeable parts of some of her jewels. > pp. 44, 80

•

LIAUNG-CHUNG YEN | Taiwanese
liaung@yahoo.com / *www.liaungchungyen.com*
After studying at the National Taiwan Academy of Art, Liaung-Chung Yen received an MFA in Metal and Jewelry from the Savannah College of Art and Design. A winner of New York Foundation for the Arts Fellowship 2005, a 2013 NICHE Award and a second place in the 2012 MJSA Vision awards, he has been featured in *Art Jewelry Today 2*, *Metalsmith* magazine's *Exhibition in Print*, and in ten titles in Lark Books' *500* series. Important exhibitions include SOFA Chicago, Philadelphia Museum of Art Fine Craft Show, Smithsonian Museum Fine Craft Show, the Museum of Contemporary Craft in Portland, Oregon, and the National Museum of Art, Design and Architecture in Oslo. By arranging similar forms in repetition, Yen tries to create a sense of rhythm in space. He sees his work as

exploring three-dimensional sculpture in jewelry form, documenting the time in which he lives and his emotions. > pp. 143, 174

•

LINDA SÁNCHEZ MÉNDEZ | Colombian
afrolindainfo@gmail.com / www.afrolinda.com
Linda Sánchez Méndez studied art jewelry at the Massana School in Barcelona. Her work has been featured in group exhibitions in Barcelona and Colombia and in the touring exhibition 'Think Twice: New Latin American Jewelry', which visited locations including the Museum of Arts and Design in New York, the Estonian Museum of Applied Arts and Design in Tallinn, and Franz Mayer Museum in Mexico City. She has also taken part in jewelry fairs in Colombia and the US. Linda runs her own jewelry atelier, where she creates personalized collections on themes including love, freedom, lightness, decisions, and the power of action. She later produces these collections in limited runs. > p. 190

•

LISE SCHØNBERG | Norwegian
lise.a.schoenberg@gmail.com / www.liseschonberg.com
Lise Schønberg studied goldsmithing at the Oslo Vocational College. Her work has been displayed in Oslo's Kunstnerforbundet, at the Sørlandets Art Museum in Kristiansand, and at COLLECT London at the Victoria and Albert Museum. She has been honoured for her work in her homeland by the region of Vest-Agder and received the New Materials Integration Award at the International Cloisonné Jewelry Contest in Tokyo. Lise's work often speaks out for social causes. A notable examples of this is the 'Who Cares?' exhibition at the Agder Regional Centre for Arts, Kristiansand, where she addressed the prevalence of malaria and AIDS, the struggle for women's rights, the environment and the fight for food and survival. > p. 113

•

LITO | Greek
www.lito-jewelry.com
Lito Karakostanoglou's ability to roam between the realms of modernism, romance, futurism, science, ancient tribes and tradition is a rare skill that few visual artists can match. Her meticulous craftsmanship and sense of taste have been honed by studying sculpture at the École Nationale des Beaux-Arts in Paris and technical drawing at the École de la Chambre Syndicale de la Bijouterie, Joaillerie et de l'Orfèvrerie. From India to Mexico and from Japan to Africa, Lito travels the globe in search of magnificent gemstones and uncommon materials. Her curious eye seeks out new ways of translating her sensitive yet bold view of the world into jewelry that a woman can wear as a symbol of who she is, where she came from and what her dreams are made of. Her highly collectable pieces have been included in couture and ready-to-wear shows by Jean Paul Gaultier and Kenzo. Since 1999, Lito has run Cabinet des Curiosités, an atelier-boutique in central Athens. In 2011, Lito launched her own wholesale distribution company and has gradually reached global markets through carefully planned collaborations. Her pieces have been featured in galleries and stores in France, the UK, Italy, Austria, Portugal, the US and Japan. > pp. 49, 195

•

LULU TEHILA FEINSILVER | Israeli
lulutake5@gmail.com / www.lulufeinsilver.com
Lulu Tehila Feinsilver is an Israeli jewelry designer. She is a graduate of the Bezalel Academy of Arts and Design in Jerusalem and a former student of the

Geneva University of Art and Design. She currently works as an associate designer and right-hand woman to luxury Judaica designer Emil Shenfeld in Jerusalem. Lulu's pieces are mostly created using precious metals, although she enjoys seeking the right materials for each project. Her jewelry is a means of expressing feelings and opinions. Lulu uses a wide range of themes in her work, ranging from the deeply personal to the universal. She uses her pieces and the fine details of her craft to emphasize the thoughts and sensations she wishes to convey. > pp. 81, 216

•

LUZIA VOGT | Swiss
info@luziavogt.ch / www.luziavogt.ch
Luzia Vogt studied at the University of Pforzheim in Germany after completing a goldsmithing apprenticeship in Basel. She has exhibited at the Museum Bellerive in Zurich, Schmuck in Munich, the Emilia Cohen Gallery in Mexico City, and Gallery Ornamentum in Hudson, NY, and was showcased in solo exhibitions at the Beatrice Lang Gallery in Berne in 2008 and at Galerie Ra in Amsterdam and Galeria Reverso in Lisbon in 2014. She is the recipient of a Swiss Federal Design Grant as well as many awards, including the Innovation Prize at Inhorgenta and first prize at Form Forum Switzerland. Luzia questions the value of materials, changing by-products into featured parts by altering their context and meaning. Through her jewelry, she seeks to catch the eye of the spectator. > p. 176

•

MANUELA URIBE PIEDRAHÍTA | Colombian
manuela.uribe@gmail.com
Manuela Uribe Piedrahíta studied graphic design and art jewelry at Le Arti Orafe School and the Quasar Institute in Italy as well as at the Colegiatura Colombiana and EAFIT University in Colombia. Her independent collections include Il Bosco, Fabula and Caja de Sorpresas. Using silver, gold, precious and semi-precious stones, natural elements, and enamel, Manuela explores themes related to nature. Her simple designs help underscore the colour and shape of the gems she uses, and her pieces are graced by minute, carefully elaborated details, textures and embossing as well as original shapes which bring to mind woods, animals, and the memories of a charming past. > pp. 44, 177

•

MARC MONZÓ | Spanish
marc@marcmonzo.net / www.marcmonzo.net
Marc Monzó studied jewelry at Barcelona's Massana School. His work has been showcased in galleries, publications and museums across Europe, the US and Asia, and is included in the permanent collections of the Françoise van den Bosch Foundation, the SM Stedelijk Museum and the CODA Museum in Apeldoorn in the Netherlands as well as the Museum of Decorative Arts in Barcelona and the National Gallery of Australia. In 2006, he won the Design Prize of the Catalan Federation of Jewelers, Goldsmiths and Watchmakers, and in 2008, he was featured in a monographic volume, *Marc Monzó Jeweler*. Marc's pieces are founded on a base of strong craftsmanship using jewels as his tools, although his larger projects revolve around his attempts to understand gemstones. > pp. 158, 159

•

MAREEN ALBURG DUNCKER | German
mail@mareenalburg.de / www.mareenalburg.de
Mareen Alburg Duncker studied jewelry-making at the Burg Giebichenstein University of Art and Design

in Halle, Germany. She was invited to participate in the Talente 2004 exhibition at the International Handicraft Fair in Munich, was one of the finalists for the Bavarian Craft Council's BKV Prize in 2009 and received a bursary from the Sachsen-Anhalt Art Foundation and the Kloster Bergesche Foundation in 2012. Her pieces have been exhibited in Germany, Austria, Belgium, the Netherlands, Japan and the US, and have been featured in *The Marzee Collection*, *Collection Feldversuch*, *500 Earrings* and *New Earrings*. Looking at reflections of light on materials leads Mareen to sense the inherent possibilities of objects, which she later crafts into finished pieces. > p. 216

•

MARI ISHIKAWA | Japanese, lives in Germany
mi@mari-ishikawa.de / www.mari-ishikawa.de
An art graduate from Nara University of Education, Mari Ishikawa first trained as a jeweler at the Hiko Mizuno College of Jewelry in Tokyo before attending the Academy of Fine Arts in Munich. Her works have been displayed in Germany, Austria, Belgium, the Netherlands, Luxembourg, Italy, France, Portugal, Spain, Sweden, Poland, Denmark, the UK, the US, Australia, Chile, Thailand, Vietnam, China, South Korea and Japan. She won a special award at Inhorgenta Munich in 2014, second prize at the 2012 Elizabeth R. Raphael Founder's Prizes, the 2010 Bavarian State Prize for Young Designers, and the Herbert Hofmann Prize in 2000. Since 1994, Mari Ishikawa has lived and worked in Munich, Germany. She is attracted by the perfect shapes of plants and seeks to explore the effect they have on people and preserve the fleeting nature of their beauty in her pieces. > p. 63

•

MARIA AVILLEZ | Portuguese
maria.avillez@netcabo.pt
With a background in graphic design, Maria was attracted by the manual and artistic possibilities offered by jewelry-making. She completed a professional course at Lisbon's Contacto Directo School, where she obtained a young creators' prize. This was followed by short courses on silversmithing, Japanese lacquer, Rhinoceros 3D design software and cast setting. Maria has exhibited at a number of international fairs, including Bijorhca in Paris, Inhorgenta in Munich and Portojóia in Portugal, and her pieces have been published in several magazines and Lisbon city guides. Although not defined by them, Maria likes to follow fashion trends. Influenced by day-to-day life and exploring a range of materials, her work is characterized by simple graphic forms. > p. 65

•

MARIA CRISTINA BELLUCCI | Italian
mcb@mcbjewellery.com / www.mcbjewellery.com
Maria Cristina Bellucci graduated in Stage Design from the Academy of Fine Arts in Rome. She studied metalsmithing at Rome's San Giacomo School of Ornamental Arts, before attending Le Arti Orafe in Lucca and the Alchimia School in Florence. For several years she worked making theatrical costumes and accessories, as well as creating a wide range of jewelry for stage use. She then developed a strong interest in contemporary jewelry and has been a freelance jewelry designer since 1999. Maria Cristina's recent work – produced using silver, coloured pencils, ebony and other woods – is characterized by the interplay between solid-looking elements and colour. She enjoys imbuing everyday objects with new meaning, deconstructing and

decontextualizing them and transforming them into pieces of jewelry. > p. 34

MARÍA GOTI FERNÁNDEZ | Spanish
info@mariagoti.es / www.mariagoti.es
María Goti studied jewelry design, stone setting and lost wax casting at the European Centre of Jewelry Making and Gemmology in Oviedo, Spain. Silver, including textured and oxidized variations, gold, natural stones, pearls, resin, ebony, druse and fossilized coral are just some of the materials María handles. Her minimalist pieces reflect an interest in nature, the sea and abstraction. María is inspired by her surroundings, her experiences and her memories, creating personal jewels that leave the wearer feeling comfortable and attractive. > p. 137

MARIANA VISO ROJAS | Venezuelan
mvisorojas@yahoo.es / mvisorojas.blogspot.com
Caracas-born Mariana Viso Rojas moved to Barcelona nearly 20 years ago, attending the School of Arts and Trades and the Barcelona Guild of Jewelers and Watchmakers. She has studied techniques such as enamelling, hand engraving and Berber filigree, and her pieces have been shown at galleries and shops across the city, including Hipòtesi, Ignia, La Basílica and Àurica. She was a finalist in the Best Technique category in the professional division of the Enjoia't Contemporary Jewelry Awards. Mariana's jewels, principally made of silver, are the synthesis of the various cultures amid which she has spent her life. This background fuels a deep-rooted curiosity, which leads her to find inspiration in almost anything, in particular her emotions. > p. 26

MARIA PAOLA BARROTTA | Italian
paolabarrotta@gmail.com / www.mariapaolabarrotta.com
For Maria Paola Barrotta, the artist is a mediator who takes the internal language of an object and translates it into a final form representing a sensation, emotion or memory. Once finished, the jewel tells its own story but also becomes part of the story of its wearers and viewers: the piece is in constant transformation as it creates communicative links between these different worlds. > p. 191

MARIE MARCANO | Venezuelan
marie.marcano@gmail.com
Marie Marcano is a Venezuelan visual artist based in the US. She creates contemporary jewelry and limited-edition artist's books. Her work has been exhibited at the Noble Museum, the Corcoran Museum of Art and the Bienes Museum of the Modern Book. Marie conceives of art as a multidisciplinary practice. Her jewels seek to rouse the senses, evoking pleasurable sensations through fine textures and forms. She is committed to experimentation in order to fashion striking, original pieces. Her inspiration comes in the shape of exotic aromas, the ocean, and the processes of transformation. > p. 93

MARIE PENDARIÈS | French
mariependaries@yahoo.fr / mariependaries.blogspot.com
Marie Pendariès did an undergraduate art degree at the Paul Valéry University in Montpellier and graduated with an Advanced Diploma in Design and Art from Strasbourg Higher School of Decorative Arts. In June 2010, she participated in 'Un peu de terre sur la peau', a ceramic jewelry exhibition at the Bernardaud Foundation in Limoges, France. Her work was selected for the Talente 2009 International Handicraft Fair in Munich, Germany and the Contemporary Jewelry exhibition in Vilafranca del Penedès, Spain. Marie greatly enjoys working with cheap or ephemeral materials, which she converts into jewels, thereby inverting commonplace codes of value. Her recent body of work explores the world of couples and in particular married life. > p. 200

MARIELLE DEBETHUNE | French
coucou.marielou@gmail.com / www.marielledebethune.com
Marielle Debethune studied art jewelry at the Massana School in Barcelona, graduating in 2009. Since then, her work has been exhibited in shows in Paris, Lille, Padua, Valencia and Barcelona. She sees her work as a poetic interpretation of a world that is overwhelming, based on the concept of placing emotions inside shells, membranes and walls. In a time in which people are anxious to shield themselves from real or imagined dangers, her shell-like forms become a kind of double skin, simultaneously protective and confining. The shell becomes a hindrance that must be dragged along or a sarcophagus from which people must struggle free, casting off their outer skin. > p. 44

MARILÈNE MORENCY | Canadian
info@marilenemorency.com / www.marilenemorency.com
Marilène Morency is a self-taught jewelry artist. Since starting out in 2004, her work has been shown in North America, Europe and Asia. Having travelled to North Africa in her early childhood, Marilène has always been fascinated with the ancient art of filigree. Inspired by the complex ornamentation of this type of work, she combines filigree with textile and paper techniques to create unique jewelry pieces in sterling silver. These wearable art sculptures often explore the notions of presence and absence. > p. 81

MARINA MASSONE | Argentinian
info@marinamassone.com / www.marinamassone.com
Marina Massone trained as an industrial designer, but it was in jewelry that she found a place to merge her earlier studies with her need for artistic expression. In 2011 she founded her own contemporary jewelry studio. In her works, Massone explores the formal and technical possibilities of materials: their curves, movements and volumes. Every collection begins with the design of a single module, which is then repeated and articulated to form flexible metallic structures that move on the body. Her work has been featured in many national and international exhibitions and design fairs and has won several awards, as well as featuring in national and international magazines and books on contemporary jewelry. She also curates exhibitions and conferences. She has taught classes in industrial design at the University of Buenos Aires, and currently leads a workshop in the design and production of contemporary jewelry. > p. 75

MARINA MOLINELLI WELLS | Argentinian
marinamw@yahoo.com
Marina Molinelli Wells apprenticed at the La Nave studio while studying industrial design at the University of Buenos Aires. The many workshops she has attended have made her highly proficient with materials such as glass, enamel and latex, as well as techniques including sand, wax and cuttlefish casting. In 2005 she co-curated a contemporary jewelry selection hosted at the Museum of Latin American Art in Buenos Aires (MALBA). From 2004 to 2011, alongside with Francisca Kweitel, Marina ran Metalistería, an online store selling contemporary work by several Latin American artists. > p. 242

MARJORIE SIMON | American
marjoriesimon@aol.com / www.marjoriesimon.com
Marjorie Simon is a former chairperson of the editorial advisory committee for *Metalsmith* magazine, to which she regularly contributes, and was a juror for Lark Books' *500 Brooches*. The Mint Museum of Craft and Design, North Carolina, the Newark Museum, New Jersey, and the Racine Art Museum in Wisconsin all include pieces by Marjorie in their permanent collections. 'Housing and Warehousing', an installation of her new enamelwork, is included in 'Heat Exchange 2', an exhibition touring the UK and Germany in 2015–16. Over the last ten years, Marjorie's jewels have explored botanical and floral themes, making use of copper, sterling and fine silver along with vitreous enamel, altered photographs and mild steel. > p. 88

MARTA FERNÁNDEZ CABALLERO | Spanish
mfcjoyas@gmail.com / martafernandezcaballero.wordpress.com
Marta Fernández Caballero completed a degree in Fine Arts at the University of the Basque Country, Bilbao, where she later pursued a PhD in CAD-CAM-CAE tools applied to sculpture. She holds a degree in microbiology from the same university and has also studied jewelry at the AFEDAP school in Paris and arts at Muskingum College in Ohio. Marta has twice taken second prize at the International Pearl Design Contest in Japan and won third prize in the Tahitian Pearl Trophy competition. She is currently head of the art jewelry department at the EASO Polytechnic Institute in San Sebastián. > p. 245

MARTACARMELA SOTELO | Mexican
maca@martacarmela.com / www.martacarmela.com
Martacarmela Sotelo's work is the outcome of her search for a language of self-expression. After gaining a BA in Architecture and an MA in Fine Arts, Martacarmela started to explore construction processes and began to create wearable art pieces, constantly switching between different materials and techniques. Her work has been exhibited at locations including the Museum of Arts and Design in New York, the Bellevue Arts Museum in Seattle, the Fine Art Museum in Tallinn, the Franz Mayer Museum and CONARTE in Mexico City, and at Mexico, New York and London Design Week. In 2012 she won the Quorum Award for Mexican design, and in 2015 she received an honourable mention at the Hugo Salinas Price National Silver Awards. She has also worked with the Mexican silver brand TANE as an freelance designer. > p. 170

MASAKO HAMAGUCHI | Japanese / British
hamaguchi.masako@gmail.com
After earning a BFA from the University of Michigan, Masako Hamaguchi went on to Gerrit Rietveld Academy in Amsterdam, graduating in 1988. She participated in showcase exhibitions such as 'Jewelry USA' (American Craft Museum, 1984), 'ORNAMENTA' (Schmuckmuseum Pforzheim, 1989) and 'De Main à

Main' (Museum of Design and Contemporary Applied Arts in Lausanne, 2008). She has received various awards in international competitions, most recently an honourable mention at the Itami International Craft Exhibition in 2013. Her work is included in the Bollmann Collection, Austria, and the Angermuseum in Erfurt, Germany. Masako's mixed media pieces question the idea of 'preciousness' from different angles. Her jewels are the material manifestation of her theories and investigations, which seek to get to the bottom of what jewelry is. > p. 40

MEIRI ISHIDA | Japanese
meiriishida@gmail.com / www.meiri-ishida.com
Meiri Ishida attended the Tama Art University in Tokyo, Japan, where she has also lectured, before taking courses at the Alchimia School in Florence, Italy. Her work has been shown at Schmuck 2006 in Munich, the Object Gallery in Sydney, the National Museum of Modern Art in Tokyo, and the Sculptural Felt International at the Museum de Kantfabriek in the Netherlands and Wollongong Art Gallery, Australia. She also participated in COLLECT London 2015 with Yufuku Gallery. She has been published in *The Compendium Finale of Contemporary Jewellers* and Lark Books' *500 Bracelets, 500 Necklaces* and *500 Plastic Jewelry Designs*. Meiri's pieces shed light on the parallel world hidden in daily life. Her jewels are not complete until they are worn on the body, when their form, colour and feel come together with the wearer's personality. > p. 59

MEL MILLER | Australian
melmillerjewellery@gmail.com / www.melmillerjewellery.com
Mel Miller completed a Master of Arts in Fine Art at RMIT University in Australia and a Bachelor of Fine Arts at Arizona State University. Her work has been showcased in the US, Australia, and Europe, with notable exhibitions including 'Jewellery Topos' at the Marzee Gallery and 'New Traditional Jewellery' in Amsterdam. The recipient of the 2008 Small Beautiful Objects Award, she has been featured in Lark Books' *500 Enameled Objects* and *Showcase: 500 Rings*. Mel's pieces explore the transformative effect on memories of storytelling and the act of remembering. Her series of objects with removable and wearable components explore the interaction between experience and memory. > p. 60

MELINDA RISK | American
mrj@melindajewelry.com / www.melindajewelry.com
Melinda Risk holds a BFA in Jewelry/Metals from Kent State University in Ohio and was a finalist in the Signity Colored Gemstone Design Award 2000. Her creations, which bring together gold, silver, bronze, gemstones, enamel, wood and porcelain, were selected for Lark Books' *500 Gemstone Jewels*. Melinda derives her inspiration from nature and her life experiences. Her deeply personal pieces – each jewel a small sculpture with its own story – aim to forge a personal relationship with the people who own them. > p. 41

MELISSA BORRELL | American
me@melissaborrell.com / www.melissaborrell.com
Melissa uses modern machines and industrial processes as well as traditional craft techniques to create pieces that challenge our expectations. A native Texan, Melissa has lived in many cities around the globe. With a background in jewelry design, she worked as a studio artist in San Francisco for several years before moving to Providence for graduate school. She received an MFA from Rhode Island School of Design in 2005. Melissa currently lives in Austin, Texas, where she creates her jewelry designs and sculptures. She is always thinking about new ways to use technology to create art. > p. 67

MELODY ARMSTRONG | Canadian
melodymetaldesign@hotmail.com / www.melodyarmstrong.com
Melody Armstrong graduated with distinction from the Alberta College of Art and Design in 1999, majoring in jewelry and metal. Working with traditional and non-traditional metals, enamels and stones, Melody describes her style as industrial-organic. This design philosophy is demonstrated through a mix of natural shapes and geometric structures, with great attention to detail and quality of workmanship. Melody maintains a professional studio and is a jewelry instructor and resident artist at the Neil Balkwill Civic Arts Centre. Her recent accomplishments include being selected as part of the Dimensions 2015 touring exhibition, receiving an Independent Artists Grant from the Saskatchewan Arts Board, having a solo exhibition at Affinity Gallery and having articles published in *Art Jewelry* magazine. She is represented by Mata Gallery in Regina, Saskatchewan. > p. 193

MIA HEBIB | American
mia@oblik-atelier.com / www.oblik-atelier.com
After attending the School for Applied Arts and Design in Zagreb, Croatia, Mia Hebib graduated with distinction from the Savannah College of Art and Design. She has taken part in major exhibitions in Bosnia and Herzegovina, San Diego, Savannah, Korea and Croatia, and she has been featured in *City, Z, T Magazine* and *Vogue*. Mia's work range from limited editions in precious metals and stones to combinations of metals and wood. She is currently focused on creating an alliance between fashion and art through her Brass Band collection. These pieces are handcrafted in brass with precious metal platings. This collection is about moving lines in metal, creating visually simple forms that withstand passing trends and fads. > p. 185

MICHAEL BERGER | German
info@atelier-berger.de / www.atelier-berger.de
After serving an apprenticeship as a goldsmith in Münster, Germany, Michael Berger continued his training in Koblenz and Düsseldorf, qualifying as a master craftsman in 1998. Now living and working in Düsseldorf, he won the Bochum Design Prize in 2005, the Tahitian Pearl Trophy 2007–2008, and the North Rhine-Westphalia State Prize for Arts and Crafts in 2009. He has exhibited for many years in cities all over the world, including London, New York and Barcelona. Inspired by the body and by his period as assistant to Friedrich Becker, the inventor of kinetic jewelry, Michael's kinetic jewels feature individual elements that can rotate, swing or be turned. > p. 133

MICHAL OREN | Israeli
michaloren7@gmail.com / michaloren.wordpress.com
Michal Oren completed a BFA in the Department of Jewelry and Metalwork at Jerusalem's Bezalel Academy of Arts and Design, followed by a master's degree in Art History. Since 2002 Michal has exhibited her work internationally, and in 2008, she was awarded the Israeli Ministry of Culture's Prize for Design. Michal is one of the members of Inyanim, a group of nine leading Israeli artists and designers working in the field of contemporary jewelry. They have presented their work together in places such as Gallery Loupe in New Jersey, the B-Side Festival in Amsterdam, and in Tallinn, Lisbon, Munich and Tel Aviv, and continue to share their thoughts on personal, political and social issues through their jewelry. Michal's pieces deal with the moving human body, moulding it to the patterns of geometry and nature. > p. 234

MICHELL GALINDO | Mexican
info@galaislove.com / www.galaislove.com
Michell Galindo Temores is an excellent craftswoman who quickly learnt how to manipulate silver. Her pieces have been showcased at 'TNT: Thursday Night Thing' at the Museum of Contemporary Art in San Diego, as well as in fashion magazines including *Vogue, ELLE, Harper's Bazaar* and *L'Officiel*. A fervent believer in love, Michell explores her romantic streak in her Gala Is Love series. These jewels are designed to bring out a smile, to make their wearers feel beautiful, and to radiate happiness. > p. 25

MICHELLE KRAEMER | Luxembourgian
info@michellekraemer.com / www.michellekraemer.com
Michelle Kraemer was born in Luxembourg. After obtaining a degree in Three-Dimensional Design at the University of Portsmouth, she continued her studies at Alchimia, the contemporary jewelry school in Florence, with Manfred Bischoff and Ruudt Peters. Since 2009 she has lived and worked in Vienna, where she is a member of Atelier STOSSIMHIMMEL, a studio for contemporary jewelers. She sees jewelry as something that needs to be touched, and always begins by intuitively manipulating material. Her challenge is to transform the material in such a way that it changes completely, until it becomes something else entirely: a piece of jewelry. > p. 19

MIGUEL ÂNGELO DURO GROMICHO | Portuguese
miguel.gromicho@gmail.com
Miguel Ângelo Duro Gromicho studied at the Contacto Directo School in Lisbon, taking part in the school's end-of-year exhibition in 2009. Miguel's organic pieces, which employ silver, gold, titanium, gems, stones and pearls, unite fluid forms with geometric accuracy. Based on the conflation of jewelry with identity, each jewel is conceived for people who appreciate wearing it in their real life and above all enjoy actively participating in the creative process, suggesting features and details that help the artist forge something that is at once different, unique and extremely personal. > p. 150

MIKALA MORTENSEN | Danish
contact@mikalamortensen.dk
Mikala Mortensen attended the Royal Danish Academy of Fine Arts and the Institute of Precious Metals in Copenhagen. Her work has been displayed at the Caractère Gallery in Switzerland, Scandinavia House in New York and the Trapholt Museum in Denmark. She has received travel grants from various Danish institutions, including the Ministry of Culture, and contributed to the book *500 Pendants & Lockets*. Mikala's pieces – which she groups into the poetic, the playful, the graphic, the architectural and the industrial – evidence her diverse background as a concept designer at LEGO, a precious metal artist

and an architect. Weaving together silver and gold with Plexiglas, thread and leather, her creations tell stories through colour and light. > p. 39

MI-MI MOSCOW | Russian
mimimoscow@gmail.com / www.mi-mi.ru
The members of mi-mi moscow, Mila Kalnitskaya and Micha Maslennikov, graduated from the Moscow Higher Art and Industrial School, formerly the Stroganoff School. They participated in 'Romancing the Stone' at Manchester Town Hall, are published in Lark Books' *500 Earrings* and have exhibited across Europe, Asia and the US. Mi-mi moscow have received both the Judge's Award and the Grand Prize at the International Craft Exhibition in Itami, Japan. Their striking, life-inspired work forms part of collections at the Kremlin Armoury, the All-Russian Museum of Decorative, Applied and Folk Art in Moscow, the Espace Solidor in Paris, the Pforzheim Jewelry Museum in Germany, and the Cominelli Foundation in Italy. > pp. 64, 65, 116, 117

MIRIAM VERBEEK | Dutch
miriamverbeek1@hotmail.com / www.miriamverbeek.nl
Miriam Verbeek is an award-winning graduate from Amsterdam's Gerrit Rietveld Academy, taking the school's Jury Award in 1993. She has been featured in several books, including three titles from Lark Books' *500* series as well as *1000 Rings*. In her homeland, her work has been shown at the Textile Museum in Tilburg, CODA Museum in Apeldoorn and Gorcums Museum in Gorinchem, while she has also exhibited abroad in Belfast, Madrid, Montreal and Munich. Using English and Dutch bereavement rituals as a departure point, Miriam was initially fascinated by mourning jewelry. Her more recent pieces, mixing hand-felted wool with, silk and thread, take their cue from an observation of nature within its cultural and historical context. > pp. 65, 184

MOTOKO FURUHASHI | Japanese
motokofuruhashi@gmail.com / motokofuruhashi.com
Motoko Furuhashi was born in 1982 in Tokyo, Japan and moved to the US to pursue a career as an artist and educator. She received her MFA from the University of Illinois at Urbana-Champaign. Currently she is an assistant professor at New Mexico State University. Her work has been exhibited nationally including at the Museum of Contemporary Art Chicago, the Houston Center for Contemporary Craft, Gallery K in Tokyo, and the Oakland Museum of California. Stretching her imagination in order to fathom things that she does not possess or which do not yet exist, Motoko uses her mixed-media creations to establish bridges between these novel concepts and the objects and elements in her everyday environment.
> pp. 101, 129, 157, 224

NANCY NEWBERG | American
nancy@nancynewberg.com / www.nancynewberg.com
Los Angeles-based designer Nancy Newberg has created a fine jewelry collection that elevates the modern wardrobe. Trained in fashion, Nancy uses strong architectural shapes and surface textures, lending new relevance to classic designs. Precious metals, white diamonds and pearls combine to form jewelry that can be layered and worn in a variety of ways. Modern and timeless, Nancy's pieces are continually evolving but the primary focus remains on the women who wear them. > p. 82

NATALIA MILOSZ-PIEKARSKA | Australian
natalia925@gmail.com
After graduating with a BA in Visual Communication, Natalia Milosz-Piekarska completed a BA in Gold and Silversmithing at RMIT University in Melbourne. Recent awards include the 2015 Lynne Kosky Jewellery Award and the 2013 Australia Council New Work Grant. Some exhibitions of note include 'Lucky Fool' at E.g.etal in Melbourne; 'Immortal Morsels' at the Pieces of Eight Gallery, Melbourne; Talente 2011 in Munich; 'Unnatural Acts' at Velvet da Vinci, San Francisco; and 'Touch, Pause, Engage' at Objectspace Gallery, Auckland. Natalia's work has recently been collected by the Musée des Arts Décoratifs in Paris, and she is also a sessional lecturer in the School of Fine Art at RMIT University, Melbourne. Natalia's amulet-like and talismanic adornments delve into superstition, folklore and ritual, exploring human inclinations towards charmed objects and the power of belief. Her playful pieces, employing silver, gold, timber, stones, resin and found materials, emanate a sense of character and spirit. > p. 220

NEVIN ARIG | Turkish
nevin.arig@yahoo.com / www.nevinarig.weebly.com
Born in Turkey, Nevin Arig studied at the Fine Arts Academy in Istanbul, where she found herself inspired by the contrasts of her vast homeland, divided between Europe and Asia, with its mixture of Byzantine and Ottoman cultures. After graduating with a BA in graphic design, she went to Europe to work in design studios. In 1995, she started studying jewelry design, and since then, she has enjoyed every moment of the learning and working process. Her work emanates from the intricacy of nature, the traditions of Turkey and the duality of two cultures. She likes to combine metal with natural elements such as wood, coral and stones, as well as with resin, glass and pigments. > p. 192

NICOLAS ESTRADA | Colombian / Spanish
nicolas@amarillojoyas.com / www.amarillojoyas.com
Born in Medellín, Colombia, in the early 1970s, Nicolas Estrada has lived and worked as a jeweler in the city of Barcelona since 2000. Raised in a period of great social conflict, Nicolas draws upon the memories of his youth, pursuing recurring themes throughout his work. Originally, Nicolas studied business administration, and after working as a marketing executive for several notable companies, he moved to Barcelona to take a master's degree in marketing at the IDEC-UPF. However, during his studies, Nicolas discovered the art of jewelry, an event that led to a change of career. Nicolas attended Trier University of Applied Sciences in Idar-Oberstein, a city famed for its gemstones, earning his MFA in July 2015. On his return to Barcelona, he reopened his studio and launched a new line of pieces: wearable art characterized by precious stones. Nicolas's work has received widespread recognition, including the German Prize for Jewelry and Precious Stones. His work has been featured in many international publications, including *ELLE* and the book *New Directions in Jewellery*, and been exhibited in prestigious museums and galleries including the Museum of Arts and Design (MAD) in New York, and the Marzee Gallery in the Netherlands. Nicolas Estrada is an artist with his own distinct voice. His artistic direction stems from a foundation of irony combined with a profound sense of reflection. He remains respectful of his sources

of inspiration and is a passionate artisan, always seeking new interpretations for the mundane. Nicolas operates as a high-end art jeweler under his own name, preferring to trade his commercial jewelry under the brand name Amarillo Joyas.
> pp. 130, 131, 179, 214, 219

NICOLE DEUSTER | German, lives in Spain
nicki_deuster@hotmail.com
Nicole Deuster studied jewelry at the Massana School in Barcelona, where she learned the techniques of Japanese lacquer, chasing and repoussé, and sculpture. In 1987 she was given a placement at the workshop of Gerd Schröder in Munich. Since 2008, she has been part of the project Joyas Sensacionales, which is coordinated by the artist Silvia Walz. Nicole's pieces have been exhibited in national and international galleries. A two-time finalist at Enjoia't, the international contemporary jewelry awards run by FAD in Barcelona, she has also been featured in *Märkische Allgemeine*. Nicole's work explores life's constant motion and transformation, building on the contributions of past and present generations. Her pieces, imbued with symbolism and vivacity, integrate the body into their aesthetic in order to achieve their full effect. > p. 148

NIKI ULEHLA | American
nikiulehla@gmail.com / www.nikiulehla.com
The holder of a BA in Drawing and Painting from Stanford University, Niki Ulehla studied puppetry in Prague and jewelry-making at the Revere Academy of Jewelry Arts in San Francisco. Her work in painting and puppetry influences her jewelry: images, shapes, and techniques cross disciplinary lines and are juxtaposed to create memorable pieces, which feature eclectic materials such as found metals, plastics, pantyhose, teeth, nails, enamel, horn and bone. Niki won the Award of Excellence from the American Craft Council. Her work has been showcased at Velvet da Vinci Gallery and Houston's Museum of Fine Arts and published in *500 Pendants & Lockets* and *500 Enameled Objects* as well as *Art Jewelry* magazine. > p. 146

NILS PETERS | German
info@sonnenschmuck.de / www.sonnenschmuck.com
Nil Peters's jewelry represents the pure joy of life. These luminous and creative works of art are inspired by nature and carefully crafted by hand to be powerful companions. > p. 136

NILS SCHMALENBACH | German
nils.schmalenbach@web.de / www.nilsschmalenbach.de
German-born Nils Schmalenbach studied goldsmithing in Dortmund before attending Hanau Design Academy in 2005. From 2009 onwards, he pursued further studies at Trier University of Applied Sciences in Idar-Oberstein and at Offenbach University of Art and Design. His work has been shown at the German Goldsmith's House in Hanau, the Gallery of Art in Legnica, Poland, the Museum of Applied Arts in Cologne, and Aaron Faber Gallery in New York. Today he lives a simple and happy life near a forest somewhere in Germany. > p. 68

NINA SAJET | Dutch
info@ninasajet.nl / www.ninasajet.nl
Nina Sajet likes to look attentively at the things around her and express that reality in a poetic way through her work. Like in a fairytale or a surrealist dream, the objects may become really

big or extremely small or change their context. In her world, cages turn into rings, birds into pipes, Brussels sprouts into beads. She sees every new object as part of a new reality into which she draws her audience. > p. 172

NOEMÍ FOGUET LORCA | Spanish
info@noemjoies.com / www.noemjoies.com
Noemí Foguet Lorca graduated from the Tarragona School of Art and Design and has since taken classes at the Barcelona School of Arts and Trade. She has presented her work at 'Joyas à la Carte', Inhorgenta and Eurobijoux, and won second place in the latter's young designers gallery and third prize at the Avantguarda Jewelry Exhibition in Altafulla, Spain. In 2007, Noemí established her own business and brand under the name Noem Joies. Her creations, which employ fine metals and precious stones, seek to unite the simplicity of form and beauty of modernity. > p. 164

NORA PATRICIA SOLARTE | Colombian
ps@patriciasolarte.com / www.patriciasolarte.com
An architecture graduate from the Bogotá-based Pontifical Xavierian University in Colombia, Nora Patricia Solarte Guerrero pursued postgraduate studies at the Polytechnic University of Catalonia in Barcelona. She took up jewelry-making at the Catalan Federation of Jewelers, Goldsmiths and Watchmakers and the Massana School, where she completed courses in casting and Berber jewelry. She has exhibited at the Marzee Gallery in Nijmegen, the Netherlands, JOYA 2009 in Barcelona, and the 2010 International Jewellery Competition in Legnica, Poland. Nora Patricia's pieces create a nexus of terms, concepts and objects, forging new modes of expression that explore the sensitive, transgressive boundary between what something purports to be, what it really is and what it might become. > p. 231

PAMELA RITCHIE | Canadian
pritchie@nscad.ca / pamelaritchie.ca
Pamela Ritchie creates jewelry that draws on links between the past and the present, relating to both mythology and personal identity. Following postgraduate research work in Norway, she received her MFA from the Nova Scotia College of Art and Design, where she is currently a professor in the Jewellery Department. The winner of multiple awards, she has had her work showcased in many solo and group exhibitions throughout North America, Australia, Asia and Europe. She has also been featured in Canadian, American and Korean magazines, as well as in books such as *Contemporary Jewelry in Perspective*. Her work celebrates the concentrating effect of detail, and the paradox that an abundance of ideas, forms and patterns can be encapsulated in very small objects. Pamela is represented by Galerie Noel Guyomarc'h in Montreal. > pp. 60, 170

PATRICIA ALIFANO | Argentinian
patoalifano@gmail.com
Patricia Alifano studied ceramics and fine art at the National Ceramics School as well as the National University Institute of the Arts (IUNA) in Buenos Aires. She has been making jewelry since 2003, first acquiring the trade in the various workshops in which she worked and later beginning to create her own jewelry. Patricia bases her work on many sources of inspiration, including architecture, cultures, nature, plants, the sea, the wind and

music. Her unique pieces and limited-run series explore the possibilities of combining myriad techniques and materials in novel ways, creating jewels that 'speak for themselves'. > p. 129

PAULA ESTRADA MATYÁŠOVÁ | Colombian
estradapaula@hotmail.com / www.paulaestradamatyasova.com
Paula Estrada Matyášová began her career as an industrial designer after graduating from the Pontifical Bolivarian University in Medellín, Colombia. At first she specialized in furniture design, winning awards such as Colombia's Steel Pencil for the Io chair and the Mantis freestanding office system. Later, she moved onto shop window design for the fashion industry. Nowadays, Paula is a full-time contemporary jeweler. She sees jewelry-making as the perfect three-dimensional multidisciplinary field, allowing her to combine different worlds and visions, creating aesthetics, design methods and concepts. Objects may turn into jewels, and jewels may turn into objects. As well as adorning the body, jewelry is a means of communication for her: an act that has its own memory and bonds the soul to the world. > p. 115

PETER HOOGEBOOM | Dutch
hoogeboom@chello.nl / www.peterhoogeboom.nl
A graduate of Amsterdam's Gerrit Rietveld Academy, Peter Hoogeboom was nominated for the Rotterdam Design Award and the European Prize for Applied Arts and won the New Traditional Jewellery Award in 2007. He has exhibited solo at the Hnoss Gallery in Sweden, Gallery Ra in the Netherlands, Galerie Noel Guyomarc'h in Canada, Gallery Loupe in the USA and UBI in China. He has participated in many other exhibitions all over the world and his work has been featured in books such as *Sustainable Jewellery* and *Jewelbook*. The MAD in New York and the V&A in London are among the museums with works by Peter in their collections. Peter's unique jewelry utilizes motifs such as slip-cast ceramic elements interwoven with silver chain maille or small bamboo boxes, to tell a story of transitory beauty. This transience – a dropped ceramic necklace breaks easily – adds to the value of his pieces, which are inspired by everyday objects and focus on themes of ethnography and vulnerability. > p. 54

PETRA CLASS | German
petra.class@gmail.com / www.petraclass.net
A graduate of the University of Stuttgart and the State College for Glass and Jewelry in Neugablonz, Germany, Petra Class has owned her own jewelry studios – first in Berlin and later in San Francisco – since 1985. She has held more than a dozen solo shows and garnered numerous prizes, including the American Craft Council's Best of Show and Award of Excellence. Petra's work is characterized by rhythmical arrangements of multiple elements, repetition of similar forms or colours, and unexpected contrasts between different textures. At present, she is fascinated by nature's wealth of different reds and sea of blues, from lapis's opaqueness to the transparency and subtlety of a pale lilac-coloured sapphire. > p. 17

PHILIP SAJET | Dutch
philipsajet@gmail.com
Philip Sajet's celebrated career has included over 200 exhibitions in Europe, the US, and Asia. He has

won the Alatyr Competition and the Marzee Prize, and has been featured in numerous publications including *500 Gemstone Jewels*. His work can also be found in the permanent collections of fifteen different museums, including the Royal College of Art in London, the Museum of Fine Arts in Boston, and the Musée des Arts Décoratifs in Paris. Using gold, niello, silver, precious and semi-precious stones, enamel and other materials, Philip seeks to create jewels that satisfy the observer and wearer independent of culture and time, pieces that express the beauty of vanity. > pp. 36, 71, 145

PILAR GARRIGOSA | Spanish
pilar@garrigosa.com / www.garrigosa.com
The holder of a degree in gemmology from the University of Barcelona, Pilar Garrigosa completed her studies at the Massana School and School of Arts and Trades in Barcelona. She was a finalist in Inhorgenta's design competition and has exhibited at the Daniele Gallery and the Oratory of San Rocco in Padua, Italy as well as the Klimt02 Gallery in Barcelona. Pilar's pieces are impregnated with rationalism and sensuality. Their predominantly geometric metal forms contrast with the exuberance of the jewels she insets. As the protagonists of her pieces, her gems always have personality: special sizes, rarities, transparencies or opacities that imbue the piece with intrinsic beauty.
> pp. 36, 169, 236

PILAR RESTREPO | Colombian
pilirestrepo@gmail.com
Pilar Restrepo studied architecture at the Pontifical Bolivarian University in Medellín, Colombia, before moving to Bogotá to attend jewelry-making classes. Her major exhibitions in Colombia's capital city include 'Kilates de Amor' at the Portobelo Design Centre, and multiple appearances at the Expoartesanías trade show. She was nominated for the Steel Pencil Design Award in 2009. Pilar's pieces, rendered using silver, gold and semi-precious stones, take their impetus from a rigorous observation of the fine details that the artist finds in nature. > p. 245

POLLY HORWICH | British
phorwich2@aol.com / www.pollyhorwich.com
After pursuing a career in architecture, Polly Horwich continues to explore concept and design at a different scale through her contemporary jewelry practice. Inspired by human experience, she develops ideas using silver or steel combined with other everyday materials. Ongoing themes include sensory loss, memory, preciousness and the built environment. She is captivated by the simplicity of the drawn line and by grids, which impose order and security over chaos and uncertainty. Her work is bold and colourful, demanding an instant response, while at the same time seeking to reward those who choose to explore the underlying concept. > p. 47

RAIMON ALZAMORA | Spanish
info@raimonjoies.com / www.raimonjoies.com
Raimon Alzamora Sánchez entered the world of jewelry in 1989 as an apprentice in his father's gemstone-setting workshop. Since then, he has been officially recognized as an expert in natural, synthetic and transparent gemstones by the Spanish Gemmology Association. He has showcased his work at the 100th anniversary celebration of Fostering Art and Design (FAD), at the Exhibition of Contemporary

Jewelry in Altafulla, Spain, and at the annual Vermut Amb Joies jewelry event in Barcelona. Raimon's pieces, which combine silver, gold, and ebony with uncut or cut gemstones, aim to carry their wearers to places of memory: the bucolic countryside, sand-swept beaches or the ebullient sea. > pp. 138, 169

RAMÓN PUIG CUYÀS | Spanish
puigcuyas@gmail.com / www.ramonpuigcuyas.tk
Ramón Puig Cuyàs graduated from Barcelona's Massana School in 1974 and has been a member of its faculty since 1977, teaching courses on design and jewelry-making. He is a prominent internationally renowned art jeweler and has served as a visiting professor at a wide number of schools and universities in Canada, Denmark, Estonia, Finland, France, Italy, Germany, Portugal, the Netherlands and the UK. Since 1974, Ramón's work has been featured in hundreds of galleries and museums across the world. His pieces can be found in the most important public and private jewelry collections in Europe, the US, and Canada. > p. 98

RANA MIKDASHI | Lebanon
info@ranamikdashi.com / www.ranamikdashi.com
Rana Mikdashi has studied silversmithing, jewelry, and enamelling in Canada, Egypt, Italy and Spain, including at the Alchimia School and Massana School. A finalist in the Enjoia't competition in 2005, she has been part of solo and group exhibitions in Egypt, Lebanon, Italy, Spain, South Korea and the U.A.E., and has been featured in *The Compendium Finale of Contemporary Jewellers, Terra di Mezzo: il Gioiello Contemporaneo incontra il Mediterraneo, Cross Point of E to W* and *Cutting Edge*, as well as various magazines in Europe and the Middle East. Playing with materials such as silver, gold, copper, iron, wood, silk, bone, horn, Plexiglas and polymer clay, Rana allows the process of creation to lead her. Though her ideas are not always lucid in the beginning, they inevitably evolve and transform until they reach a point of balance. > p. 127

REBECCA HANNON | Canadian
rjhjewel@gmail.com / www.rebeccahannonjewelry.com
Rebecca Hannon completed her undergraduate degree at Rhode Island School of Design in 1995 and went on to work as a professional goldsmith in New York City. After a thorough professional education, she won a Fulbright Scholarship to study at the Academy of Fine Arts in Munich. Five years later, she returned to North America, where she now maintains her own workshop, participates in international exhibitions, and teaches full time at the Nova Scotia College of Art and Design in Canada. > p. 243

RIKE BARTELS | German
rike@ rikebartels.com / www.rikebartels.com
Rike Bartels studied at the University of Pforzheim and Barcelona's Massana School. She has exhibited across Europe, from the Museum of Applied Arts in Prague to the Slavik Gallery in Vienna and the Victoria and Albert Museum in London, as well as at Art Basel and Art Basel Miami Beach. She has also been featured in the books *The Compendium Finale of Contemporary Jewellers, Danner Award 2002: Vivid and Timeless, Masters: Gold, Art Meets Jewellery* and *New Earrings*. Rike's many inspirations include volcanic shards littered on a Stromboli beach, a Palermo window graced by Moorish designs, the leaves of an olive tree, or the fantastical forms of homemade

gnocchi. Her pieces are designed to possess not only beauty but also personality, inspiring curiosity in those who behold them and encouraging them to dream. > pp. 121, 135

ROB JACKSON | American
jacksonr@uga.edu
Rob Jackson studied at the Penland School of Crafts in North Carolina before receiving his BFA and MFA from the University of Georgia. The winner of awards from the Rocky Mount Arts Center, Wichita Center for the Arts, and Zoller Gallery at Penn State University, he has exhibited across the US, including at Velvet da Vinci, Signature Contemporary Craft, and the National Ornamental Metal Museum. Using found objects embedded with a former history, Rob addresses time and erosion's influences on surface and form, investigating how surface texture informs content. His work can be found in books including *The Penland Book of Jewelry, On Body and Soul: Contemporary Armor to Amulets,* and *The Compendium Finale of Contemporary Jewellers*. > p. 42

ROBEAN VISSCHERS | Dutch
robeanvisschers@hotmail.com
Robean Visschers trained at both the Vocational School in Schoonhoven and the Alchimia School in Florence. In addition to shows in the Netherlands, Israel and Japan, his pieces have been featured in *The Compendium Finale of Contemporary Jewellers*. He was one of only five winners at the second SIERAAD New Traditional Jewellery contest. Robean's jewelry incorporates gold, silver, platinum and semi-precious stones. His highly rhythmic and geometric pieces seem reasoned but actually reflect the instinctive and sometimes irrational choices of the artist's creative process. > pp. 24, 96

ROBERT W. EBENDORF | American
ebendorfr@ecu.edu / www.ecu.edu/cs-cfac/soad/metals/ebendorfwork.cfm
The co-founder and former president of the Society of North American Goldsmiths (SNAG), Robert Ebendorf received the American Craft Council Fellowship in 1995. He has taught throughout the US and in the UK, and is currently teaching at East Carolina University in Greenville, North Carolina. He is represented in worldwide collections including the Metropolitan Museum of New York, London's Victoria and Albert Museum and the British Museum. The Racine Art Museum in Wisconsin hosted a retrospective of his work in 2010. In 2010 he was awarded the North Carolina Award for the Arts. In 2015 the Smithsonian acquired his archives. Robert devises engaging uses for discarded materials, casting familiar objects in an astonishing new light. His pieces explore the nature of adornment, often reversing ideas of what is precious. > p. 151

ROBERTA FERREIRA & LAURA JENER | Argentinian and Spanish
info@dterra.es / www.dterra.es / dterrablog.blogspot.com
After completing their studies at Llotja, Barcelona's Higher School for Design and Art, Roberta Ferreira López and Laura Jener Roca set up the Dterra Gallery and Atelier in Sant Cugat del Vallès, a space where they could pursue their artistic careers in ceramics and jewelry respectively. Together they began to experiment with the field of jewelry,

combining precious metals with ceramics to create a line of pieces with its own distinct identity. Their creations reflect influences and motifs from art history, reinterpreted with a contemporary sensibility that takes each piece to the borderline between art object and body ornament. Roberto and Laura use the same space to stage a programme of temporary exhibitions, talks and workshops, led either by themselves or other established artists who share their knowledge of jewelry, ceramics and related topics. Their own work has been widely exhibited, including at JOYA, Barcelona's contemporary jewelry week. > pp. 43, 110

ROBERTO CARRASCOSA | Spanish
roberto@roberto-victoria.com / www.roberto-victoria.com
Roberto Carrascosa studied at Barcelona's Massana School and pursued his graduate studies at Elisava. The winner of the Catalan Federation of Jewelers, Goldsmiths and Watchmakers' Design Trophy, he regularly exhibits his work under the brand name Roberto & Victoria, both in Spain and abroad. Roberto's pieces are begun through an intellectual process of reflection but truly take shape when he takes his materials – including gold, silver, enamels, and precious and semi-precious stones – into his own hands and starts to create. Exploring memory and seeking to build a bridge between past and present, his lively, handcrafted work tries to highlight the artisanal process that brings it into being. > p. 97

ROC MAJORAL & ABRIL RIBERA | Spanish
info@majoral.com / www.majoral.com
Roc Majoral and Abril Ribera learned their trade under Enric Majoral, in whose studio they have worked since 1994. Since 2003 they have actively collaborated on the design of new Majoral collections, providing their own creative vision and establishing a thread of continuity without losing sight of the firm's hallmark and spirit. They also produce their own distinct pieces, which they exhibit independently. The duo have participated in regular shows at the Formentera Artistan Association (AFA) and the Sa Nostra Cultural Space in Formentera, Spain. Other notable contributions include the touring exhibition 'Anti-War Medals', held at Barcelona's Alea Gallery and organized by San Francisco's Velvet da Vinci Gallery. > pp. 70, 73, 122

ROOS ARENDS | Dutch
info@roosarends.nl / www.roosarends.nl
Roos Arends followed up jewelry-making studies in Schoonhoven with a degree in visual marketing, graduating in 2003. This mixed background informs her interaction with materials such as gold, silver, diamonds, pearls and precious stones. Citing various sources of inspiration, many of Roos's pieces arise out of the desire to transform an old piece of jewelry, such as a well-worn string of pearls with a story. Roos sets out to create classy yet modern pieces that fit people on a personal level, eschewing wider trends. In this way she is able to fashion jewels that stay with people throughout their lives and become friends along the way. > p. 185

SALIMA THAKKER | Belgian
salima.thakker@skynet.be / www.salimathakker.com
Salima Thakker attended the Royal Academy of Fine Arts in Antwerp and the Royal College of Art

in London. The winner of Design Flanders's Henry Van de Velde Award and an award for fashion jewelry from Goldsmiths' Craft and Design Council, she was a finalist at the Diamond High Council Awards. She has presented her work in various galleries around the world, and is represented annually at SOFA New York and Chicago by Charon Kransen Arts. For several years she has run her own store in the heart of Antwerp, where she shows her pieces. Inspired by everyday surroundings, Salima's pieces strive to intrigue wearer and viewer. Her work relies heavily on graphic and modular patterns, coming alive when worn and changing according to the wearer's profile. > pp. 27, 165

SAMUEL SAAVEDRA | Spanish
operajoies@telefonica.net
Samuel Saavedra specialized in metalsmithing at Barcelona's Llotja School. He has displayed his creations in Barcelona and León in Spain and at 'Ojo!', an exhibition of Spanish contemporary jewelry in Manchester. Officially certified a Master Artisan by the Catalan Government, he received the Jury's Prize at Enjoia't 1994–95 in Barcelona and the Catalan Federation of Jewelers, Goldsmiths and Watchmakers' Design Trophy in 2009. Employing cement, paint, metals and precious stones, Samuel's jewels reveal our inner contradictions, exploring the absorbing interplay between harmony and contrast. His figurative and sometimes geometric work reflects critically on the world around him, expressing his thoughts in the form of visual poetry. > pp. 169, 238

SANDRA DUARTE | Portuguese
du.art4u@ymail.com / www.duart4u.com
Sandra Duarte initially pursued a degree in fashion design at the Faculty of Architecture at Lisbon Technical University (FAUTL). After discovering contemporary jewelry design in 2004, she went on to study at Lisbon's Contacto Directo School, whose prize she won in 2006, and where she took part in the 'Jóias Recíprocas' show. Her pieces were selected for the Portojóia annual jewelry fair in 2005. Experimenting with materials such as silver, plastic, rubber and wood, and harking back to all kinds of art, spiritual traditions and esoteric subjects, Sandra's jewelry expresses the most playful part of her personality – her inner child. > pp. 110, 122

SANNI FALKENBERG | British
sanni@sannifalkenberg.co.uk / www.sannifalkenberg.co.uk
Sanni's life-long passion for rocks and crystals started when she was a little girl with an innocent collection of stones and minerals. It grew into a passionate fascination, and she still feels incredibly awed to be working with materials formed hundreds of millions of years ago. From her childhood, the long dark winters of her homeland offered Sanni an unparalleled view of the night sky and the aurora borealis. These observations led to questions and inspired dreams and visions. Sanni's unique imagination takes her through the galaxies, nebulae and stardust to faraway star systems. There she finds inspiration and returns to express it in the form of cosmic jewelry. > p. 172

SARAH DE GASPERIS | Canadian
sarahdg2@hotmail.com / www.sarahdegasperis.com
Sarah is a trained goldsmith, passionate about her craft. She is a native of Toronto whose love of

travel led her to study in Córdoba, Spain where she completed a two-year goldsmithing programme and received a study grant apprenticeship in Hamburg, Germany. Sarah draws her inspiration from nature, ancient civilizations, mythical creatures and all things magical. She enjoys working instinctively, allowing each piece the opportunity to unfold on its own, creating the intimate feel of a treasured jewel rediscovered. > p. 95

SARAH HOOD | American
sarah@sarahhoodjewellery.com / www.sarahhoodjewellery.com
Sarah Hood first discovered metalsmithing at Cabrillo College in California, and later went on to receive her BA from Parsons The New School for Design in New York and her BFA in Metalsmithing from the University of Washington. Her jewelry is included in both private and public permanent collections including the Tacoma Art Museum in Washington, and has been shown nationally and featured in publications including *Metalsmith* magazine, *The Rings Book* and *500 Necklaces*, among others. Disparate interests – including gardening, botany, literature, children's toys, Eastern philosophy, and travel – all make their way into Sarah's creations, often inspiring compelling tangents which present the original ideas in a new light. > pp. 166, 203

SARAH RHODES | British
sarah@sarahrhodesdesign.com/ www.sarahrhodesdesign.com
Dr Sarah Rhodes completed her practice-based PhD at Central Saint Martins, which culminated in the exhibition 'The Craft of Ubuntu: An Exploration of Collaboration Through Making', shown at both the Iziko South Africa National Gallery and also in London. Sarah's jewelry has been exhibited internationally including at the London Design Festival, Sotheby's and Talents, Frankfurt. She has contributed chapters on southern African design for two books: *Contemporary Jewelry in Perspective* (2013) and *Cultural Threads: Transnational Textiles Today* (2014). Her consultancy work includes designing a collection for fair trade jewelry company Made and developing the curriculum for Botswana's first jewelry design and manufacture course. Previously based in Africa for many years, Sarah grounds her work in ethical practices and social sustainability. > p. 210

SARAH ROBINSON | Spanish
sarahrl@hotmail.com / imthegirloftherings.blogspot.com
Sarah Robinson trained at the Higher School of Art and Design (EASD) in Valencia. Her award-winning organic pieces are inspired by nature and primitive metalwork techniques. Sarah's work expresses her relationship with her surroundings, evoking the minutiae of places which are meaningful for her, simultaneously aiming to create a connection with the observer and to reinforce the wearer's identity. Sarah acknowledges the influence of Mari Ishikawa, whom she admires for her naturalism and fine detail, and Karl Fritsch, whose work stands out for his irreverence towards raw materials and the primitive quality of his finishes. However, by far Sarah's biggest source of inspiration comes from small Iberian figures, bronze ex-voti representing animals or humans. > pp. 39, 244

SAYUMI YOKOUCHI | Japanese
Sayumi6@gmail.com / www.sayumiyokouchi.com
Sayumi Yokouchi was born and raised in Tokyo, Japan. She moved to the US in 1990 and began her practice in metalsmithing at Cabrillo College in California. She earned her BFA in Metal Arts from California College of the Arts, followed by an MFA in Metal Arts from the State University of New York in New Paltz. Her work has been exhibited in museums and galleries in the US, Japan and Europe, and has been featured in publications including *New Earrings*, *American Craft*, *Metalsmith*, Lark Books' *500* series and *The Compendium Finale of Contemporary Jewellers*. She is currently a faculty member in the Art Department at New York University, and Brooklyn Metal Works in New York. > p. 153

SEAN O'CONNELL | Australian
sean@oneorangedot.com / www.oneorangedot.com
A former student at Sydney University's College of the Arts, Sean O'Connell has participated in many exhibitions both in his native Australia and internationally, holding five solo shows in ten years. He has received numerous Australia Council grants, and in 2009 won the Itami Award at the Itami International Craft Exhibition in Japan. Sean is inspired by the beauty of the natural world, whirring gears inside machines, old fairy tales, black and white movies, and even the materials he uses – especially the cold, clear perfection of stainless steel. He cannot stop himself from buying useless toys, and indeed, it is this sense of play, function and over-stimulation that characterizes his jewelry. > p. 187

SEBASTIAN BECK | German
seb-beck@web.de
Sebastian Beck originally studied metalworking and worked for the German furniture manufacturer Sedus Stoll. He produced ceramics and handicrafts for trade fairs throughout Germany as well as the Jürgen Blank Ceramics Atelier in Happingen, Germany. He then retrained at the Goldsmiths' School in Pforzheim, where he became a goldsmith and gemsetter. He subsequently worked for Bernhard Haas in Dietlingen-Pforzheim, where he came in contact with several high-end jewelry firms. Currently he is a goldsmith for Miquel Barbera at Hàbit jewelry atelier in Barcelona. He also teaches at the Massana School. Sebastian's work has been included in numerous shows organized by the Jewelers and Silversmiths' Guild of Pforzheim. In 2008, his pieces won special recognition from this association. > p. 97

SELDA OKUTAN | Turkish
info@seldaokutan.com / www.seldaokutan.com
Selda Okutan first set up a jewelry workshop in 2008. She subsequently opened Selda Okutan Studio and Gallery in Istanbul in 2011, where she works on jewelry designs alongside other disciplines. Design is her passion and she loves to incorporate figurative motifs into her creations. She sees pieces of jewelry not only as forms of wearable beauty but also as sculptural art objects. She has also designed her own equipment to aid her in her quest for perfection, and regularly researches new techniques, tools and materials. > pp. 54, 208, 229, 233

SENAY AKIN | Turkish
info@senayakin.com / www.senayakin.com
Born in 1976, Senay Akın studied photography at

Mimar Sinan Fine Arts University. During her studies she discovered a passion for wearable objects and subsequently took courses from the jewelry masters at the Grand Bazaar. She then went to Italy to further her education, training in jewelry design and gemmology at the School of Arts and Crafts in Vicenza and completing an internship at the Alberta Vita atelier. In 2007 she launched her first solo exhibition, 'Onlar' (Them), and has taken part in many group exhibitions. Her work has appeared in various publications, including *New Earrings*. She is often inspired by the many cities she has visited and the layers of history that seem to lie beneath their surfaces. Senay continues to create jewelry and offer training at the atelier she founded in Istanbul in 2008. Her works can be found in Turkish and international jewelry galleries. > pp. 168, 215, 218

•

SHU-PING (JOANNE) HUANG | Taiwanese
info@joanne-huang.com / www.joanne-huang.com
Joanne Huang commenced her education at the Fu-Shin Trade and Art School in Taipei, Taiwan, where she majored in package design. She subsequently pursued studies in fine art, industrial design, painting and metalwork in Melbourne, Australia, first at RMIT University and later at Monash University, before finishing with a jewelry-making course at the Alchimia School in Florence, Italy. Her pieces have been shown at the Mangold Gallery in Leipzig, Germany, at the Alchimia Graduate Exhibition in Florence's Antonella Villanova Gallery, and at the V&V Gallery in Vienna, Austria. Joanne's work explores the productive dialectic between covering up and revealing, expressing and concealing, turning this tension into art. > pp. 43, 61

•

SILVIA WALZ | German, lives in Spain
silviawalz@gmail.com / www.silviawalz.com
Silvia Walz studied at HAWK University in Hildesheim, Germany and the Massana School in Barcelona. She has lived and worked in Spain since 1988 and has been a teacher at the Massana School since 1994. Her numerous solo exhibitions have been held at galleries including the Biró Gallery in Munich, Aurum Gallery in Frankfurt, Velvet da Vinci in San Francisco, Galerie Noel Guyomarc'h in Montreal, Museo González Martí in Valencia and Mirada Expandida in Barcelona. Silvia was honoured for her work at the International Amber Biennial in 2007. She is featured in books including *Jewelbook*, *The Sourcebook of Contemporary Jewelry Design*, *Éclat: The Masters of New Jewellery Design*, *500 Brooches*, *Maker-Wearer-Viewer* and *Challenging the Chatelaine*, and has been a guest lecturer in Canada, the Czech Republic, Estonia, Poland, Portugal and the UK. > p. 197

•

SIM LUTTIN | Australian
simluttin@gmail.com / www.simluttin.com
Sim Luttin is a contemporary jeweler living and practising in Melbourne. The holder of a BFA in Goldsmithing and Silversmithing from RMIT University and a Master's in Metalsmithing and Jewelry Design from Indiana University, Sim has exhibited throughout Australia, Japan and the US. Her work can be found in the collections of the Marzee Gallery in the Netherlands and the Art Gallery of South Australia, and has been featured in Lark Books' *Wrap, Stitch, Fold & Rivet*, *Modern Jewelry from Modular Parts*, and *500 Pendants & Lockets*. Currently, she is also the gallery manager and curator at Arts Project Australia. Sim is an artist

and object maker who plots a course across time. Examining notions of ritual, personal authenticity and materiality, she inserts meaning at each point on a highly personal internal map. Her practice is grounded in daily ritual and the first charted position is her gaze. A still or moving image is taken, uploaded, printed and then distilled. A brief pause allows ideas, motifs and shapes to emerge that may then be translated into objects. > pp. 41, 197, 239

SOFIA BJÖRKMAN | Sweden
sofia@platina.se / www.sofiabjorkman.se
Sofia Björkman is an MFA holder from Konstfack University College of Arts, Crafts and Design in Sweden. She has received several grants from her country's Art Grants Committee as well as a City of Stockholm Culture Grant. She regularly exhibits in Europe and has been selected several times for the show Schmuck in Munich, but also exhibits around the world in places such as the US, South Korea, China, New Zealand and Brazil. She is the founder and owner of Platina Gallery in Stockholm. > pp. 34, 92

•

SONIA LEDOS | Venezuelan
sonia.ledos@gmail.com
Sonia Ledos attended the Cristobal Rojas Visual Arts School in Caracas, Venezuela. She subsequently studied contemporary jewelry at the Association for the Training and Development of Visual Arts (AFEDAP) in Paris, graduating in 2003. She has shown her work at the Caractère Gallery in Neuchâtel, Switzerland, in the Galerie Noël Guyomarc'h in Montreal, Canada, and at the Contemporary Jewelry Biennial in Nîmes, France. A member of the jewelry association Contrepoint, her pieces have been published in *Metalsmith* magazine. Sonia's work reflects the interaction between her thoughts and the world around her. She turns her feelings into physical reality by exploring the potential present within her materials as they respond to the body in motion. > p. 202

•

SOPHIA HIPPE | German
sophia.hippe@gmx.de
Sophia Hippe received her BA in Gemstones and Jewelry from Trier University of Applied Sciences in Idar-Oberstein. In 2010 she presented her first collection, and since then, her works have been shown at many different events in Germany. She prefers not to explain what her pieces mean to her, instead encouraging viewers to connect their own thoughts and emotions with her jewelry. Her work brings her joy and inspires her to move beyond precious metals and use new materials. > p. 196

•

SOPHIE BOUDUBAN | Swiss
sbouduban@sunrise.ch
Sophie Bouduban trained in Geneva at the School of Decorative Arts and the School of Applied Arts. She has held solo exhibitions at the viceversa Gallery in Lausanne, Switzerland and was represented by Charon Kransen Arts at SOFA 2010 in New York and Chicago. A past winner of Switzerland's Federal Award for Applied Arts, her work appears in publications including the *Dictionnaire international du bijou* and *Le bijou en Suisse au 20ème siècle*. For Sophie, creating means discovering materials, seeking new techniques and exploring shapes and volumes in relation to the body in a tactile way. Her pieces establish an intimate relationship between jewel and wearer, in which the jewel may become a

shell, a second skin or even a protective shield that conceals the body yet creates a puzzle. > p. 118

SOYEON KIM | South Korean
soysky@gmail.com / www.studiosoyeon.com
Soyeon completed an MFA in Metal/Jewelry at the University of Illinois at Urbana-Champaign. She is the recipient of numerous awards and scholarships, including the 2008 Educational Endowment Scholarship from the Society of North American Goldsmiths. Soyeon's latest pieces, employing gold, lace, sponge, porcelain, paper and found objects, hinge on an investigation into the value of objects. She is increasingly interested in reassessing and transforming values that are seen as innate or inviolable, and therefore often enjoys working with pre-owned jewelry made from precious metals. She currently lives in Korea. > pp. 61, 182, 194

STEFANIA LUCCHETTA | Italian
stefania@stefanialucchetta.com / www.stefanialucchetta.com
Stefania Lucchetta initially studied in Venice, at the Academy of Fine Arts and Ca' Foscari University. She combined working in her family's jewelry company with graduate studies, pursuing a master's in Industrial Design from the Italian Design School in Padua. Her creations have been showcased at the Milan Triennial, Milan's Sforzesco Castle and Berlin's Museum of Decorative Arts. She has twice been selected for the ADI Design Index, and in 2009 was shortlisted for the Best Young Italian Jewelry Designer Award. Stefania exploits her proficiency with stamping, casting, laser-cutting and etching and her mastery of CAD/CAM systems and rapid prototyping in order to fashion up-to-date pieces that create a new idiom in contemporary jewelry. > p. 66

STEFANIE BAUER | German
funkysteffi@hotmail.com / www.stefanie-bauer.com
Stefanie Bauer followed up goldsmithing apprenticeships in the German town of Schwäbisch Gmünd with studies at the Massana School in Barcelona. In 2007 she set up her own atelier in Ellwangen, Germany. She has exhibited at the Marzee Gallery in the Netherlands, and in Barcelona at the Poble Espanyol and La Capella exhibition space. She took third place in the 2002 Swarovski Crystal Awards. Stefanie draws on materials ranging from polyester and nylon threads to oxidized silver, Swarovski crystals and pearls. She enjoys employing materials and techniques in contexts for which they were not intended: for instance, making jewelry using the crochet technique she originally learned at a school workshop. > p. 161

•

STEPHANIE JENDIS | German
schmuck@stephanie-jendis.de / www.stephanie-jendis.de
Stephanie Jendis studied goldsmithing, jewelry-making and object design in Pforzheim, Germany. She was awarded a one-year fellowship by the German Academic Exchange Service (DAAD), and won a 2005–6 grant from the Amsterdam-based Netherlands Foundation for Visual Arts, Design and Architecture. In 2008 she opened her shop Einzelstück in Berlin. Her work has been displayed in galleries across Europe, and published in the books *Choice: Contemporary Jewellery from Germany* and *500 Gemstone Jewels*. Stephanie's pieces are the product of processes of sorting and grouping,

creating regularities, disorder and exceptions, and examining differences and contrasts between natural and artificial materials. Her abstract yet lucid jewels tell stories based on her own special memories, but remain open enough to allow other interpretations. > pp. 71, 211

SUSAN MAY | British
susan@susanmay.org
www.susanmay.org
Rings have figured prominently in Susan May's jewelry ever since she graduated from Middlesex University (formerly Hornsey College of Art) in 1976. Recent exhibitions have included 'Rings' at the Mobilia Gallery, Cambridge, MA; '200 Rings' at Velvet da Vinci, San Francisco; and 'The Ring' at the Ruthin Craft Centre, Wales. One of Susan's rings was selected for the 2015 exhibition 'A Sense of Jewellery' at the Goldsmiths' Centre, London. She has shown regularly at COLLECT London, and her work has been featured in many publications. Susan spends much of her time drawing from life, particularly the urban environment; the drawings are not used for direct visual reference but this practice informs and supports her work in metal. Her jewelry has been described as three-dimensional drawings in silver. > pp. 178, 216

TANIA SKLYAR | Ukrainian, lives in Germany
contact@tania-sklyar.de / *www.tania-sklyar.de*
Recycling and breathing new life into used objects are key motifs in the work of Berlin-based Tania Sklyar, who started out as a set designer at the Odessa Film Studio in her hometown in Ukraine. Deviating from the beaten track, Tania creates unconventional items with a vintage flair, inspired by childhood secrets and memories. She feels particularly influenced by the photographer Joel-Peter Witkin's explorations of physical deformities and death. Over the years, Tania has contributed to several magazines and catalogues, including *Art Ukraine* and *Jewelry Lookbook*. Her work has been showcased at JOYA, Barcelona's Contemporary Jewelry Week, RestCycling Art Festival in Berlin, Tendence in Frankfurt, Bijorhca in Paris, Frauenmuseum in Bonn, Dymchuk Gallery in Kiev, and Winzavod Centre for Contemporary Art and ArtStrelka in Moscow. > p. 41

TERESA KLEINEIDAM | German
teresakleineidam@web.de
Teresa Kleineidam has exhibited her work throughout Germany, including at Inhorgenta and the IHM International Crafts Trade Fair in Munich and the Kestner Museum in Hanover. She has also been honoured with first place in the Junge Cellinis jewelry contest. Made from silver, gold and paint, Teresa's pieces seek to express new points of view and are at times peppered with irony. Her goal with each piece differs: some are designed to be beautiful with no deeper intention than to make their wearer happy, while others seek to offer a tiny insight into their owner's soul. > pp. 141, 227

TERRY WARE | American
terry@terryware.net / *www.terryware.net*
Having formally studied art history, Terry Ware is self-taught in the making of jewelry and has had a studio practice since 1998. She believes that something magic occurs in the reincarnations of earthly materials. Time and matter are mysteriously forged to become something else. Just as a leaf

regenerates back into soil or a nest is built from twigs, the minerals, places and ideas form a substance that she utilizes in her process. This, along with the value of culture and history as it relates to fine art, informs her practice. > pp. 43, 192

THEO SMEETS | Dutch
post@theosmeets.com / *www.theosmeets.com*
Theo studied at the Gerrit Rietveld Academy in Amsterdam and specialized in gold and silversmithing at the Vakschool Schoonhoven. Since 1992 he has been a freelance jeweler. He is professor of Jewelry and Object Design at Trier University of Applied Sciences in Idar-Oberstein. He feels that his work reflects the people around him and the passage of time. > p. 48

THERESA BURGER | South African
tweebi@gmail.com / *www.theresaburger.com*
Theresa Burger is a jewelry designer based in Cape Town. In 2009 she graduated from Cape Peninsular University of Technology with a BTech degree in Jewelry Design and Manufacture. She completed her MA in Design at NCAD, Dublin, in 2012. Her master's project focused on merging rapid prototyping technologies such as 3D printing with traditional jewelry-making skills. The collection was inspired by the rich heritage and symbolism of Zulu beadwork and draws from its patterns and motifs. Along with her partner, Theresa is currently the co-owner of a contemporary jewelry design company called Pistol & Peach and is a full-time practising jewelry designer. Recent exhibitions include 'BIJOUX!' at the Norton Museum of Art in Vail, Colorado, in February 2015. > p. 192

TING-CHUN ARA KUO | Taiwanese
ara11ara@hotmail.com
Ting-Chun Ara Kuo received both her BFA and master's in Metal and Jewelry from Monash University in Melbourne, Australia. Since 2008, she has been continuing her training with specialized courses at the Alchimia School in Florence, Italy. Ting-Chun's work has been showcased at galleries and exhibitions in Australia and Europe, including the Marzee Gallery in the Netherlands and Galerie Sofie Lachaert in Belgium. Her creative, modern pieces have been featured at Inhorgenta as well as in the magazine *ELLE*. > pp. 69, 237

TITHI KUTCHAMUCH | Thai
Info@tithi.info / *www.tithi.info*
When Tithi Kutchamuch was growing up, her family always seemed to have some sort of animal in the house: at one point, they even had peacocks, hedgehogs and a gibbon. She created her first jewelry collection, A Secret Friend, when she was living in London, just a few months after finding out that her dog, who had been living with her family in Bangkok, had passed away. All of her collections are designed to tell stories. From an early stage, she has treated her jewelry as a medium to document her thoughts and experiences in three-dimensional form. > pp. 23, 86, 217

TOBY COTTERILL | British
toby@tobycotterill.co.uk / *www.tobycotterill.co.uk*
Toby Cotterill studied Design: Crafts at Staffordshire University, graduating in 2002, and has exhibited at various locations across the UK and abroad including Art in Action and Velvet Da Vinci in San Francisco. Toby's creations in gold, silver, resin

and natural pigments investigate the motifs of evolution, form and function. His work attempts to draw attention to the overlooked and inconspicuous; here, his exploding ring reveals a hidden layer of fine gold. Inspired by his childhood on a farm in Wales, his work is driven by the beauty of the natural world. > p. 90

TOM FERRERO | American
tom@tomferrerostudio.com / *www.tomferrerostudio.com*
Tom Ferrero received a BFA in Jewelry Design from the Rochester Institute of Technology and an MFA in Metalsmithing and Jewelry from Indiana University. In 2003–4 he was awarded a Fulbright Scholarship to study visual arts at the Manukau Institute of Technology of the University of Auckland in New Zealand. A two-time NICHE Award winner and a first-place Saul Bell Design Award winner, Tom has had his work exhibited at home and abroad and published in books including *1000 Rings* and *Fabulous Jewelry from Found Objects*. His work is held in notable private collections including the Kamm Teapot Foundation. He is currently an Assistant Professor of Jewelry at NSCAD University in Halifax, Nova Scotia. > p. 69

TOMOYO HIRAIWA | Japanese
tomoyo-hiraiwa@ksh.biglobe.ne.jp /
tomoyohiraiwa.com
Tomoyo Hiraiwa studied at the Tokyo National University of Fine Arts in her native Japan. She has exhibited extensively in Europe, North America, Australia and Asia, including at Schmuck, SOFA New York and the 12th International Lace Biennial. Tomoyo received a Japanese Government Overseas Study Scholarship for Artists to continue her training at New York's Museum of Arts and Design. She took first prize at the Friedrich Wilhelm Müller International Jewelry Competition in Germany and the International Craft Biennial in Cheong Ju, Korea. She is the author of a book about metalworking, released in Japan, and also contributed to Lark Books' *500 Bracelets*. She admires the beauty of simplicity and likes to explore the dynamic potential of her chosen materials. > pp. 94, 225

TORE SVENSSON | Swedish
tore.svensson2@comhem.se / *www.toresvensson.com*
Tore Svensson trained in his native Sweden, first at Västerberg Art School and later at Gothenburg University. The winner of the 1999 Bavarian State Prize and the 2012 Herbert Hofmann Award, he has exhibited in numerous locations including London, Gothenburg, Philadelphia, Munich, Tokyo and Nijmegen. An eponymous book about his work, *Tore Svensson*, was released in 2000, and he has also been featured in the publication *Raising the Bar: Influential Voices in Metal*. Tore's work is principally non-narrative, opting instead to explore materials and geometric forms. He mainly utilizes paint and steel, which is etched and fired with linseed oil. His projects often stretch over long periods, with some merging into one another and others remaining undefined and incomplete. > pp. 182, 206

TOVE KNUTS | Swedish
info@toveknuts.se / *www.toveknuts.se*
Tove Knuts attended Ädellab, the Metalwork Department at the Konstfack University College of Arts, Crafts and Design in Sweden. She spent a semester at the Academy of Art, Design and

Architecture (AAAD) in Prague, and has also studied at the Hungry Creek School of Art in Auckland, New Zealand. A participant in the 5th Tallinn Applied Art Triennial in Estonia, the 2010 edition of MINIMUM and the 2015 edition of BOUNDARIES at the International Jewellery Festival in Legnica, Poland, she has also been showcased at the Röhsska Design Museum in Gothenburg, Malmö Konsthall and Gustavsbergs Konsthall in Sweden. She has also had two solo exhibitions in Stockholm: in 2012 at DAUGHTERS and in 2015 at Gallery Movitz. Tove enjoys working with a range of materials, including plastic and bone, but metal (especially silver) remains her medium of preference. > p. 180

•

VICTOR SALDARRIAGA | Colombian
victor@lasierpe.net / www.lasierpe.net
Victor Saldarriaga Tomic's training included studies in industrial design, gemstone setting and wax casting at both the Pontifical Bolivarian University in Medellín, Colombia and the Guild of Jewelers, Goldsmiths and Silversmiths in Valencia, Spain. His work has been showcased in Medellín at the Castle Museum and the Medellín Museum of Modern Art and in Mexico City at the Gray Area Symposium. Victor is a poet in the guise of a jeweler, using fire and metal instead of pencil and paper. He translates sight and the other senses into physical form in metal, just as he would do if writing, creating a novel and personal way to see the world. > p. 101

•

VICTORIA ALTEPETER | American
*victoria.altepeter@gmail.com /
www.victoriaaltepeter.blogspot.com*
Victoria Altepeter is a metalsmith and educator who calls Tempe, Arizona home. Born and raised in St Louis, Missouri, she finds endless inspiration in the the landscape and skies of the American West, especially the bright night sky. It is the microcosm of our planet juxtaposed with the vast grandeur of the universe that drives her metal sculptures, installations and wearable pieces. She endeavours to create 'snapshots' of moments in time and space

through the use of metals, minerals and cast organic objects. Victoria earned a BFA with an emphasis in metals at Northern Arizona University and a MFA at Arizona State University. Following this, she spent a year at Arrowmont School of Arts and Crafts as an artist-in-residence, and went on to teach metals at NAU from 2010–12. She is currently area head and visiting lecturer in metals at Arizona State University. Her work has been exhibited nationally and included in a variety of books and publications, including *500 Silver Jewelry Designs*, *American Craft* and *Wrap, Stitch, Fold & Rivet*. > p. 22

•

VIKTORIA MÜNZKER | Slovakian
*office@viktoriamuenzker.eu
www.viktoriamuenzker.eu*
Born in Bratislava, Viktoria Münzker currently lives and works in Vienna. In 2007 she received a Master of Arts from the Academy of Fine Arts and Design in Bratislava. Over the last ten years, she has participated in many international exhibitions, winning the Gioielli in Fermento 2013 prize at the Torre Fornello Awards, as well as first prize in the Azur Jewelry Art Contest 2012 at the AmberTrip International Baltic Jewellery Show. > p. 49

VINA RUST | American
verust@hotmail.com / www.vinarust.com
Vina Rust earned a BFA in Metals from the University of Washington. Her work has been shown across the US, including at the Sienna Gallery in Lenox, Massachusetts and the Velvet da Vinci Gallery in San Francisco. She took second place in the Society for Midwest Metalsmiths' 2008–9 METAL Inclinations Contest, and has been featured in *Metalsmith* magazine and the books *500 Earrings* and *The Penland Book of Jewelry*. Vina's many inspirations include the *fin-de-siècle* English illustrators Arthur Rackham and Aubrey Beardsley and the jewelry of Southeast Asia and Oceania. An acute observer of natural forms, she appreciates the tension between beauty and menace so often found in nature's defences. > p. 109

YAEL KRAKOWSKI | Israeli
yael@yaelkrakowski.com / www.yaelkrakowski.com
Yael Krakowski earned her BFA from the Bezalel Academy of Arts and Design in Jerusalem. A past winner of the BC Creative Achievement Award from the British Columbia Achievement Foundation in Canada, she has exhibited in Israel, Europe, the US and Canada, including at SOFA in New York, Chicago and Santa Fe, OBJECToronto, and in a solo show at the Bielak Gallery in Poland. Her work has been featured in the books *500 Enameled Objects*, *500 Pendants & Lockets*, and *Jewellery Using Textile Techniques*. Yael's work is inspired by the constant changes in nature. She avoids synthetics in favour of natural materials, which infuse her pieces with vibrant designs and colours. > p. 98

•

YUKI KAMIYA | Japanese
kiyuyamika@gmail.com / www.yukikamiya.com
Yuki Kamiya studied jewelry-making at Le Arti Orafe in Florence. Yuki's silver, bronze and gold pieces are marked by smooth, flowing lines. They aim to invoke the ideas that she herself most values: harmony, simplicity and spontaneity. > p. 190

YUYEN CHANG | Taiwanese
yuyenona@gmail.com / www.yuyenchang.com
Yuyen Chang received her MFA from University of Wisconsin – Madison. She has exhibited at the Penland Gallery, Delaware Center for the Contemporary Arts, Kentucky Museum of Art and Craft and the Milan Triennial. She was also the recipient of Art Jewelry Forum's Emerging Artist Award and the Society of North American Goldsmiths Educational Endowment. Her work has been featured in *1000 Rings*, *500 Necklaces*, *500 Brooches*, *Art Jewelry Today* and *Chasing and Repoussé*. Both jewelry and the human body attract attention, especially when they deviate from the norm. Yuyen's work attempts to bridge these two kinds of attention and the social rules that govern them. > p. 20

NICOLAS ESTRADA

Nicolas Estrada (Medellín, 1972) set out on his path as an artist in Barcelona, where other, very different motives had taken him. Until then, he had been a businessman working in the field of marketing. Destiny, however, had other things in store for him, ultimately leading Nicolas down different roads to the creation of jewellery filled with meaning, unique pieces of art replete with moving stories.

It was at Barcelona's Escola Massana where Nicolas first encountered the world of jewellery, one in which he discovered a galaxy of infinite expressive possibilities. An indefatigable researcher, his curiosity and passion for this discipline have taken him all over the world. Guided by a sense of balance and refinement, Nicolas has pursued diverse courses of study ranging from gemmology, setting and carving techniques to research and work in such fields as traditional Berber Kabyle jewellery and filigree techniques in the Colombian town of Santa Cruz de Mompox.

Nicolas Estrada draws inspiration for his pieces from simple subject matter that touches directly on the humanity of those who observe his creations. The pieces do not seek to defend or take a position on situations that undoubtedly carry weight and importance for Nicolas's native country and continent. Rather they represent the pure and clear gaze of an artist deeply moved by these phenomena who with the tools of his trade attempts to shed new light on and offer fresh interpretations of them. For Nicolas, each piece of jewellery possesses great power and value. An artistic proposal such as the one contained in the work of Nicolas Estrada is crystallized in a creative reflection full of meaning and strength, one that translates into an intimate dialogue between the object and the gaze of the other. Nicolas offers us nothing less than the possibility of seeing something extraordinary and provocative, an ode to irreverence, a reflection within the aura of a judiciously executed and deeply contemplated discipline.

THE AUTHOR

ACKNOWLEDGMENTS

New Rings was my first adventure in the world of books, a huge endeavour that demanded a lot of work but produced great results. It's now my pleasure to present this revised and updated version, which includes the work of some forty new jewelers as well as the very best from the previous edition.

It's so exciting for me to see pages and pages filled with such fascinating and beautiful pieces, many of which have been made by people I have the great privilege of knowing personally. Many of the contributors have attended jewelry fairs, exhibitions and other events with me. The world of artisan jewelry remains a small one, but it is thrilling to know what a book like this can do to spread awareness of this amazing work.

I would like to thank Thames & Hudson for entrusting me with this project and having faith in my selections to add to this new edition. I would also like to thank Joaquim Canet and his team at Promopress, who opened the door to the world of publishing for me. Thanks must also go to Sophia Hippe, whose work appears in these pages and who helped me to come up with inclusion criteria and find stunning and unique pieces to feature. My immediate family have always supported me in everything I do, and they encouraged me to embark on this project and gave me lots of ideas that helped me to make it a reality.

I am grateful to Carles Codina, who was my teacher some years ago and subsequently became a great friend. Carles's work appears in these pages and he has also contributed a text on the role of rings in the world of jewelry. Elizabeth Shypertt, one of the first gallerists to exhibit my work and now a great friend, allowed me to revise her original essay for this book, to enrich it with the benefit of her opinions and experience.

Finally, I would like to thank all the artists whose work appeared in the original book and those who are included in this new edition: it is their wonderful work that allows the book to exist and inspires readers to take it home with them. And of course, my thanks to everyone who bought the first edition of this book and made this revised volume possible.